The Origins of International Economic Disorder

FRED L. BLOCK

The Origins of
International Economic Disorder

A Study of United States International
Monetary Policy from World War II
to the Present

UNIVERSITY OF CALIFORNIA PRESS
Berkeley · Los Angeles · London

University of California Press
Berkeley and Los Angeles, California
University of California Press, Ltd.
London, England
Copyright © 1977 by
The Regents of the University of California
ISBN 0-520-03009-5
Library of Congress Catalog Card Number: 75-7190
Printed in the United States of America

For Carole

CONTENTS

PREFACE

The common attitude toward international monetary matters is embodied in the old joke that only two people really understand the workings of the gold standard and they disagree. This perspective is not only inaccurate but anachronistic in a world where international economic realities increasingly impinge on our daily lives. The reality is that there are in international economics a number of highly technical issues of great complexity, as in any area of specialized knowledge. However, one does not need to understand these arcane details to develop an adequate understanding of the basic workings of the international monetary system.

Much of the blame for convincing people that international monetary issues are hopelessly complex rests with the discipline of economics. Economists have generally described international monetary arrangements as purely technical expedients to maximize certain collective goods. Yet it is quite obvious today that any set of international economic arrangements means that some collectivities (nations, classes) get more goods than others. The protestations of the economists have served both to obscure these inequalities and to justify them as natural and inevitable. To prove that an existing set of social institutions is natural and inevitable, the economists have been forced to develop a set of arguments that are rich in obscurantism and obfuscation. It is this set of arguments that has persuaded so many people that these matters are beyond their intellectual grasp.

When it is recognized that international monetary arrangements are social creations that tend to reflect and maintain the distribution of power among nations and social classes, many of the artificial complexities disappear, and the issues become comprehensible to the nonspecialist. But the fact that we continue to repeat, in reference to international monetary arrangements, the now almost hackneyed sociological insight that a specific social institution may be structured in very different ways is testimony to the damage that has been done by dividing social science knowledge into different disciplines. The relative backwardness of our understanding of international monetary arrangements points to the need for a unidisciplinary intellectual approach that brings together the now separate studies of politics, economics, sociology, and history. It is hoped that the present work makes some contribution to the advancement of such a unidisciplinary approach.

As with other efforts to write contemporary history, I have encountered a great unevenness in available sources. For the earlier periods, a wide variety of sources are available, and I have attempted to make use of as many of them as possible. I did not, however, make use of archival materials because the time-consuming nature of such work would have forced me to abandon the project of analyzing both the rise and the fall of the post-World War II monetary order. For the more recent periods, the sources on policy-making are often quite limited. The consequence is that the analysis necessarily becomes more speculative as it moves closer to the present.

My greatest intellectual debt is to William Appleman Williams and Gabriel and Joyce Kolko. I have drawn from their works far more than is indicated in my footnotes. Their contributions, and the contributions of their students, to the understanding of twentieth-century American foreign policy is the foundation on which I have tried to build. While some of my interpretations diverge from theirs, my work would not have been possible without theirs.

I am especially grateful to David Matza and Larry Hirschhorn. David Matza, as chairman of my dissertation committee, provided me with continuous encouragement and support, as well as countless substantive suggestions. Larry Hirschhorn's intellectual stimulation was very important in starting me on this project, and he was always there when I needed to discuss a particular nuance of the argument. I also found particularly valuable the suggestions of Steven Cohen, Carole Joffe, Karl Klare, Magali Larson, Franz Schurmann, Susan Strange, Ann Swidler, and Bob Wood.

I would also like to thank Robert Triffin and Charles Kindleberger—two of the giants of international economics—for their kindness in answering a number of questions about policy decisions in which they played a part. I should hasten to add that their answers to those questions and what I learned from their extensive writings are the full extent of their participation in this project. I am grateful as well to the North American Congress on Latin America for giving me access to their newspaper files. Marcy McGaugh and Ann Richter patiently and skillfully typed various drafts, and Jerome Fried provided invaluable editorial assistance.

Carole Joffe, to whom I am married, has helped me in every imaginable way, except with the proverbial wifely protection from the chores of daily life. For what she did and for what she didn't do, I am hard pressed to express the extent of my gratitude and appreciation.

ABBREVIATIONS

BIS	Bank for International Settlements
CRU	Composite Reserve Unit
ECA	Economic Cooperation Administration
ECSC	European Coal and Steel Community
EDC	European Defense Community
EEC	European Economic Community
EFTA	European Free Trade Area
EPC	European Political Community
EPU	European Payments Union
ERP	European Recovery Program
FRUS	Department of State, *Foreign Relations of the United States*
GAB	General Arrangements to Borrow
GATT	General Agreement on Tariffs and Trade
IBRD	International Bank for Reconstruction and Development
IEPA	International Economic Policy Association
IET	Interest Equalization Tax
IMF	International Monetary Fund
ITO	International Trade Organization
MLF	Multilateral Force
NACIMFP	National Advisory Council on International Monetary and Financial Policy
NATO	North Atlantic Treaty Organization
NSC	National Security Council
OECD	Organization for Economic Cooperation and Development
OEEC	Organization for European Economic Cooperation
OPEC	Organization of Petroleum Exporting Countries
SCB	Department of Commerce, *Survey of Current Business*
SDRs	Special Drawing Rights
WEU	Western European Union

ONE. *Introduction*

The Bretton Woods international monetary order now lies in ruins, while the world's finance ministers and their deputies meet incessantly to create a reformed international monetary order. Yet their deliberations drag on year after year without tangible results. Even if an agreement on paper is finally achieved, there are grounds for profound skepticism that a new set of rules would succeed in restoring a stable international monetary order. The purpose of this study is to illuminate the obstacles to the contemporary efforts at international monetary reform by examining the rise and fall of the Bretton Woods system. But the history of Bretton Woods that I will recount differs from most accounts of international monetary history in that it is not primarily concerned with the technical aspects of international economic arrangements nor with the evolution of international organizations. My interest is in examining historically the ways in which specific international monetary arrangements both reflect and influence the distribution of political-economic power among the major capitalist countries. In short, my intent is to use international monetary history to illuminate the relationship between the United States and Western Europe in the period since World War II.

THE NATURE OF INTERNATIONAL MONETARY ORDER

The international monetary system is simply the sum of all of the devices by which nations organize their international economic relations. The nature of these devices can be understood by looking at the theoretical range of alternatives available to any particular nation. The crucial dimension in organizing a nation's international transactions is the role of the market in determining the flows of economic resources across the national boundaries. Nations that allow the market to play a major role can be termed "open," while those that allow market forces little or no role in determining international transactions can be termed "closed."[1] There is a continuum between pure closedness and pure openness on which all nations can be located, since all nations use some combination of controls and market freedom. A country's location

1

on the continuum is significant because, over any period of time, a nation can spend internationally only as much as it has available through past savings, current earnings, or current borrowing. If the nation's expenses and income diverge too much, it will be forced to adjust one or the other to balance its international accounts. The way in which this adjustment is achieved depends greatly on the openness or closedness of the economy.

The process of adjusting international income to international expenses is straightforward for countries with closed economies. For example, they can simply reduce or increase their imports of certain commodities by fiat. Countries with relatively open economies can do the same—impose import restrictions or capital controls—but that has the effect of making their economies significantly less open. Nations committed to maintaining the openness of their economies have two major means to make adjustments—changing the level of domestic economic activity or changing the exchange rate of their currency. Both of these techniques of adjustment leave the market unimpaired, but each can have a major impact on the fabric of social life. If, for example, a country has a balance-of-payments deficit, either lowering the level of economic activity—deflating—or lowering the exchange rate—devaluation—is designed to reduce the country's international expenditures while increasing its international revenues. However, deflating the economy means putting people out of work and applying downward pressure on real wage levels. Similarly, an effective devaluation will also reduce real wage levels. In short, these adjustment techniques work by affecting the level of employment and the level of income. This can lead to a breakdown of social order and an intensification of class conflict.

The costs of this type of adjustment can be extremely high in capitalist countries where the political integration of the working class depends on high levels of employment and stable or increasing real wage levels. But the dilemma is that moving toward a more closed economy, one that is less influenced by international economic forces, has serious drawbacks for the capitalist class. First, as long as an economy is open, it is possible for those with wealth to invest their capital abroad for the sake of higher returns or greater security. As an economy begins to be closed off, the risk is great that the freedom to export capital will be restricted. Second, capitalist firms that export or have foreign investments have an interest in maintaining the openness of the world economy to assure the largest possible market. If their own economy begins to close itself off, it is likely that other countries will retaliate and these capitalists will lose foreign markets and investment opportunities. Finally, the openness of an economy provides a means to combat the demands of the working class for higher wages and for economic and social reforms. Dramatic wage increases or radical reforms cause balance-of-payments difficulties because of diminished international competitiveness and the withdrawal of capital from the economy by citizens and foreigners. Usually, this kind of balance-of-payments crisis, or the threat of one, is sufficient to discourage or reverse any such radical actions. In short, the evident need to protect the balance of payments in an open economy serves to reinforce the capitalist class's resistance to reforms that might damage its interests.

The drawbacks for the capitalists of both an open and a closed economy create one of the central problems for contemporary capitalism. The more open an economy, the greater the likelihood that painful adjustments will be necessary, and these painful adjustments create a risk of intense social conflict. The more closed an economy, the greater the likelihood that the prerogatives and interests of the capitalist class will be impaired. To some degree, national societies work out their optimal place on the open/closed continuum depending on particular national conditions. However, this freedom is at times circumscribed by the existence of rules of international economic behavior. During certain historical periods, the international monetary system is governed by a definite set of rules and procedures. There exists in these periods an international monetary order.[2]

The structure of such an international monetary order tends to reflect the influence of the most powerful capitalist nations. Their military superiority and control of key economic resources—capital, advanced technology, raw materials, and access to their own large domestic markets—makes it possible for them to exercise leverage over other nations. This leverage is generally used to create an international order with a high degree of openness so that capitalists from the strongest economy will be able to take advantage of opportunities for profit in other countries. In short, a world order in which the flow of goods and capital is determined largely by market forces will maximize the advantages for the country with the highest level of technical development and with the most enterprising and strongest firms.

While the most powerful nations or nation will have the greatest influence in shaping the international monetary order, they will also have a special responsibility to see that the system works within those particular rules. Crucial is their ability to mobilize large sums of capital to aid countries facing balance-of-payments deficits, because international credit is a lubricant for the adjustment process. When a country can borrow abroad, it can extend the adjustment process over a longer period of time to make it less severe and less painful. In fact, when international credit is unavailable, it is harder for weaker countries to resist domestic pressures for a more closed economy.

But if the interests of the most powerful nation or nations determine the outlines of a particular international monetary order, there is a possibility that the order will be jeopardized by shifts in the relative power of different capitalist countries. Nations that were relatively weak when the order was first established can undergo a period of rapid economic advance and find that the existing order fails to reflect adequately their economic power and interests. That order might, for example, place too much of a burden of adjustment on the late arrival's economy. In such a case, the late arrival might agitate for a revision of the arrangements, attempting to create a new and more equitable order. Alternatively, a major power might find that rising competition from other powers makes it difficult to achieve all of its national goals within the existing rules. It might attempt to use its economic power to force other countries to accept a bending of the rules. The outcome of these efforts to revise the order could be the evolution of a new international monetary order that reflects the new power alignment while safeguarding the vital interests of the old dominant powers, or it could be the complete breakdown of international monetary order. In the latter case, economies might increasingly be organized on a closed basis, if nations find it necessary to protect themselves from the possible collapse of international trade and flow of capital.

THE GOLD STANDARD VS. "NATIONAL CAPITALISM"

Although some scholars have traced the existence of international monetary orders back to the ancient world, it is the nineteenth-century gold standard that has been the touchstone in most subsequent thinking about the subject. The period from 1875 to 1914[3] is a kind of mythical "golden age" of international monetary arrangements when all major nations lived within the rule of international monetary behavior and balance-of-payments adjustment proceeded smoothly and virtually automatically. The reality was somewhat different from the myth, and researchers are still attempting to separate the actual mechanics of the nineteenth-century system from the received wisdom about the mechanics. Despite the exaggerations of the myth, the years from 1875 to 1914 were characterized by a high level of international monetary stability, particularly in comparison to what would come later. However, the twentieth-century advocates of a return to the "golden age" have generally failed to realize that the stability of that order was intimately linked to the special circumstance of Great Britain's dominant international role.[4] Great Britain's special role in the stabilizing and eventual destabilizing of the gold standard will be explored in the next chapter. But it is important here to examine the basic rules of the nineteenth-century gold standard because so many twentieth-century efforts at international monetary reform have been based on some version of recapturing that "golden age."

The core mechanism of the gold standard was the setting by most major countries of fixed values for their currencies in relation to gold. These countries also allowed the relatively free movement of gold across their boundaries and agreed to convert their currency into gold at the established price. The exchange rates between currencies were allowed to fluctuate in response to market demand. This meant that if Country A were spending more abroad than it was taking in, the overabundance of its currency abroad might lead to a fall in its price relative to the currency of Country B. If this fall were large enough, it would be profitable for bankers and others to buy Currency A at its reduced exchange rate, convert it into gold at the fixed price in Country A, and then transport that gold to Country B where it could be exchanged back into Currency B at the fixed rate. The possibility of these gold movements served to limit the fluctuations in exchange rates, because the purchase of Currency A to convert it to gold might help reverse the original decline in Currency A's exchange rate. More fundamentally, the gold movements contributed to balance-of-payments adjustment because the loss of a share of a country's gold supply would reduce the total supply of domestic money and credit. This, in turn, would deflate the economy and might lead to a gradual improvement in the country's payments balance. If a country were running a balance-of-payments surplus, the inflow of gold might accelerate the growth of money and credit, which could lead to an acceleration of imports, a slowing of exports, and the elimination of the surplus.

This control mechanism was lubricated by substantial international capital movements that helped to ease the adjustment process. Countries in good credit standing could simply increase their short-term borrowing to weather a short-term outflow of gold, and other countries relied on a continuing inflow or outflow of long-term capital to keep their accounts in balance. The gold-standard mechanism protected the value of these foreign loans because it kept exchange rates relatively constant among the principal countries, and it also effectively operated to discourage any inflationary policies that could undermine the value of a currency. While the gold standard facilitated the free flow of goods and capital across national boundaries in response to market forces, governments did depart from strict laissez-faire by using a variety of techniques to blunt the impact of international market forces at various times. These interventionist techniques, however, generally involved efforts to influence the market forces rather than to block their operation. Such market-disrupting techniques as the use of exchange controls, the suspension of gold convertibility, or the imposition of import controls were of little importance in the gold-standard world.[5]

While the high level of openness that characterized the gold-standard world clearly benefited Great Britain—the world's leading exporter of goods and capital during the 1875-1914 period—the openness was justified on more universal grounds. The idea was that openness made the world market for goods and capital more extensive, and this would speed the pace of economic advance everywhere as nations took advantage of the possibilities of a more developed international division of labor. The classical economists had demonstrated that each nation gained through the specialization that extensive international trade facilitated, and vigorous international trade competition accelerated the pace of technical advance in all nations. A critique of this justification for maximum international openness emerged in the nineteenth century that emphasized the benefits of extensive protection of infant industries. However, that critique generally fell short of a rejection of the value of an open world economy.[6] In short, the theoretical justification for an open world economy remained basically intact and continued to provide the underpinnings of the twentieth-century efforts to restore the openness of the gold standard epoch.

It is not difficult to understand why the universal benefits of international openness remained largely unquestioned in the capitalist world. We noted earlier than an open economy generally serves the interests of the capitalists in resisting working-class demands for improved wages and social services, while movement toward a more closed economy poses a threat to the freedom of capitalists to dispose of their wealth as they wish. Another important element is that the theory of the universal gain from the free flow of trade and capital internationally has served historically to justify and obscure the exploitation of underdeveloped countries. The theory of comparative advantage has served to hide the unequal exchange between developed and underdeveloped countries, and the maintenance of openness to capital flows has allowed capitalists in the developed countries to dominate the most profitable sectors of the underdeveloped economies. Of course, in the past fifteen years, a powerful critique of the open world economy has been developed that argues that underdevelopment has often been perpetuated by the international division of labor among nations.[7] In recent years, this critique has given rise to concrete actions by underdeveloped countries, such as the OPEC nations, to improve their position in the world economy by challenging the workings of the international market.

Yet there was another critique of the benefits of an open world economy that long predated the current Third World position. Now largely forgotten, it was developed within Western Europe and the U.S. during the Great Depression of the 1930s.[8] The effort to restore the gold standard and an open world economy after World War I had failed to re-establish the stability of the prewar period. In fact, the openness of the international economy had only served to transmit deflationary pressures from one country to another after 1929 and had acted as an obstacle to national recovery programs in the early 1930s. This reality led some analysts to argue that an open world economy in which international market forces dominated was inconsistent with domestic economic welfare. The proponents of this heretical view argued that the free flow of capital across national boundaries was far more disruptive than it was beneficial. They also argued that while a certain quantity of international trade was necessary, foreign trade should be carefully controlled by governments to assure that its fluctuations did not interfere with domestic economic objectives. Keynes' article, "National Self Sufficiency," published in 1933, attacked the orthodoxy of an open world economy directly, and he suggested that: "Ideas, knowledge, science, hospitality, travel—these are the things which should of their nature be international. But let goods be homespun whenever it is reasonably and conveniently possible, and, above all, let finance be primarily national."[9]

Implicit in the views of Keynes and his co-thinkers was the conception of a "national capitalism" in which state intervention and planning would be used to maintain full employment of labor and of industrial capacity. Even if certain goods might more cheaply be produced abroad, the beneficial employment effects of producing them domestically would justify restricting imports. Hence, foreign trade would be oriented toward trading exports for only those goods that could not reasonably be produced at home. This kind of foreign trade could be organized through a series of bilateral trading arrangements that would assure other countries a stable market for certain of their commodity exports or through some type of state trading monopoly. Either of these approaches to the organization of trade would eliminate the need for extensive financing of trade through short-term lending. This would make it possible to eliminate most international capital flows, except some long-term investments organized through national or international authorities. Underlying this vision was the simple argument that, over the long term, whatever diseconomies might result from the failure to pursue international specialization would be more than outweighed by the gains that resulted from continuous, uninterrupted full employment and full capacity utilization.

The validity of this argument cannot be tested because national capitalism has not been seriously tried by any of the developed capitalist countries, either in the 1930s or later. Yet there seems little reason to doubt that national capitalism could be a perfectly viable economic form if it were attempted across a reasonably broad area. There would be a difficult period of transition as national self-sufficiency was expanded but, assuming that other nations would be willing to trade on the terms of the national capitalist countries, it is quite possible that, after the transition, the full employment benefits would outweigh the other costs. The most serious problem would be in achieving long-term dynamism of such an economy, since the use of trade controls would eliminate much of the external pressure for economic modernization. If internal competition were also weak, there would be little pressure for increased efficiency and industrial modernization. Yet even this prolem could be effectively minimized through vigorous government policy. If efforts were made to encourage internal competition, to monitor other nations' technical progress, and to provide government subsidies for research and development in critical sectors, it should be possible to create functional equivalents to the modernizing pressure of international trade.

It is the political viability of such a system that seems most problematic. Important sectors of the capitalist class would likely exert pressure to establish a more open system so that they could take advantage of foreign business opportunities and regain their freedom to send capital abroad. At the same time there would likely be pressure from the left for the state's intervention in the economy to be expanded even further. While those pressures might balance in the short term, they would probably become explosive over the long term. It seems that to maintain full employment and to manage foreign trade optimally, there would have to be a steady expansion in the power and size of the state. Sooner or later, this expansion would be perceived as threatening to overwhelm the already attenuated private sector, and this could easily generate a more intense struggle between the alternatives of a return to liberal capitalism or the elimination of the private sector. Since a return to liberal capitalism would threaten the security of the working class, it is conceivable that the political forces in favor of the elimination of the private sector would triumph. In sum, it is altogether possible that national capitalism would serve simply as a stopping point on the road to some type of socialism.[10]

Analyzing the viability of national capitalism is not simply an academic exercise. Although little was actually done before World War II to implement national capitalism, there is good reason to believe that after the war, there might have been substantial experiments with national capitalism among the developed capitalist countries. In fact, in the immediate postwar years, most of the countries of Western Europe resorted to the whole range of control devices associated with national capitalism—exchange controls, capital controls, bilateral and state trading arrangements. The reason these controls were not elaborated into full-scale experiments with national capitalism was that it became a central aim of United States foreign policy to prevent the emergence of national capitalist experiments and to gain widespread cooperation in the restoration of an open world economy. When one observer wrote in 1944: "The United States is, in effect, as concerns leadership, very nearly single-handed, trying to reverse the whole trend of policy and practice of the world at large in the field of economic relations since 1914, and especially in the ill-fated years since 1929,"[11] he was referring precisely to the effort to restore an open world economy against the powerful drift of other countries toward a national capitalism that would impose severe restrictions on international economic transactions.

The struggle by the United States to restore an open world economy after World War II encountered serious resistance both at home and abroad, but United States policy-makers used a series of brilliant political expedients to outmaneuver their opponents. By the late 1950s, their efforts to establish a new international monetary order that was characterized by a high level of openness were crowned with success, and the threat posed by national capitalism had been largely eliminated. But to understand the American struggle to restore an open world economy, it is necessary to know what the United States was struggling against. It is on this issue that the Cold War has seriously distorted much historical analysis of the post World War II period. The traditional Cold War perspective obscures the fact that both before and after the intensification of the Cold War, the struggle to prevent the emergence of national capitalism in Western Europe was central to U.S. foreign policy.[12] In short, American policy-makers were more concerned about national capitalism in Western Europe than they were with a possible invasion by the Red Army or successful socialist revolution. Of course, the struggle against national capitalism and the conflict with Soviet Communism were linked. First, the threat of national capitalism was greatest in those countries where the left was strongest, and it was feared that national capitalism would simply be a transition to socialism. Second, it was thought that national capitalist regimes would be vulnerable to political domination—"Finlandization"—by the Soviet Union because of their tendency to develop trade and friendship ties to the Soviet Union. But the point remains that it is necessary to place the Cold War in the context of the American effort to create a certain type of world economy.

This perspective shapes the emphasis of my study. My focus is on the relationship between Western Europe and the United States because those areas were the center of the choice between national capitalism and an open world economy. I touch on United States-Soviet relations only when they are relevant to the development of United States-European relations. This approach also means that I neglect United States policy toward other parts of the world, particularly toward the underdeveloped countries. Fortunately, this omission is not serious, because a number of recent studies have explored in depth the impact of the United States-designed international monetary order on the fortunes of Third World nations.[13]

PART I. *The Making of an International Economic Order*

TWO. *The Decline of the Nineteenth-Century Gold Standard*

The international monetary disorders of the interwar years shaped the outlook and strategies of the men who sought, during World War II, to plan for a different postwar world. The disorders of the 1920s and 1930s were rooted in the effort to restore the gold standard after World War I. The effort failed because it rested on the assumption that simply re-establishing the gold standard rules would automatically bring a return of the international monetary stability of the "golden age" between 1875 and 1914.[1] However, the relative stability of that earlier era had been based on a particular political and economic reality—Great Britain's dominant international position and special role in organizing the international monetary order. As that domination began to slip, the international monetary order that rested on it also began to decline. After World War I, Great Britain's diminished international position made it impossible for her to exercise effective international monetary leadership, and no other country was willing to assume Britain's responsibilities. The consequence was a prolonged period of international economic chaos, and this chaos gave rise to extended discussions of international monetary reform.

THE GOLD STANDARD AND BRITAIN

The nineteenth-century gold standard can be understood only in relation to Britain's unique role in nineteenth-century world economy. It was not simply that Britain provided the long-term and short-term capital necessary to keep the system going, but that the specific evolution of the world economy in the nineteenth century was integrally related to Britain's own economic development. As the world's strongest industrial and mercantile power, Britain used its diplomacy and military strength to create a world economy that gave maximum freedom to trade and investment. The gold-standard mechanism assured freedom of trade and the security of foreign investments. The use of sterling as the main international currency and the pivotal role of British bankers were, in turn, indications of the success of Britain in making the entire world its trading area.[2]

Because Britain benefited the most from the openness of the nineteenth-century world economy, it was logical for her to take the most responsibility to make the system work. While French and German bankers often insisted that recipients of foreign loans buy French or German goods, British bankers attached no such conditions because of their confidence that, in the long term, they would benefit, regardless of where the money was spent.[3] When Britain faced a balance-of-payments deficit, the Bank of England simply raised the bank rate, increasing British domestic interest rates. This drew short-term capital from the rest of the world and slowed the outflow of new capital. It often also slowed the pace of economic activity in Britain, resulting in increased unemployment.[4] But this was a price the British bankers were willing to pay to keep the international system working; and given the extreme dependence of British capitalism on the health of the world economy, this was a logical sacrifice. The fact that Britain imported more than she exported during much of this period, while logical for an island nation with limited natural resources, was also important for the health of the world economy. It provided other countries with a means to earn sterling, while continually expanding the size of the world market.

But Britain's economic supremacy was both the strength and the weakness of the nineteenth-century gold standard. As Britain's economic lead diminished with the rise of American and German competition, so too did the sturdiness of the gold standard. The actual mechanism continued to function up until the explosion of World War I, but signs of instability began to appear long before that. International progress toward freer trade was dramatic in the period from 1860 to 1880, but then it came to an end as country after country began imposing tariffs to protect emerging industries. The rush by the European powers to divide Africa at the end of the nineteenth century was a sign that Britain's "imperialism of free trade" was on the decline. Most significantly, the intensifying economic and political rivalry between Britain and Germany meant that "the loose federation of independent powers" that had dominated Europe since the Congress of Vienna was replaced by "two hostile power groupings; the balance of power as a system had now come to an end."[5]

While there was no discernible crisis in the gold standard in the period immediately preceding World War I, a system that was centered in Britain was obviously of questionable appropriateness to a world increasingly divided into hostile alliances.[6] There is also evidence that after 1900 the British had begun to abuse their unique role in the international monetary order. The British seem to have used their ability to run balance-of-payments deficits to avoid adjustment, rather than continuing to accept the sacrifice of domestic unemployment.[7] But it took the war itself to deal the gold standard a series of blows from which it would never recover. The outbreak of the war halted the flow of credit from London, and some loans were called in from other centers. The result was financial chaos: many countries declared moratoria on debt repayments or established exchange controls. While almost all countries continued to define their currencies as equal to certain quantities of gold, they acted to halt international gold shipments and close down free gold markets. This meant that a gold standard continued to exist only in the trivial sense that currencies were based on gold.[8] Over the long term, the enormous costs of the war for Britain diminished her economic superiority further, thus eroding the specific conditions that had sustained the nineteenth-century gold standard.

THE INTERWAR YEARS

With the end of the war, efforts were begun to restore the workings of the gold standard. But restoration could only mean re-establishing the old forms bereft of their substance. Britain lacked the economic power to fulfill the role she had played in the prewar system, and the United States, her major economic rival after the defeat of Germany, was not prepared to fill the vacuum. Nevertheless, politicians and bankers acted as though there were no obstacles to the re-creation of the smoothly functioning monetary system of the prewar period. This failure to perceive the changed circumstances proved very costly: the malfunctioning international monetary system was a major cause of the world depression of the thirties.

Even the restoration of the forms of the gold standard was not a simple matter in the chaotic aftermath of World War I. The immediate postwar years were years of worldwide inflation fueled by the backlog of consumer and business demand from the war years, the rapid expansion of money in circulation during the war, and the most intense period of Europe-wide class conflict since the revolutions of 1848.

Fixed exchange rates, for currency as in the prewar period, were not possible. Most currencies were allowed to float—their exchange rates relative to other currencies were determined by the foreign exchange market without a fixed gold parity. This experiment in floating exchange rates was accompanied by massive movements of flight capital and intense speculative pressure against weaker currencies.[9]

For advocates of gold standard restoration, the monetary chaos of the early twenties simply reinforced their view that Europe badly needed the stern discipline of the gold standard and fixed exchange rates. International conferences were convened to pressure national governments to take steps to halt inflation, including the balancing of governmental budgets. In addition, a number of means were devised to build up national monetary reserves to levels at which the currencies could be stabilized in relation to gold. But since total gold supplies appeared insufficient to provide adequately large reserves for all of the European countries, a deliberate effort was made to substitute currency reserves for gold.[10] And some countries did significantly increase the share of their reserves held in the form of balances in foreign countries, particularly in Britain.[11] In addition, a series of stabilization loans were floated by consortia of private and central bankers to provide additional resources to support new gold parities in a number of countries. Even with these measures, the stabilization of European currencies in relation to gold dragged on through much of the 1920s: the German mark was stabilized in 1924, the pound in 1925, the French franc in late 1926, and others even later.[12]

Once stabilization of a currency appeared practical, another problem emerged. At what exchange rate should the currency be fixed? As long as other currencies were still fluctuating wildly, it was difficult to calculate an exchange rate that would balance a country's accounts. Returning to the prewar rates was unimaginable for the countries of continental Europe because inflation had reduced these currencies to a fraction of their prewar values. But some currencies, particularly the dollar, had remained unchanged in their gold values since before the war. This meant that severe deflation would be necessary before high-inflation countries could stabilize at a new parity, or else their currencies would be wildly undervalued. There were also political limits to the amount of deflation that could be tolerated. France and Belgium, for example, carried out extremely painful deflations but still ended up fixing new parities that left their currencies substantially undervalued. The undervaluing of the French franc, in particular, would contribute to later international instability by creating the illusion of French financial strength.[13]

The British responded to the dilemma of choosing an appropriate exchange rate by deciding to return to the prewar parity. In contrast to the French franc, which had lost 60 to 70 percent of its prewar value by 1920, the pound had lost only 20 percent of its value at its postwar low. And by 1923, the pound had returned to within 10 percent of its prewar rate, so that restoration of the old rate seemed plausible. The motivations for returning to the old price were primarily considerations of international financial confidence. It was thought that, while return to prewar parity might well have serious domestic costs, it was necessary to bear those costs to set an example for other countries that were being pressured by the British to exercise greater monetary discipline. Many also argued that the prewar parity was necessary to restore levels of international confidence in British currency and British banking high enough for Britain's prewar role to be resumed. There were also very hard financial considerations behind the establishment of a high price for sterling. A reduction in the price of sterling from the prewar parity would mean that the holders of Britain's still massive foreign investments would receive their interest and profits in pounds that were worth less than those they had originally invested.[14]

The key point, though, is that American cooperation and assistance were of great importance in making the British return to the old rate possible. For American international bankers, the stabilization of the pound was seen to be in America's interest because it was a major step toward the stabilization of the general European monetary situation, a prerequisite for the attainment of American financial and trading ambitions.[15] Two lines of credit to Britain—one of $200 million with the Federal Reserve Bank of New York and the other of $100 million with a syndicate headed by J.P. Morgan & Co.—were negotiated in 1925 to assure that sterling could be maintained at the prewar parity once that parity was fixed. Benjamin Strong, the governor of the New York Federal Reserve Bank, and Montagu Norman, the autocratic and eccentric governor of the Bank of England, also reached agreement on the coordination of British and American interest rates. American interest rates were to be kept below British rates, an agreement which had some benefits for both sides. It was hoped that the higher British rates would exercise a downward pressure on British prices, which were still on the average 10 percent higher than American prices for goods in international trade. But the interest rate differential would also discourage a movement of short-term funds from London to New York, since such movement of funds would prove destabilizing for the pound. Finally, the Americans hoped that the lower rates in New York would divert a certain share of long-term international borrowing from London to New York, increasing New York's share of a profitable business.[16]

The British, with this American assistance, succeeded in re-establishing the prewar parity in May 1925. The achievement was immediately and devastatingly criticized by John Maynard Keynes. He argued that the prewar parity was too high and would impose painful and useless deflation on the British economy. British goods would be priced out of world markets, resulting in widespread unemployment in Britain. Keynes believed, contrary to classical doctrine, that the working class would successfully resist a direct reduction in its wages, so that even a high level of unemployment would fail to bring British wages and prices down to an internationally competitive level. He anticipated that the main results of the new parity would be intensification of class conflict in Britain and persistent unemployment.[17] He did not have to wait long for his predictions to be vindicated: 1926 brought a bitter coal strike that escalated into Britain's first twentieth-century general strike. Furthermore, throughout the 1920s Britain experienced continuing high levels of unemployment—"the intractable million" remained unemployed despite booming economies elsewhere in the world.

THE UNITED STATES' ROLE IN THE 1920's—

The American role in stabilizing the pound was only the most obvious sign that the United States was exercising successful leadership in the world economy. During the twenties the United States was the major supplier of capital internationally, providing funds for relief, for currency stabilization, and for a variety of other productive and nonproductive purposes. Britain's domestic capital needs made it impossible for her to continue exporting capital at the prewar rate, but the United States had sufficient capital to take up the slack.[18] The problem was that the United States was not prepared to take on all of the responsibilities that Britain had assumed earlier. The subordination of domestic economic interests to the health of the world economy was not practical for the United States. Whereas Britain's domestic economic health had been completely dependent on the world economy, the

United States' position was different. Although the United States had the economic power to play a central role in organizing the world economy, the role was not forced upon her; she was much less dependent than Britain on either exports or imports to make her economy work. The result was that the United States played its international economic role haltingly and irresponsibly.[19]

The forces that pushed the United States into a world economic role were the largest industrial firms and the banking interests centered on Wall Street. The close of the American frontier in the 1890s and the rise of the national corporations in the period from 1880 to 1916 had created a sizable business interest oriented toward foreign markets. The major American banks that had organized or emerged from the great industrial combines of the pre-World War I period were envious of the international role played by the British banks and eager to get a piece of the international banking action. Although there were divisions over the best means to displace the British, these bankers were united in a vision of an American international banking empire.[20]

Though these economic groups controlled the "commanding heights" of the American economy and had a powerful impact on the national leadership of both political parties, there were very real limitations on their power to shape American foreign policy. A variety of interests in the society opposed an internationalist foreign policy for different reasons. Most of the economy was organized in small and medium-sized businesses and farms, and the men who ran these gave little thought to foreign markets and were generally wary of foreign political entanglements. Many of these businessmen and farmers organized to lobby for protectionist tariffs and against internationalist policies. Organized labor was also generally protectionist, and its left wing (far more formidable before, during, and immediately after the war than in the later twenties) was vocally opposed to an internationalist foreign policy. Beyond these organized groups was public opinion, which tended to be isolationist—resistant to a policy of sustained involvement in foreign affairs.[21]

The clash between internationalists and anti-internationalists resulted in a foreign policy of limited internationalism.[22] The internationalists could build mass support for certain kinds of policies at specific times, but they could not build support for a sustained or consistent internationalist policy. They often had to settle for partial measures, since organized groups and public opinion would not tolerate what would have been the rational and sensible move. This meant, specifically, that the United States would become involved in European economic and political problems, often by providing credits, but then find itself unable to carry through on its original involvement. Whereas British diplomacy and military power could usually be relied on to support British finance in the prewar period, American finance often found itself floundering with partial and inadequate support from Washington.

U.S. involvement in World War I can be understood in this context, as can the bitter legacy of that involvement. Opposition to American entrance into the war was widespread and deeply rooted, and it persisted despite deliberate and devious efforts to create a war mood. But entrance into the war was seen as essential by internationalist groups, and they eventually succeeded in building a pro-war coalition with a uniquely American blend of jingoistic (especially anti-German) and idealistic ("The war to end wars") propaganda. Still, severe repression against anti-war forces was necessary to prevent the Left from capitalizing on popular hostility to the war.[23] Fortunately for the internationalists, the war was settled after a relatively brief, albeit costly, American involvement. But it was in the period after the war that the costs of a widely unpopular foreign involvement began to accumulate.

The most obvious cost was the defeat of American participation in the League of Nations. Wilson's vision that the United States would play a central role in European and world politics through the League was destroyed by anti-internationalist opposition. However, Wilson's position had been weakened by the opposition of other internationalists to some of the economic provisions of the Versailles Treaty. These tactical differences among the internationalists strengthened the position of the anti-internationalists, and the resulting defeat of the League broke whatever momentum toward an American world role had been generated by the war effort.[24]

Ultimately more important than the fate of the League was the issue of war debts and reparations. Throughout the twenties the United States insisted on repayment of the loans made to Britain, France, and other allies during the war. As long as France and Britain were obligated to repay these debts, they insisted that Germany pay to them the enormous reparations agreed on at Versailles. But the strain on the German economy of paying the reparations was serious, and it threatened to disrupt the German political and economic order and weaken European stability in general. Hence, the American insistence on repayment of war debts was a major source of international instability in the twenties and early thirties. But the American refusal to reconsider the war debts can only be understood as a result of the fear by successive administrations that American public opinion would not stand for a writing-off of those debts. Because many Americans still felt that the war had not been their war, they would not accept the idea of letting France, England, and other countries off the hook for the aid that they had been given.[25]

Since cancellation of the war debts seemed impossible, the American internationalists coped with the problem through a number of ad hoc arrangements that probably did more harm than good over the long term. Starting in 1923, debt-funding agreements were negotiated that allowed for repayment of the war debts over sixty years at an average interest rate of 2.1 percent. "While these debt-funding agreements gave the 'appearance of repayment' they in fact reduced the combined outstanding indebtedness of the Allied nations by approximately 43%."[26] This was partial cancellation behind the public's back, but it did little to relieve the situation because the European powers were not pressured to make parallel concessions on reparations. The American contribution to the reparations part of the problem was to lend Germany huge sums of capital, which were then used to finance the reparations payments. The Dawes Plan in 1924 and the Young Plan in 1929 both established schedules for German reparations payments linked to new international loans to Germany. In both plans American initiative was crucial, though American participation in the negotiations was nominally nongovernmental in deference to anti-internationalist sentiment. Aside from the American shares of the Dawes and Young plans, huge quantities of U.S. direct and portfolio capital flowed into Germany between 1924 and 1929.[27]

However, when the New York stock market boom of the late twenties absorbed all available funds, the halt in the movement of capital to Germany placed severe pressure on the German economy, because it had become dependent on the American capital flow. Since many of the loans had not been used for productive purposes in Germany, the result was an intensification of Germany's difficulties; she still had heavy reparations obligations along with now sizable debts to U.S. bondholders.[28]

The German experience was the most blatant example of the shortcomings of New York as an international capital market. The problem was not simply that the funds for foreign investment dried up during the stock market boom, but that foreign investments were often highly speculative and irresponsible. New York, as an international financial center, lacked the wisdom of London—gained through past speculative disasters—in deciding on the soundness of foreign loans. Foreign lending became a fad in the United States, and American underwriting houses pressed foreign governments to borrow more because new bond offerings meant large new commissions. To make matters worse, there was virtually no governmental regulation of American offerings of foreign bonds. Herbert Hoover fought for a policy of government review of foreign lending, but his efforts were frustrated by business opposition and interagency conflicts.[29]

In two other areas the use of American economic power fell far short of the British example. The first was trade policy, where the weakness of the internationalists was most evident. Campaigns by the internationalists to open foreign doors to American goods required some reciprocal American effort at tariff liberalization, but these efforts were consistently blocked by protectionist domestic interests. The internationalists attempted to take the tariff issue out of politics by reliance on a tariff commission and on flexible tariff rates, but these ploys did not fool the protectionists, and tariffs moved even higher. Where Britain in her creditor years had run a consistent import surplus, the United States in the twenties and early thirties ran a consistent export surplus. The fact that the Europeans could sell hardly any manufactured goods in the U.S. market meant that there was no easy way for them to earn dollars to pay interest on dollar loans and the Allied war debts.[30] Furthermore, U.S. protectionism was an obstacle to tariff liberalization elsewhere, because European countries were reluctant to make tariff concessions to each other that would have to be passed on to the United States under the most-favored-nation principle.[31] In short, it was not simply that the United States failed to lead in tariff reduction in the interwar period, but that the United States was a major obstacle to trade liberalization.

Finally, the U.S. Federal Reserve Board refused to manage the economy according to the gold standard. While this refusal made sense in terms of the health of the domestic economy, it served to intensify the adjustment problems of other economies. During much of the twenties, but particularly in the period 1919-1924, the Federal Reserve authorities acted to neutralize the expansionary effects of large gold imports into the United States. In so doing, the Fed prevented a domestic price rise which might, in turn, have slowed the gold inflow by weakening the American competitive position internationally. Much of the gold that flowed into the United States during this period was a consequence of capital flight from unstable social and economic conditions in Europe. Nevertheless, by sterilizing the gold inflows, the United States placed an even greater burden of adjustment on European economies already facing severe economic problems.[32]

THE CRISIS

If Britain's economic weakness and America's inability to use its economic power to bolster the international economy were the sources of the structural weakness of the interwar gold standard, it still took the American stock market crash and the gathering international depression to destroy the experiment of gold standard restoration. While economists continue to debate the precise relationship between the stock market crash and the beginning of the industrial depression,[33] it seems clear that American economic problems contributed significantly to the European financial crises of 1931. Those crises, in turn, led to a worsening of the world depression by destroying the existing international monetary order.

The German and Austrian economies were particularly vulnerable to financial crisis because of the size of their short-term foreign obligations. Germany alone owed $2.5-3 billion on short term in 1931, most of it to Britain and the United States. Because the depression led to a drying-up of the flow of international capital, and a decline in prices, production, and income that placed banks and governments in an increasingly precarious position, the danger of a cumulative financial panic increased. The failure in May 1931 of Austria's largest commercial bank that had sizable short-term debts to Britain, the United States, and Germany made the threat clear: "A chain of deposit withdrawals, panicky runs on the banks, and moratoria could spread from Austria to Germany and even to Britain and the United States."[34]

An effort was made to avert this chain reaction by international action first to defend the Austrian schilling and later the German mark. Standstill arrangements were negotiated under which Austria's creditors agreed not to withdraw their funds, and two $14 million loans were floated by a group of central banks to protect the schilling. But these efforts were too little and too late to halt the accelerating crisis. The standstill arrangements increased suspicion of other currencies because the freezing of liquid assets increased the likelihood that other countries would be unable to cover their own international obligations. So, while the Austrian banks did remain open and the schilling remained at parity, the crisis moved on to Germany. Rumors of a German debt moratorium led to intense pressure on the mark, with the Central Bank losing some $250 million in gold and foreign exchange in the first three weeks of June 1931.[35]

Again, efforts were made to organize an international credit to defend the mark, but these efforts became hopelessly entangled in the issues of reparations, war debts, and Franco-German relations. The Germans had been agitating for years for an end to the reparations burden, but American intransigence on the inter-Allied debts had blocked any revision of the reparations settlements. In the context of the deepening financial crisis of 1931, Hoover finally made a compromise offer. He called for a one-year moratorium on Allied debt payments, conditional on similar action on reparations payments. But by this time the French, whose financial position was quite strong because of an inflow of gold in response to the undervaluation of the franc and the as yet mild impact of the world depression on France, were determined to force German political concessions quid pro quo for actions to alleviate Germany's financial problems. The French were reluctant to accept Hoover's moratorium proposal. They feared that an agreement on a halt in reparations would rob them of the lever they were using to force Germany to abandon her plans for a customs union with Austria and to stop German agitation for a revision of her eastern frontiers. By the time the French agreed to the Hoover moratorium, Germany was in need of another major international credit to defend the mark, and the French pressed the same demands as a condition for their participation in the loan.[36]

The French felt that the Germans had no choice but to accede to their political demands to avoid a currency debacle. The British were far more sympathetic to Germany's plight, and they were eager to push through a solution to the crisis that would destroy all the remnants of the harsh peace agreement of Versailles. The problem was that the British lacked the resources to come to Germany's aid alone; Britain needed the cooperation of the United States and France. But the U.S. position was closer to France's than to Britain's, because the United States was still unwilling to accept anything more than a one-year moratorium on debts. The United States was not prepared to accept the "new start" in Europe that the British wanted. This configuration of positions gave the French effective veto power over a loan agreement, since the United States would not participate in a loan effort without France. But the German government could not accede to the French demands because of pressure from the Nationalist and National

Socialist right wing. When no loan was forthcoming, the Germans did not allow a currency debacle. Instead, they began building up a structure of exchange controls that prevented a further outflow of gold and capital. They began closing their economy off from the rest of the world economy.[37]

In retrospect, the German violation of the rules of the gold standard is hardly surprising, but at the time it came as a bolt from the blue. For the first time, techniques that had previously been used only during war and the aftermath of war were being used in peacetime. To men whose consciousness had been shaped by gold standard orthodoxy, it was such a radical departure that their failure to anticipate such a response by Germany is understandable. In fact, even after Germany's first resort to exchange controls during the 1931 crisis, it was widely thought that Germany would abandon the controls after a brief interval. However, the ever-worsening international depression made such a return to orthodoxy unattractive, and instead the exchange controls of 1931 were the first step in Germany's construction of a closed economy—insulated from the rest of the world economy by controls, bilateral trading arrangements, and manipulated currency values.

The freezing of foreign assets in Germany in July 1931 served to move the focus of the financial crisis to Britain. The freezing of British liquid assets in Germany led to doubts about the strength of the pound. In addition, the German and Austrian crises had led other Continental countries to withdraw funds from London to bolster their own liquidity. To make matters worse, the British budget deficit increased suspicion that the Labour government was not committed to, or capable of, defending the pound's parity. Once again, the response to the crisis was to seek international credits to defend the pound. The quid pro quo, however, was severe action to cut the budget deficit, including reductions in unemployment benefits. The debate over the budget cutbacks split the Labour government, and MacDonald, the Prime Minister, with Snowdon, his Chancellor of the Exchequer, allied with the Conservatives to form a National Government that would defend the pound by any means necessary. Nevertheless, the pressure against the pound continued, despite further domestic deflation and additional foreign loans. By September 1931, the National Government was forced to abandon the gold standard, and once again the pound was allowed to float.[38]

The British action decreased available international liquidity further and led to significant withdrawals of gold from the United States. Central banks throughout the world raised their interest rates to defend diminished reserves, pushing the level of economic activity even lower. Fluctuating exchange rates made international trade more difficult, as did the growth of tariff barriers designed to protect national markets from cheap imports. The value of world exports fell a third from 1931 to 1932. In addition, the abandonment of the gold standard in its traditional center dealt a serious blow to international business confidence, already at a dangerously low point. In sum, the financial crises of 1931 had the effect of pushing the world economy deeper and deeper into depression.[39]

NATIONAL RESPONSES

Despite the worsening of the world economic crisis, efforts to find international solutions continued. The Lausanne Conference in June 1932 resulted in British endorsement of the German decision to repudiate all further reparations payments, disregarding an American plea for a three-to-five-year postponement, after which reparations payments would resume. No decision was reached on Allied debts, and progress on other fronts was minimal, but another conference was called for, to be held in London in 1933. This was to be a world economic conference that would include official American representation. But when the conference convened, it was dominated by a desire to return to the gold standard, and those countries that had maintained fixed gold parities pressured countries with floating rates for stabilization. It was hoped that stabilization of currency values would restore the international trade that had been disrupted by fluctuating exchange rates. Even this modest, and no doubt insufficient, proposal was defeated when Franklin D. Roosevelt made clear the American refusal to accept any restrictions on United States freedom of action in financial matters.[40]

Whether or not the United States could have played a productive role at the London conference, the fact was that Roosevelt had opted by this point for a nationalist solution to America's economic problems.[41] His message to the London conference made clear his belief that "a sound internal economic system" would contribute more to world economic recovery than any international agreement. Roosevelt and his chief advisors had come to the conclusion that the gold standard and the international economy in general were having a deflationary impact on the American economy. They believed that cutting the dollar loose from gold, a step that had been taken in April 1933 when gold exports were halted, was necessary for domestic prices to rise and for economic recovery to get under way.[42]

Roosevelt and Henry Morgenthau, his chief economic confidant, were notoriously inept in their grasp of economics. In those early New Deal years, they were strongly influenced by eccentric economic theories and theorists. Their motivation for devaluing the dollar relative to gold was apparently based on a belief that this would automatically lead to inflation of domestic prices, considered a precondition for domestic recovery. But the devaluation did make some contribution to economic recovery for reasons quite different from the initial theoretical justification. The devaluation provided an American response to the 30 percent decline in the value of the pound and the depreciation of other currencies. It maintained the competitiveness of American goods, so as to protect the continuing U.S. export surplus. More importantly, the devaluation made it easier to pursue a program of domestic reflation. It is possible that if Roosevelt had attempted to carry out the New Deal programs while maintaining the old parity, the threat of inflation and of the loss of business confidence would have led to a major run on the dollar far more serious than the brief panic that occurred after the British went off gold. Such a dollar crisis would have been a major blow to recovery and to the stability of the New Deal political coalition.[43]

Roosevelt and Morgenthau essentially stumbled onto a sound Keynesian foreign economy policy. Throughout this period, Keynes argued that the only way toward international recovery was for nations to pursue expansionary domestic economic policies while defending themselves from the deflationary impact of the world economy. Since gold standard mechanisms operated to discourage the pursuit of domestic policies of deliberate expansion through deficit spending that Keynes advocated, he favored some measures to insulate the nation's or region's economy from the world market. For Britain, partial insulation was accomplished by the consolidation of a sterling trading area with a system of preferences and relatively fixed exchange rates. For the United States, already much less dependent on the world market than Britain, the dollar devaluation accomplished the same function.[44]

The domestic policies of the Roosevelt administration, however, were less consistently expansionary than Keynes would have liked.

The administration generally avoided resort to deliberate deficit spending, and a loss of nerve in government intervention led to a new economic decline in 1937. Nevertheless, government actions to expand available credit, to increase payments to the unemployed, and to carry out an extensive public works program did succeed in expanding the economy between 1933 and 1937. That these policies failed to restore full employment is hardly remarkable in light of the failure of business investment to return to predepression levels. In fact, the degree of recovery that was achieved was almost entirely attributable to government policies, since the expected recovery of business investment failed to materialize.[45]

Britain's domestic policy response to the depression was even less Keynesian or expansionary than the American, but the British went much further in reshaping their foreign economic policy to resist the pressures of international deflation. The major domestic move by the British government was an effort to cheapen credit through a lowering of interest rates, but little was done by way of public works. This was consistent with the largely external origins of the depression in Britain, which made the government's prime concern the improvement of the country's international economic position. As with the United States, devaluation was a major step, because it increased the competitiveness of export goods while protecting the home markets from imports. This protection of the home market was augmented by the imposition of a general tariff and the inauguration of a system of imperial preference. Imperial preference was designed to expand Britain's trade with the dominions and the colonies: the tariff advantage would make it possible for British suppliers to displace other suppliers in those markets. Britain also negotiated a number of bilateral trading arrangements in which other countries agreed that all the sterling they earned by selling to Britain would be used either to buy British goods or to repay previously defaulted loans. Finally, the British embargoed long-term capital exports, except within the Empire, and almost all the capital that was exported was used to finance British exports.

Restrictions on capital exports were a necessary consequence of the government's cheap money policy. Freedom to export capital and a policy of cheap credit to stimulate domestic recovery could not coexist. The other measures—devaluations, imperial preference, bilateral agreements, and an expanded system of export credits—fitted together as parts of an effort to reverse the 30 percent decline in British exports from 1929 to 1931 that had brought the depression to Britain's already stagnant economy. Even if full export recovery was not attained, the system of preferences and trading arrangements could protect Britain from a further precipitous drop in its exports.[46] Since most countries were responding to the depression by building high tariff walls and by depreciating their currencies, the British policies were defensive efforts to create a stable market for British exports.

Other nations went even further than Britain in making their international transactions secure against further disruptions. Germany, under the Nazis, developed an elaborate system of exchange controls, managed currency rates, and bilateral trading arrangements that assured her continued export markets and allowed her to pursue an extensive program for domestic recovery and mobilization. The German domestic program was more far-reaching and more successful than those pursued elsewhere: between 1933 and 1938, six to seven million unemployed German workers went back to work, virtually eliminating unemployment. The feat was accomplished by an enormous expansion in the government's expenditures for public works and, of course, for armaments, made possible by the government's terroristic control of the economy. But the more radical domestic measures that the fascist government implemented required much more extensive controls over foreign economic transactions than had previously been attempted. The Nazi policy was essentially one of complete closure; domestic economic conditions came to have almost no relation to foreign transactions.

Exchange controls dated back to the mark crisis of 1931, but they became progressively more elaborate and more general. All foreign exchange earned by private capitalists was turned over to the government, and a system of import licenses operated to assure that the foreign exchange would be used only for essential goods. In addition, a system of bilateral clearing was initiated with certain countries to conserve foreign exchange and to protect export markets. The bilateral trading agreements involved government intervention to assure that the transactions with another country would balance. Germany was able to manipulate these clearing arrangements with weaker countries, especially those in southeastern Europe, in such a way as to force the weaker countries to buy German goods at an inappropriately high mark-exchange rate. While the Germans did not devalue the mark, their exercise of market power through a highly centralized trading system proved to be as effective as, or more effective than, devaluation in improving the country's foreign trade position.[47]

In general, the actions during the depression years by individual countries to protect their economies and to defend their shares of international trade had the inevitable effect of shrinking the total quantity of international trade.[48] The thirties began with the enactment of the notoriously protectionist Smoot-Hawley tariff in the United States, and as other countries began feeling the impact of world depression they responded either with new tariffs or increases in existing tariff levels. International efforts at negotiating tariff truces or reductions were largely ineffective. In 1934, the U.S. Congress passed the Reciprocal Trade Agreement Act, which gave authority for bilateral tariff reductions that would be generalized under the most-favored-nation principle. While the act was a significant departure from traditional American protectionism, the negotiations under the act's authority did little to liberalize international trade.[49]

At any rate, by 1934, tariffs had become increasingly less significant as an obstacle to international trade as more countries imposed quantitative restrictions or initiated bilateral clearing arrangements. These devices became more general because some countries resorted to competitive depreciations to push sales of their exports while limiting imports. The pattern of devaluations, beginning with Britain in 1931 and the United States in 1934, reinforced the use of nonmarket controls by making international prices significantly less realistic. Again, efforts were made through the thirties to reach international agreement for the dismantling of controls, but generally nothing resulted other than detailed studies of the problem.[50] One of the few positive achievements of international cooperation during this period was restricted to exchange rates. In 1936, France, England, and the United States approved the Tripartite Monetary Agreement, which called for the three countries to assist each other in stabilizing their currencies on a daily basis. This did not constitute a full stabilization, since the British and French currencies were still floating, but it meant that the three nations would cooperate in managing the degree of day-to-day fluctuation.[51] This mutual cooperation acted to discourage further competitive devaluations, and since Belgium, the Netherlands, and Switzerland subsequently joined the agreement, it did provide some stability for a portion of the world economy.[52] It did nothing, however, to ease mounting international tensions. As the rush to war gained momentum through the late thirties, nothing was done to build on the foundations of the Tripartite Agreement. In a world divided into increasingly antagonistic blocs, there was no possibility of negotiating a new international monetary order that could satisfy both the status quo powers—France, Britain, and the United States—and the new imperialist powers that were seeking a redistribution of international resources—Germany, Italy, and Japan.[53]

LESSONS OF THE INTERWAR PERIOD

The central problem of the international monetary system during the twenties and thirties was the inability or unwillingness of the United States to take on the responsibilities that Britain had carried in an earlier epoch. However, even when one accepted this diagnosis, it was still possible to draw quite different lessons for the future. One lesson was that the attempt to return to the pre-World War I level of international openness was utopian, because no country had the resources or freedom to stabilize the world monetary order in the way that Britain had during the nineteenth century. In this view, the increasing necessity of stable domestic economic conditions required a much diminished level of international openness, so that the future called for the development of a system of "national capitalisms." A second lesson also accepted the impossibility of any single country filling Britain's role, but it argued that this function could be internationalized. The creation of an international institution for stabilizing the international monetary order would make possible more openness than the proponents of the first lesson assumed to be possible. A third lesson also accepted the critique of American policy, but its adherents insisted that U.S. failures were not inevitable. If given a second chance, the United States could stabilize an international order with a high level of openness. All of these conclusions figured prominently in the planning of a new international monetary order for the post-World War II world.

There were several formulations of the first lesson, some placing more emphasis on the shortcomings of U.S. policy and others concentrating on the impossibility of organizing an open world economy in light of changes in capitalism.[54] But the conclusions essentially come to the same thing: the major responsibility of a national government is to maintain high levels of domestic economic activity. Once this goal is reached, countries can then worry about international cooperation, but international measures must never interfere with domestic full employment. If domestic economic recovery and maintenance of high levels of demand require extensive use of controls over trade and capital flows, that is a price that must be paid.[55] On the other hand, if a structure of international cooperation can be created that can reconcile domestic stability and high levels of international trade, so much the better.

It is not far from the first lesson to the second: the advocacy of an international mechanism for stabilizing the world economy. In fact, Keynes himself moved away from his earlier advocacy of national capitalism when he proposed the creation of an International Clearing Union for the post-World War II world. Keynes' idea was that the clearing union would operate to protect national economies from deflationary pressures by providing free access to an international pool of credit. With the clearing union making deflation unnecessary, it would be possible to dismantle some of the structure of controls imposed during the period of depression and war. Keynes' plan recognized the difficulty of creating an international organization that would have independent powers; his clearing union was essentially a bookkeeping device that allowed countries to build up international debts or credits within certain generous limits.[56] Other plans did emerge for a more active international agency whose actions would be analogous to those of Britain in the pre-World War I gold standard, but these plans also recognized the necessity of avoiding deflationary pressures.[57]

The third lesson was based on a less fundamental critique of the organization of the world monetary system in the twenties and thirties. While recognizing the failure of the gold standard in that period, the proponents of this view argued that the failure was due to the unfortunate legacy of World War I and to errors in American and British economic policies. The idea was that the system could be made to work again without fundamental changes, provided the United States played a responsible role. The United States had the capacity to stabilize the world economy as well as Britain had in the earlier period. This was the position of the American internationalists who wanted a second chance to fill Britain's shoes by making the United States the financial center of the world economy. But the American internationalists were acutely aware that the strength of the anti-internationalist forces in the United States had contributed to the first failure. Their intention was to see to it that American political and military internationalism, thrust upon the nation once again by the Japanese attack on Pearl Harbor, would continue long past the end of the war and would provide a sound underpinning for U.S. economic internationalism.[58]

THREE. *Bretton Woods and the British Loan*

Those who wanted a "second chance" for the United States to manage an open world economy had to defeat their national capitalist opponents both abroad and at home. Both sets of opponents posed formidable problems. It is one of the stranger ironies of international monetary history that the men who actually dominated U.S. international monetary policy during World War II were far more sympathetic to national capitalism than to the idea of an open world economy. In fact, the International Monetary Fund, designed to be the central institution of the postwar monetary order, was shaped initially by national capitalist assumptions. This meant that the proponents of a second chance had a double problem. They had to find ways to blunt the efforts of their domestic antagonists, while they continued the struggle against foreign resistance to their vision.

Both "second chancers" and their domestic opponents held positions of power within the wartime American government. That different views on such a critical issue could coexist in the same administration can be explained by the complex nature of the Roosevelt administration's political base, particularly during the war. The administration was a coalition of two different sets of interests. One included the traditional centers of power in the Democratic party—the primarily agricultural South, the urban political machines, and representatives of the dominant business and financial interests. The other comprised the newly emergent industrial unions and representatives of Midwestern agrarian progressivism. During the war, when the cooperation of the industrial unions in maintaining production was absolutely essential, the political power of the second set of interests was enhanced. The industrial unions had not yet been politically tamed, and the political-economic problems of the Great Depression had not yet been solved. This meant that there were substantial differences on fundamental issues of domestic and foreign economic policies between the two basic elements of the Roosevelt coalition.[1]

THE UNITED STATES POLICY DEBATE
DURING WORLD WAR II

The U.S. foreign policy debate during the war did not center on the traditional issue of opposition or support for a U.S. international role. The shock of Pearl Harbor and reports of Nazi atrocities silenced most of the advocates of non-involvement in foreign, particularly European, conflicts.[2] (That debate would, however, re-emerge with the end of the war when once again Americans realized that military efforts alone had failed to guarantee a generation of peace.) The wartime debate concerned the nature of the international role that the United States would play. The foreign policy alternatives can be described as business internationalism and idealistic internationalsim, but the meaning of these terms can be understood only in the context of differences over domestic economic policies.

The central issue facing American society at the end of the war was the future health of the economy. Only the mobilization for war had finally dragged the U.S. economy out of depression, and anxiety was widespread that high levels of unemployment would return with the end of huge government expenditures for military goods. To make matters worse, the United States had enormously increased its industrial capacity during the war, so that it was capable of producing many more goods than before the war.[3] If purchasing power had been inadequate to keep factories running at full capacity before the war, what would happen after the war when a much higher level of demand would be necessary to keep the factories running? It was widely recognized that this danger of postwar depression would not fully emerge until a few years after the war was over. High levels of foreign demand for U.S. goods and the backlog of domestic consumer and industrial demand would probably sustain the economy for a couple of years.[4] But what would happen once foreigners became capable of supplying their own needs and domestic consumers had completed their long deferred purchases paid for with the savings that they had accumulated during the war?

A debate over the best way to maintain high levels of employment had begun during the New Deal, but the Roosevelt administration had not resolved the issue. Rival factions within the New Deal coalition had effectively blocked the pursuit of any one particular economic strategy, so the New Deal economic policy was an amalgam of different policies. Proponents of business self-management, antitrusters, and advocates of national economic planning co-existed within the Roosevelt administration, although the relative strength of the different groups varied at different periods. The advocates of national economic planning were often Keynesians, and they believed that a greatly expanded government role in managing the economy was a prerequisite for full employment. They tended to favor deficit spending by the government for social services and industrial infrastructure projects—such as TVA—and the coordination and regulation of private business investment by the government. The weakness of the national economic planners was revealed during the 1937-38 recession when the strength of conservative opinion forced a premature cutback in government expenditures and then blocked for a period the use of the most modest pump-priming measures. In short, business interests both within and outside the New Deal were able to block the programs of the national planners until World War II armament-spending produced full employment again.[5]

The end of World War II, however, and the possible need for strong antideflationary measures to maintain high levels of employment threatened to bring the triumph of national economic planning.[6] The business community was almost unanimous in its opposition to such an outcome. There were several strands to this opposition. One was the deeply held commitment to fiscal conservatism: governments were obliged to balance their budgets and live within their means. This, in turn, grew out of a belief that "the government that governs best, governs least." An expanded government role would mean higher taxes, which endangered profits, and it would increase the likelihood that government would limit the sphere of profit-making activity. The entrance of the government into producing electric power or building housing would tend to displace the capitalists already providing these services. The national economic planners would, furthermore, create a planning apparatus that businessmen feared would reduce them to mere functionaries with little sphere for independent decision-making, free of outside interference.[7]

The national economic planners tended to have close links with the labor movement, particularly with the new industrial unions, and this was another source of business hostility. The business community feared that a national planning apparatus would increase the power of the labor movement and make it impossible to roll back some of the gains made by labor during the depression and the war. Redistributive taxation was seen as a threat to existing wealth and to the maintenance of an adequate pool of relatively cheap labor. Businessmen feared that if all the reforms of the national economic planners were carried out, the combination of high corporate taxes and reduced power of capitalists over their employees would cause American goods to be priced out of the world market.[8]

Certain elements in the business community realized, however, that if the economy did slip back into depression conditions, the triumph of the national economic planners or even something worse was inevitable. These elements favored some government action to bolster the economy, but their preference was for measures that maximized business freedom. They favored tax incentives to encourage business investment, an emergency public works program, and government spending that could stimulate private investment without encroaching on traditional business activities. But it is striking that, even among the strongest advocates of high or full employment in the business community, there was a lack of clearcut programs.[9] They hoped that somehow the dire predictions of the stagnationists[10] would be proved false and that business investment would shoot up strongly enough to sustain the economy without a greatly expanded governmental role. But they were unable to provide a coherent argument for why this was likely to happen, and they seem to have doubted that it actually would happen.

In the context, the idea of an export surplus took on a special importance. If the United States could export to the rest of the world $5-10 billion dollars worth of goods more than it imported, this would have a stimulating effect on the domestic economy. It would be the equivalent roughly of the same amount of business investment or new government spending. Such a surplus might make an equivalent amount of government spending unnecessary, and it would avert an enormous expansion of the government's economic role. In short, the combination of strong investment in new housing, a reasonably high rate of new business investment, and a large export surplus conceivably could assure a return to high levels of employment.[11] Furthermore, a high level of exports could avert painful reorganization for certain sectors of the economy that were overbuilt during the war. The export of large numbers of machine tools, for example, could prevent a crisis in that critical industry that had dramatically expanded its capacity during the war.[12]

There were, however, a number of difficulties involved in maintaining a substantial export surplus. In fact, the U.S. export surplus had been one of the major elements of U.S. international irresponsibility in the interwar years. Because of this experience, it was widely recognized that the United States could not maintain an export surplus forever. The repayment of the loans that had been granted to finance the export surplus would make it necessary eventually to run an import surplus. It was generally argued, however, that the United States could run an export surplus for a long as ten to twenty years, and hopefully over that period of time it would be possible to reorganize the economy so that full employment could be maintained even with an import surplus. Another problem was the need to finance the surplus year after year. It was expected that American direct investment abroad could account for a small part of the flow, but there would be a need for greatly expanded portfolio investment. But it was unclear whether private investors would be willing to put their money into foreign bonds in the quantities necessary to finance the export surplus. Finally, the most basic problem was assuring the availability of foreign markets on a scale large enough to make this kind of export surplus possible.[13]

For this final reason particularly, the idea of an export surplus was very closely intertwined with the idea of an open world economy. The vision of an open or multilateral world economy had informed the policies of American governments since the turn of the century. The focal point of the vision was that all countries in all areas of the world would be open to trade and investment flows from elsewhere. The privileged access of imperial countries to their colonies would be eliminated, as would the bilateral payments and trading systems created in the 1930s by Germany, Japan, and, to a lesser degree, Great Britain. A multilateral world economy would be one in which trade and capital flowed across national boundaries in response to the law of supply and demand without political interference favoring one nation or another. The cheapest producer would triumph in trade regardless of the nation of origin. Multilateralism would also eliminate the necessity to balance international accounts with particular countries or regions. For example, a U.S. deficit with raw-material-producing countries could be offset by surpluses with other industrialized countries, so long as those industrialized countries were able to earn surpluses somewhere else. A world economy organized along these lines would create the markets and investment opportunities needed to assure both a large export surplus and the continued growth of the largest American banks and industrial firms.[14]

The national economic planners tended to have little sympathy either for the export surplus or for the multilateral vision. They favored a world system made up of national capitalisms because of the priority they gave to the pursuit of full employment. They believed that the maintenance of high levels of employment and the development of national planning throughout the world should take precedence over the opening of economies to the free flow of investment and trade. The national economic planners were suspicious of private foreign investment, which they considered to be more destructive than constructive, and they were eager for foreign countries to be relieved of the deflationary bias of the gold standard. In short, they wanted all countries to be able to pursue expansionary Keynesian policies.[15]

While the national economic planners opposed the internationalism of the internationally oriented business community, they did not favor a return to the irresponsible international role that the United States had played in the twenties and thirties. The national economic planners understood that the enormous productive capacity of the United States guaranteed it a central role in the world economy, but they hoped that U.S. economic resources could be used to promote global economic and social reform. These radical Keynesians favored not only a second New Deal at home, but an international extension of the New Deal as well. They believed, for example, that the United States should move to reduce its tariffs so that other countries would be able to sell more of their goods in the United States. They also hoped for the creation of international institutions that would funnel capital into underdeveloped areas without the strings of private capital.[16]

The irony of the idealistic internationalism of the national economic planners was that it ultimately served to strengthen the business internationalists. For both foreigners and Americans, the images of global reforms that sprang from the national economic planners served to legitimize the exercise of U.S. power on a global level. At home, many who had resisted the idea that the United States should extend its power internationally were convinced by the images of an international New Deal. Abroad, the reality of U.S. foreign economic policy was effectively hidden by the skillful invocation of the rhetoric of the idealistic internationalists. The clearest example of this was the International Monetary Fund itself. It was originally conceived as an instrument to facilitate expansionary domestic economic policies, but it eventually became another means to impose the deflationary discipline of the gold standard.[17]

While the eventual defeat of the national economic planners in the struggle to shape domestic and foreign economic policy was a result of the weakness and disorganization of the social forces—particularly the labor movement—that stood to gain from their programs, there was also a serious flaw in their vision of a reformed capitalism. The idea that government spending for social services and social infrastructures—urban reconstruction, transportation, education, health facilities, electrification, and so on—could maintain demand at high enough levels to maintain full employment was based on a static view of the economy. Government spending in these areas would serve to increase productivity in the rest of the economy dramatically, so that even more government spending would be necessary to absorb the ever-increasing flow of goods and services if high employment were to be maintained. Only if an increasing portion of government spending was wasteful could this continuous expansion of the government's role be averted. In short, national capitalism in the U.S. would have required a progressive narrowing of the private ownership of the means of production.[18]

TREASURY VS. STATE

Within the Roosevelt administration, the foreign policy conflict between business internationalists and the national economic planners manifested itself in a struggle between the Treasury Department and the State Department.[19] In most twentieth-century administrations, the top position in the Treasury Department has generally been held by a key banker or industrialist. FDR's administration followed this pattern at the outset but, when top Treasury officials (including Dean Acheson) objected to some of his financial policies, FDR elevated his long-time friend from Dutchess County, New York—Henry Morgenthau—to the secretaryship. Morgenthau is a difficult person to analyze as an economic or political thinker. Although a man of wealth and a firm defender of capitalism, he shared in the popular antipathy of the thirties toward Wall Street and the giant corporations. He blamed the economic difficulties of the nation on the selfishness of these interests, but at the same time he believed that it was the responsibility of the private sector to set things right again. Within the Roosevelt administration he fought for the orthodoxy of a balanced budget and resisted those who believed in spending their way to recovery. At the same time, he never abandoned the New Deal commitment to the third of the nation who were "ill-housed, ill-clad, ill-nourished." His commitment to the poor can be traced back to his involvement as a young man in the settlement house movement on the Lower East Side of New York. As Treasury secretary, he was an advocate of tax reform schemes that were mildly redistributive. He was also a consistent and strong antifascist who often clashed with others in the administration whose opposition to fascism was less fervent.[20]

Morgenthau's quasi-populist perspective is captured in a passage in his diaries when he comments on negotiations that were going on with Admiral Darlan, the Commander of the French fleet, who had a record of collaboration with the Nazis.

There is a considerable group of rich people in this country who would make peace with Hitler tomorrow, and the only people who really want to fight are the working men and women, and if they once get the idea that we are going to sit back and favor these Fascists, not only in France but in Spain which is what we are doing every day . . . , these people are going to have sit-down strikes; they're going to slow up production, and they're going to say, what's the use of fighting just to put that kind of people back into power?[21]

Morgenthau drew around him in the Treasury Department a group of young economists who shared some of these political attitudes, but who were also committed to Keynesian economic theories, theories that Morgenthau continued to oppose. Nevertheless, apparently aware of his own economic ignorance, he relied heavily on these assistants and gave them a good deal of freedom. The most important of these assistants was Harry Dexter White, who carried much of the burden of formulating the Treasury Department's proposal for foreign economic policies.

White was one of the most influential national economic planners. He came from an immigrant Jewish family in Boston and had worked his way through school, earning a Ph.D. in economics at Harvard. He joined the Treasury Department in 1934 and moved up fairly rapidly. He is often described as brilliant, but pushy—an embodiment of the stereotypical aggressive Jew.[22] His position on the left wing of the New Deal, his apparently difficult personal style, and his extraordinary influence on U.S. foreign economic policy during much of the war goes far to explain his dramatic downfall. He was publicly accused in 1948 of being a communist agent by Whitaker Chambers and Elizabeth Bentley, and he died while struggling to clear his name. The charges rested almost entirely on the highly questionable testimony of Chambers and Bentley. A federal grand jury that heard some of the charges refused to indict White, and a massive FBI investigation into White's past apparently failed to turn up convincing corroboration of the Chambers-Bentley charges.[23] While there is little reason to give credence to the specific charges against him, there can be little doubt that White had close ties to other individuals in the left wing of the New Deal who were, or had been, in the Communist party. It must be remembered that during the war years, the American Communist party under Earl Browder opposed class conflict in the interests of the war effort. There was little in the relatively conservative Communist party line of that time which conflicted with the views of many non- or anti-communist national economic planners.[24]

The extent to which White's views diverged from what would become the mainstream of U.S. foreign economic policy becomes clear when one examines the State Department during the war years. Roosevelt's Secretary of State was the venerable Cordell Hull, who was a firm adherent of Wilsonian internationalism. Hull's lifework was the reduction of trade barriers, a strategy which he believed was the way forward to world peace—"unhampered trade dovetailed with peace; high tariffs, trade barriers, and unfair competition with war."[25] While others in the State Department might not have fully shared Hull's somewhat naive identification of multilateralism with world peace, they shared his commitment to reducing foreign barriers to U.S. trade and investment. Dean Acheson, who had returned to the administration for wartime duty in the State Department after having left with some bitterness in the early thirties, had considerable responsibility for economic planning. His testimony before a Congressional committee in 1944 has often been quoted:

We cannot go through another ten years like the ten years at the end of the Twenties and the beginning of the Thirties, without having the most far-reaching consequences upon our economic and social system. . . . When we look at that problem we may say it is a problem of markets. You don't have a problem of production. The United States has unlimited creative energy. The important thing is markets. We have got to see that what the country produces is used and is sold under financial arrangements which make its production possible. . . . You must look to foreign markets.

If you wish to control the entire trade and income of the United States, which means the life of the people, you could probably fix it so that everything produced here would be consumed here, but that would completely change our constitution, our relations to property, human liberty, our very conceptions of law. And nobody contemplates that. Therefore, you find you must look to other markets and those markets are abroad. . . . [26]

This amounts to a clearcut attack on the views of the national economic planners.

Another key figure in the State Department was William Clayton, who came to the administration from Anderson, Clayton, Inc., the world's largest cotton-marketing firm. Clayton was an outspoken advocate of an export surplus, as the following passage from a radio speech in 1945 indicates:

Today we are exporting over $14 billion worth of goods a year. We simply can't afford after this war to let our trade drop off to the two or three billion figure it hit in 1932 during the depression. . . . Some of our best economists estimate that we will probably have to sell $10 billion worth of goods a year abroad if we want to have relatively high level employment and a national income in the neighborhood of $150 billion. In other words, we have got to export three times as much as we exported just before the war if we want to keep our industry running at somewhere near capacity.[27]

While there were many internal divisions and conflicts within the State Department,[28] Acheson's and Clayton's views were representative; and they implied a common set of views on the future role of Russia, Germany, and Britain in the world economy. The intertwining of ideology and economic interest served to make State Department planners highly suspicious of the Soviet Union, especially as the extension of Soviet power into Eastern Europe threatened to close these areas off to American trade and investment. As to Germany, the State Department view was that the revival of its industrial strength was desirable. This was based on an assessment that German industrial recovery was a precondition for Western Europe's return to multilateral trade.[29] It also reflected a conviction that only a strong Germany could resist the extension of Russian power further into Europe. While the State Department placed great emphasis on Anglo-American ties, there was a strong desire to maintain enough leverage on British policy to force Britain to accept multilateralism in the postwar period. The State Department was committed to the opening of the British Empire to American trade and investment and was willing to use whatever means it had to assure a favorable outcome.[30]

Treasury attitudes were closest to State on policy toward Britain. White and Morgenthau were also concerned with gaining leverage over Britain, but their concern was not access to the British Empire. They wanted to assure British compliance with their own plans for organizing the international monetary system. On Germany and Russia, the differences with State's view were much greater. Morgenthau's hatred of Nazism led him to propose the pastoralization of Germany, and while White might have favored a somewhat less punitive policy, he did help Morgenthau draw up his famous plan. Morgenthau's and White's hostility toward Germany was not tempered by the consideration that influenced State Department planners. If Western Europe was going to adopt national capitalism, Germany's industrial strength would not be critical for European recovery. Furthermore, White and Morgenthau did not see a need for a strong Germany as a counterweight to Soviet power. In an ironic twisting of Cordell Hull's thinking, the Treasury planners argued that the best way to deal with the Soviet Union was by developing strong economic ties with the Soviets. Since White and Morgenthau were relatively comfortable with state trading arrangements, they believed that these economic ties could develop without forcing changes in Soviet trade practices. They proposed a substantial loan to the Soviet Union for reconstruction, to be tied to substantial Soviet exports of raw materials to the United States. In retrospect, this appears as a farsighted anticipation of the developments in U.S.-Soviet relations more than a quarter of a century later.[31]

THE ORIGINS OF THE IMF

In light of the significant differences between State and Treasury thinking, it is not surprising that Cordell Hull attempted to keep the Treasury Department out of foreign economic policy making. He did not succeed, however, and Harry Dexter White was given the go-ahead to develop a plan for an International Stabilization Fund that would have broad economic responsibilities. The inability of Hull and the State Department to maintain a monopoly over foreign economic policy planning was based on a number of factors. Morgenthau's close personal ties to Roosevelt assured him some input into foreign policy making, and FDR's distrust of the State Department probably led him to encourage competition over foreign-policy preparation. Roosevelt might have believed that this kind of bureaucratic infighting would maximize his own ability to choose among foreign-policy options. Roosevelt also understood the conflict between national economic planners and free traders and, while his own preferences remain obscure, his desire to maintain the wartime domestic political alliance would dictate a strong role for the national economic planners in the key area of foreign economic policy.[32]

White apparently began thinking about and drafting plans for some kind of international monetary agency during the spring and summer of 1941. He was formally asked by Morgenthau to develop such a plan after the attack on Pearl Harbor. During the course of 1942 and 1943, the plan went through a number of drafts, reaching its final form only at the Bretton Woods Conference in July 1944. White's influence on the plan was enormous because of the monopoly of technical knowledge that he and his assistants held. Morgenthau, in particular, was completely dependent on White because of Morgenthau's lack of economic sophistication. However, the plan that White finally devised was substantially influenced by two outside forces. The first was the input of the British, and especially of Keynes. This influence was exercised through Keynes' introduction of a rival plan and through a series of extended negotiations at which Keynes was the chief British representative. The second influence was the need for Congressional approval of the plan. "White considered himself a shrewd judge of the political mood; rather than risk rejection he would cut his plan to an acceptable pattern." Although White would succeed in maneuvering his plan through Congress, his conservative opponents had their revenge. The accommodations that White was forced to make, combined with subsequent alterations by financial conservatives, would prevent the Fund from playing the role White had envisioned for it.[33]

The evolution of White's thinking and the original premises of his plans are accessible to us because the early drafts of his plan have survived. A draft from April 1942 includes specific proposals for an international bank and a stabilization fund, as well as explanations of White's thinking.[34] The draft indicates the ambitious nature of White's project and the extent of his divergence from multilateral orthodoxy. The bank is the stronger of the two institutions in this draft:

The Bank was to have a capital stock of $10 billion, half paid in immediately by members in the form of gold and local currency. It was "designed chiefly to supply the huge volume of capital to the United and Associated Nations that will be needed for reconstruction, for relief, and for economic recovery." It was designed also to eliminate world-wide fluctuations of a financial origin and reduce the likelihood, intensity, and duration of world-wide depressions; to stabilize the prices of essential raw materials; and more generally to raise the productivity and living standards of its members. It was specifically empowered to buy and sell gold and securities of participating governments, to discount and rediscount bills and acceptances, to issue notes, and to make long-term loans at very low rates of interest.[35]

In short, the bank was to be an international central bank with extraordinary powers that were to be used to achieve global full employment. It was to be supplemented by a stabilization fund that would have resources of around $5 billion, which would be used for providing credit for countries in balance-of-payments difficulties. Instead of being forced to deflate their economies, countries would be able to draw on the fund to tide them through until their balance of payments improved.

The unorthodoxy of White's initial plan is indicated by the quantity of international credit that would have been made available. The rather modest $5 billion available in the stabilization fund was to be augmented by the bank's formidable lending power. This power was not limited to the $10 billion capital stock. The bank would have credit-creating powers; it would be able to issue loans at a multiple of its basic capital. In addition, the bank would be able to sell notes on national capital markets to raise additional funds. One analyst has computed that the bank and fund together could have added some $60 billion to international liquidity.[36] The potential inflationary consequences of such an expansion of international liquidity was sure to horrify any international banker. But even without that potential, international bankers could hardly look favorably on a plan that rendered them totally superfluous by placing all their functions in an international agency.

White intended that these institutions should prevent a return to international depression and should minimize the need for painful and disruptive balance-of-payments adjustments. His concern was to create an international monetary order in which countries would be able to pursue systematically full employment policies without the danger of exhausting their international reserves. Under the gold standard, countries that were attempting to expand their economies could face an outflow of gold that would force them to deflate. White's alternative was to assure enough international credit so that countries could continue with expansionary policies. To avoid the competitive devaluations of the thirties, White's plan made changes in exchange rates difficult. Balance-of-payments adjustment would be accomplished under normal conditions through very mild disinflationary policies in deficit countries, expansionary policies in surplus countries, and changes in the level of international lending or borrowing.

Specific aspects of White's plans are interesting for what they reveal about his perspective, and, in some cases, for the contrast with the Articles of Agreement that were eventually approved at Bretton Woods. The early vision of the fund and the bank was of institutions that would have a great deal of influence over domestic economic policies. To be sure, this influence was to be used to coerce member nations to pursue policies consistent with global full employment, but national governments would be forced to abandon some of their sovereignty over economic policy. For example, changes in exchange rates could be blocked by the fund—a significant limitation on national freedom of action. And if four-fifths of the votes in the fund indicated disapproval of "any monetary or general price measure or policy" of a member government on the grounds that it would contribute to serious balance-of-payments disequilibrium, the country involved would have to change its policy.[37] In other ways, however, White's plan was designed to enhance the power of national governments. He saw the fund as a means to improve the ability of governments to control undesirable capital exports. Here again he was responding to the experience of the interwar years, when governments were forced to contend with the massive outflow of capital caused by their own citizens seeking security from social unrest and from reformist government policies. France, in particular, suffered from massive capital flight during the period of the Popular Front, with the result that the government was forced to abandon some of its economic and social reforms.[38] White's plan made it a condition for membership in the fund that governments agree

(a) Not to accept or permit deposits or investments from any member country except with the permission of the government of that country, and

(b) to make available to the governments of any member country at its request all property in form of deposits, investments, securities of the nationals of that member country.[39]

White recognized that this "would constitute another restriction on the property rights of the 5 of 10 percent of persons in foreign countries who have enough wealth or income to keep or invest some of it abroad," but this was a step he was willing to take. The White plan also provided that the fund could deny use of its resources to countries that failed to take action to half this kind of "illegitimate" capital outflow.[40]

White argued for these capital controls on the grounds that "The assumption that capital serves a country best by flowing to countries which offer most attractive terms is valid only under circumstances that are not always present." He made a similar argument about free trade. While arguing that the fund should encourage the reduction of trade barriers, he argued against a return to laissez-faire. He pointed out that "the theoretical bases for the belief still so widely held, that interference with trade and with capital and gold movements, etc., are harmful, are hangovers from a Nineteenth Century economic creed," the soundness of which he doubted. He went on to argue:

The task before us is not to prohibit instruments of control but to develop those measures of control, those policies of administering such control, as will be the most effective in obtaining the objectives of world-wide sustained prosperity. To cast aside certain effective instrumentalities of control because they may be and have been abused, is just as foolish as it would be to rely solely on the self-interest motive of individuals as a means of solving our economic problems.

He also noted that

"Free Trade" policy grossly underestimates the extent to which a country can virtually lift itself by its bootstraps in one generation from a lower to a higher standard of living, from a backward agricultural to an advanced industrial country, provided it is willing to pay the price.

This argument against an insistence on the universal adoption of free trade could hardly have endeared White to the advocates of an open world economy. It is not surprising that White went on to argue that membership in the fund should not be restricted on the grounds that countries had socialist economies.

There is likely to be, during the next decade or two, a variety of economic systems and it would seem desirable that these should not be discouraged from cooperating with the others so long as they are willing to agree to conduct their international economic affairs in accordance with principles acceptable to the United Nations.[41]

THE MODIFICATIONS OF THE WHITE PLAN

White abandoned the ambitious design of the international bank relatively quickly, and the fund became the major focus of his attention. When the plan for the fund was published in mid-1943, it was without a design for the bank. When the bank proposal was finally made public, it had been stripped of the trappings of an international central bank, for the bank had been reduced to a more traditional international lending agency. This change was clearly dictated by political realism; there was little chance of getting Congress to vote the large American subscription if the bank was going to be a radical departure from traditional financial principles.[42]

The other major change between the 1942 and 1943 drafts concerned the power of the fund to intervene in domestic decision-making. The fund would no longer be able to veto domestic economic measures that were thought to contribute to disequilibrium. Instead, countries were simply required to give consideration to the views of the fund on such policies. This change also probably reflected sensitivity to Congressional opinion.[43] Many in Congress would be extremely reluctant to cede any economic sovereignty to an international agency. The idea that some foreigners would try to tell Americans how to run their economy was bound to arouse the ire of many legislators. The fund's right to veto exchange rate changes was retained in this draft, but White probably reasoned that that could be slipped by Congress because of the unlikelihood of a change in the dollar-gold parity. Whether this reasoning was correct became irrelevant because this provision did not survive the confrontation with Lord Keynes.

The 1943 draft was the basis for the negotiations that took place between British and U.S. treasury experts in September and October 1943. Keynes came to these negotiations with his own plan that reflected his analysis of the needs of the British economy in the postwar period. As late as 1941, Keynes believed that the best course for Britain was some kind of bilateral trading system—national capitalism applied to the whole sterling area.[44] However, by early 1942, he had become convinced that Britain's best option was participation in a multilateral world economy. He took pains to argue that the bilateral path would not work because both the sterling area and the use of sterling as an international currency could not survive under the compulsory arrangements of a bilateral order. But he understood that there were dangers involved in a return to multilateralism, and his plan was designed to minimize those risks.[45]

Keynes worried about three problems in particular. First, he placed the greatest importance on Britain's pursuing full employment policies after the war, and he opposed any international monetary order that would interfere with this goal. Second, he recognized that the war had greatly reduced Britain's international investments and expanded her debts, so that Britain would no longer be able to rely on investment earnings to finance her extensive imports of food and raw materials.[46] This meant that Britain would have to expand her total exports dramatically or else be forced to reduce her standard of living significantly. This would make Britain dependent on international credit until exports could be expanded, and it gave Britain an interest in international trade liberalization. Finally, Keynes, like many others abroad, was concerned that the U.S. economy would be allowed to slip back into depression or that the United States would again behave irresponsibly in its international transactions. He wanted to create a monetary order that was not dependent on the vagaries of American politics.[47]

Keynes' plan was for an international clearing union. It was essentially an overdraft facility that would grant credit to deficit countries automatically when they ran payments deficits. Payments deficits or surpluses would appear as debits or credits in the books of the clearing union. The clearing union would be able to provide a total of $26 billion in credit, but each country would have a maximum credit quota determined on the basis of its share of international trade.[48] The large quantity of available credit meant there was little pressure for adjustment on deficit countries. The fact that surplus countries would simply accumulate credit balances rather than real assets, and that they would be required to pay interest on credit balances above a certain size, meant that there would be strong pressure for surplus countries to return to balance-of-payments equilibrium. In short, surplus countries would have to adjust by inflating their economies and by increasing their imports, while deficit countries would be largely free to pursue their own policies. The plan would give Britain freedom for domestic experimentation while assuring access to significant quantities of international credit. It would mean that even if the U.S. economy slipped into depression or ran a major export surplus, it would have little negative effect on the rest of the world economy.

Once serious negotiations began between White and Keynes, White's plan became the basis for discussion. There was no way that the United States Congress would accept a plan such as Keynes' under which the United States would be forced either to extend almost unlimited credit or to bear the main burden of balance-of-payments adjustment. Nevertheless, Keynes continued to fight for the principle embodied in his plan: easy access to credit for deficit countries and pressure on surplus countries to adjust. The Joint Statement by Experts which grew out of the Keynes-White discussions reflects the continuing differences between the two sides and the compromises that were made.[49]

Probably because the British remained unsatisfied with the amount of credit available in the fund, it was agreed that the fund would operate only in a limited way during the transition period after the end of the war. This way the fund's resources could be conserved, while most countries continued to resort to the use of controls during the transition period. It was only realism to recognize that the fund and a less ambitious bank could make only a relatively small contribution to the enormous tasks of relief and reconstruction. It would be at least several years before countries could move to eliminate their wartime economic controls and free transactions on current account. The Joint Statement recognized that controls would continue and simply urged that countries move to eliminate controls "as soon as possible." After three years, countries that continued to impose controls on current transactions would have to consult with the fund, but the fund would not have the power to force abandonment of such controls. For White, who had earlier defended the use of controls under certain circumstances, this did not represent a compromise with his principles. It did, however, represent another step away from his original ambitious plans that would have dealt with both the transitional and the long-term problems of the world economy.

On the issue of the obligations of the surplus countries, a complicated compromise was reached. White was probably reluctant to accept any provision that would appear to Congress as a limitation on U.S. freedom of action, but Keynes insisted that there must be some means to force adjustment on surplus countries. The result was the scarce-currency clause, which gave member countries the right to discriminate against the exports of a country whose currency had been declared scarce by the fund. If, for example, the United States ran a chronic balance-of-payments surplus, other countries would be likely to buy dollars from the fund to cover their dollar deficit. If this reduced the fund's holdings of dollars to a low enough point, the fund would begin apportioning dollars among different purchasers and countries would have the right to take discriminatory actions against dollar goods. This would presumably apply pressure on the United States to take other actions to adjust its balance of payments.[50]

The final compromise was on the broader issue of how interventionist the fund would be. Keynes' preference was, of course, for a passive fund that would grant credit without conditions. We have already seen that White had toned down some of the interventionism of his early plans, but he was reluctant to give in completely to Keynes, again because of fears of Congressional disapproval. While Congress would undoubtedly resist provisions that would limit U.S. freedom of action, there would also be opposition to paying the United States' quota if there was no guarantee against irresponsible use of the fund's resources. Because White was in fundamental agreement with Keynes' preference for an agency that would facilitate domestic economic expansion, the compromise was weighted toward free access to fund resources. A member country was entitled to buy another member's currency in exchange for its own currency on the following conditions:

(a) The member represents that the currency demanded is presently needed for making payments in that currency which are consistent with the purposes of the Fund.

(b) The Fund has not given notice that its holdings of the currency demanded have become scarce. . . .

(c) The Fund's total holdings of the currency offered . . . have not increased by more than 25 per cent. of the member's quota during the previous twelve months, and do not exceed 200 per cent of the quota.

(d) The Fund has not previously given appropriate notice that the member is suspended from making further use of the Fund's resources on the ground that it is using them in a manner contrary to the purposes and policies of the Fund; but the Fund shall not give such notice until it has presented to the member concerned a report setting forth its views and has allowed a suitable time for reply[51]

This meant, in short, that members could draw a quarter of their quota a year for five consecutive years, and that it was up to the fund to make a case that a member should be denied access to fund resources. Nevertheless, the ambiguities in this compromise became the basis for a later shift in the fund's philosophy away from the ideas of both White and Keynes.

THE FUND AND ITS CRITICS

With relatively minor changes, the Joint Statement was transformed into the Articles of Agreement of the International Monetary Fund at a conference of forty-four nations at Bretton Woods, New Hampshire, in July 1944. In fact, the major preoccupation of the Bretton Woods discussion appears to have been the size of different countries' quotas in the fund. The quotas were an issue because of the prestige involved and because a country's quota determined its voting power. The delegation from the Soviet Union made a major issue of the size of its quota, and the issue was resolved only through extensive last-minute negotiations.[52] By and large, however, the other forty-two nations had little impact on the agreement reached between Britain and the United States. As Leon Fraser of the First National City Bank noted:

We are told that 44 nations agreed to this. I think a more exact statement would be that 3 or 4 groups of very expert chaps got together and wrote a plan, and then took it up with 44 other technicians, stating that "this is what the United States and Great Britain are willing to stand for with you."

Of course, in the condition of the world as it was at the time of those negotiations, these fellows said, "Sure, why not?" They had nothing whatever to lose. They looked to us for their military salvation and for their economic salvation, and any proposal within human reason put forward by representatives of the United States would in the nature of things be acceptable.[53]

The international institution that was formally created at Bretton Woods can be described as follows:

1. It was designed to operate in the relatively stable international conditions to be reached after a postwar transition period. Members would be allowed to maintain restrictions on current transactions for five years, after which they would have to consult with the fund about continuing the use of the restrictions. Only under extraordinary circumstances, however, could the fund demand that restrictions be dropped even after the five years.

2. Member nations were pledged to maintain their currencies at a constant exchange rate relative to other member currencies. They were to do this by buying or selling their currency on their foreign exchange market. This provided an elegant compromise between government intervention to maintain stable exchange rates and the determination of exchange rates by market forces. If, for example, the exchange rate of a particular currency was unrealistically high, then a country would find its international reserves depleted in the effort to support the exchange rate. A country could change the exchange rate, but changes of more than 10 percent had to be approved by the fund.

3. Member nations would remove all restrictions on current transactions. They would be allowed, however, to maintain restrictions on the transfer of capital. Under certain circumstances, the fund could make controls over capital flows a condition for access to its resources.

4. Countries with deficits were expected to finance those deficits partly through depletion of their reserves and partly by buying the currencies they needed from the fund. Once their payments position began to improve, they would simultaneously build their reserves back up and restore their position with the fund. This way the fund's resources would be continually restored and available for other countries. In other words, the fund agreement did not require repayment of

drawings in a specific period, but it relied on repayment as a country's position improved.[54]

5. Countries with chronic deficits would eventually exhaust their right to draw on the fund. At that point the fund could impose conditions for further access to its resources. Countries with chronic surpluses would be likely to have their currencies declared scarce and would be subject to discrimination by member nations.

While the design of the fund was an ingenious attempt to establish international monetary order, the design was flawed by the fund's inability to deal with the problems of the postwar transition period. The fund would not have resources to loan to countries to speed their abandonment of exchange controls. And until other countries abandoned their controls, the dollar would be the only currency in the fund that could be used. These inadequacies of the fund were quickly recognized by its critics. The most prominent of these critics, John Williams, a Harvard economics professor and vice-president of the New York Federal Reserve Bank, polemicized widely against the IMF proposal on the grounds of its irrelevance to the actual situation of the postwar world.[55]

Williams' alternative to the fund was "The Key Currency Plan." The core of this plan was a substantial U.S. loan to Great Britain to underwrite the international role of sterling. Bolstered by the loan, Great Britain would pursue multilateral trade policies, restore London as an international capital market, and cooperate with the United States in the joint management of the international monetary order. The loan itself would represent a clearcut break by the United States with the irresponsibility of the 1920s and 1930s; it would symbolize the American determination to guarantee the health of the world economy. Furthermore, the restoration of London as an international capital market would be critical in providing the financing for trade within Western Europe and between Western Europe and the Sterling Area. This financing would be necessary to provide an alternative to bilateral trading arrangements and other national capitalist practices. Sterling financing was indispensable because it was recognized that the inevitable postwar scarcity of dollars would make it impossible to finance that trade through dollar credits.

At base, Williams' Plan was a call for the restoration of the gold standard. It reflected the interests of the American international bankers who opposed the IMF proposal, not because it would be ineffective, but because they feared it would be too effective. The international bankers opposed the Keynesian emphasis on economic expansion because they considered it to be inflationary. They preferred the discipline imposed by the gold standard, and they feared that access to the fund's resources would destroy that discipline forever. The international bankers did not want a return to international depression conditions, but they believed that this could be avoided without major efforts by governments or international agencies. They feared that extensive national or international governmental intervention would eliminate the role that private international bankers had historically played.[56]

A brief review of the workings of the gold standard makes it easy to understand the position of these bankers. Under the gold standard, countries did not impose any controls on international trade or capital transactions. If a particular government began pursuing inflationary policies or an extensive program of social reform, it might find itself facing a significant payments deficit as foreigners and domestic citizens withdrew capital from the country. To resolve the deficit without imposing controls, the government would have to take measures, usually deflationary, to regain the confidence of the international banking community. Such measures would be a precondition for gaining loans from private bankers or central banks to finance the deficit and for winning the return of the capital that was withdrawn. This provided an effective control mechanism to limit the domestic policy options of governments. As long as the control mechanism functioned, individuals and firms could invest in foreign countries with confidence that the value of their investments would not be destroyed by a rapid inflation in that country.[57]

The international bankers perceived that the fund would effectively destroy this control mechanism. The fund's toleration, and in some cases encouragement, of capital controls would make it possible for member countries to insulate themselves from the threat of capital withdrawals. And easy access to the fund's resources would provide an alternative source of short-term funds, so that governments would not be forced to borrow from private bankers on their conditions. The consequence would be that international investments would no longer be safe. For example, whenever a moderately left-wing government came to power, it would be able to pursue inflationary policies with capital controls, so that international investors would be unable to withdraw their funds. The investors would have to sit idly by as inflation threatened to reduce the international value of their assets sharply.

The international bankers lobbied hard to block Congressional approval of the fund. While there was presumably significant support for their views in the State Department and in other branches of the government, the bankers' task was difficult.[58] Considering the widespread fears in the United States and abroad about a return to depression conditions, it was difficult for these financial interests to make a case for free market ideas. In many cases they relied on arguments about the fund's effectiveness rather than confronting the issues of financial discipline and foreign investments. They did succeed, however, in gaining one important concession. The U.S. Treasury agreed to an amendment to the Bretton Woods Agreement Act that would establish a National Advisory Council on International Monetary and Financial Problems which would include the secretaries of the Treasury, State, and Commerce, the chairman of the board of governors of the Federal Reserve System, and the chairman of the board of the Export-Import Bank. This Council would be empowered to decide how the U.S. vote in the fund would be used. The idea of the Council was to counteract and minimize the power of the Treasury over the fund; the State Department, which was more trusted by the bankers, attempted unsuccessfully to gain the chairmanship of the Council.[59]

The failure of the powerful international bankers to block outright Congressional approval of the fund can be attributed to two factors. First, the fund had come to embody the hopes of many for a rationally ordered international economy. It was a symbol of America's good intentions on the international front. The defeat of the fund by Congress would be analogous to the defeat of American participation in the League of Nations after World War I, a sign that the United States was unwilling to play a responsible role in the world. The blow to American international credibility would have been enormous.[60] Second, the large American vote in the fund assured the United States of effective veto power over the operations of the fund. With the exercise of this power controlled by the National Advisory Council, there was a good possibility that the fund could be prevented from taking actions that would damage the interests of the American international business community. There was also a possibility that U.S. power in the fund could be used to transform the fund into a more traditional financial operation. In fact, Randolph Burgess, president of the American Banking Association, argued for such a strategy in his testimony before the Senate. Burgess realized that the Senate was going to approve the fund, but he urged reform of the fund so that it would act to enforce the gold standard discipline rather than subvert it:

Here is an administration in power in X country that is careless politically, that is careless economically. Now, in my judgement it isn't clear enough here that that administration might not draw funds from the fund to carry on an uneconomic policy, and I think economically it is possible to bore in a little more on our wording on that score. But the main conclusion I would draw is that you want to fence this fund in so that it is very carefully safeguarded.[61]

Other bankers made specific proposals for modification, including the elimination of the scarce-currency clause and the imposition of a requirement that all drawings be repaid within eighteen months. Though the Senate rejected these modifications as conditions for United States membership, the bankers would succeed over the next few years in their struggle to transform the fund.

THE BRITISH LOAN

Even before the Congressional debate on the IMF had gotten under way, events had unfolded that would destroy White's and Morgenthau's ambitions to shape the postwar world. The critical event was the death of FDR in April 1945. FDR's passing and Truman's accession to power led almost immediately to Morgenthau's departure from Washington. Morgenthau's power had rested on his friendship with Roosevelt; his relationship with Truman was characterized by mutual distaste. Truman replaced Morgenthau with Fred Vinson, a conservative Southern Democrat with orthodox views on international and domestic economics. White stayed on in the Treasury, but his influence was vastly diminished because of the departure of his protector. More important than the decline in Morgenthau's and White's personal fortunes was the decisive turn in American foreign policy away from the direction they had favored. It is possible, even probable, that, had Roosevelt lived, he would eventually have been forced to repudiate the Treasury's foreign policy. Nevertheless, during his lifetime, the Treasury influence on U.S. foreign policy was important, and at times dominant. With FDR's death, the influence of White's and Morgenthau's thinking on foreign policy was largely eradicated, and State Department foreign policy conceptions were triumphant.

State and Treasury thinking had diverged sharply on policies toward Germany and the Soviet Union. In the last few years of Roosevelt's administration, the State Department had been forced to fight a continuous holding action to prevent the acceptance of Morgenthau's plans for punitive treatment of defeated Germany.

While State had succeeded in reversing the apparent endorsement by Roosevelt and Churchill of the Morgenthau Plan in Quebec in September 1944, the guidelines for the military occupation of Germany still incorporated the assumption that German heavy industry would be destroyed. With Roosevelt's death, the advocates of German reconstruction could finally go on the offensive. From this point on, it was the other side—the advocates of German de-industrialization—who were forced to fight an ultimately unsuccessful holding action.[62]

The revival of Germany and the deterioration of U.S.-Soviet relations were closely connected. Since the Russians had borne the brunt of German industrial strength in two world wars, it is hardly surprising that they responded with implacable hostility to all attempts to rebuild Germany once again. So whether the State Department's motivation for reconstructing Germany was a desire to establish a bulwark against the Soviet Union or a belief that a strong Germany was necessary for Western Europe's recovery along multilateral lines, or both, the policy meant an inevitable deterioration of U.S.-Soviet relations. Accordingly, White's idea of securing U.S.-Soviet friendship through a massive loan gradually faded after FDR's death, and the Truman administration began a policy of "getting tough" with the Russians.

The policy shift was also evident in international monetary politics. The State Department planners were not happy with the IMF, both because of its departure from the gold standard and because the Bretton Woods agreements had let Britain off too easily. The agreements allowed Britain to maintain controls on current transactions for at least five years. In the State Department view, such a long delay in removing controls would be disastrous for the creation of a multilateral world economy and for assuring a U.S. export surplus. State saw a far more rapid movement by Britain toward the abandonment of controls as essential for the attainment of U.S. international goals.[63] To deal with this problem, State Department planners devised a strategy that was ingenious in its simplicity. They would simply forget that Bretton Woods had ever occurred and would pursue John Williams' alternative Key Currency Plan as though nothing else had happened. This meant offering Britain a substantial loan in exchange for British cooperation in restoring an open world economy.

The idea of using financial leverage to gain British cooperation with American plans for the postwar world was not exactly a new idea. The first such attempt dated back to the signing of the Atlantic Charter in August 1941. The United States had then attempted to gain a British commitment to end all trade discrimination against American goods as a quid pro quo for Lend-Lease aid. The British had managed to resist any concrete commitment that would have proved inconsistent with the continuation of the system of imperial preference, but they had committed themselves to joint discussions with the United States for the creation of a liberal world economy. To make sure that the British would fulfill this commitment satisfactorily, the United States manipulated the flow of Lend-Lease aid to prevent Britain's currency reserves from rising too high. American officials feared that, if Britain's reserves became too substantial, it would be possible for the British to formulate an independent policy that might conflict with U.S. aims.[64]

American aims in relation to Britain, as they were defined by the State Department, had two dimensions. The first were the policies and the structures that the United States wanted Britain to abandon. The most important of these were the system of imperial preference and the discriminatory aspects of the sterling bloc. The State Department wanted to open up the British Empire to equal access by American businessman, and this required the abolition of the preferential tariffs established in 1933. It also required the abolition of the system of dollar pooling among Sterling Area countries. Beginning with the onset of World War II, the countries in the Sterling Area placed all the dollars they earned in a central pool. These dollars were then redistributed among the Sterling Area countries according to some criteria of need, with Britain receiving the largest share. As a consequence, all countries in the Sterling Area acted to reduce their dollar expenditures by discriminating against U.S. goods. The State Department wanted to end this discrimination as quickly as possible and to prevent Britain and the Sterling Area from embarking on a bilateral course that would require dollar pooling as a permanent institution.[65]

The second dimension of U.S. plans for Britain was the State Department's vision of a positive role for the British in constructing a multilateral world economy. One element of this was the contribution to be made by the pound sterling. If Britain rejected the alternative of a closed sterling bloc, the pound sterling could play a constructive role in international trade for some time to come. American policy-makers knew that dollars would be scarce internationally in the immediate postwar years. The dollars that did get into foreign, especially European, hands would be used to buy U.S. goods, since the demand for goods in Europe would be much greater than the supply available locally. This meant that the dollar would be of little use over the short term for financing trade within Europe or between Europe and the Sterling Area. Only if sterling was convertible, and the City of London returned to its role as a financial center, would it be possible to finance that trade through market means. The alternative was that trade within Europe and between Europe and the Sterling Area would continue to be financed by a series of bilateral trading agreements. But it was precisely those bilateral agreements of which the multilateralists were most eager to be rid, since it was thought that the longer they existed, the more difficult they would be to remove. Hence, a strong pound, free of exchange controls, was necessary to begin lifting the system of trade and exchange controls from the European economies.[66]

Yet the goal of a strong pound was difficult to reconcile with the massive wartime accumulation by Sterling Area countries of sterling balances. The accumulation of these balances had been one of the main techniques by which the British financed their war effort. When Britain bought supplies in Sterling Area countries, or paid for troops stationed in those areas, the authorities agreed not to use the sterling they earned from those transactions to purchase goods from Britain. Instead, they simply added the sterling to their reserves. This was essentially a loan agreement: Britain paid for the goods and services with real money which was then lent to Britain by investing the proceeds in various London securities. The problem was that the extent of these balances greatly exceeded Britain's reserves of gold and dollars or its annual export of goods. This meant that at the end of the war Britain would have to figure out some way to prevent the holders of these balances from running them down too quickly. Without such action, Britain would be faced with the loss of its meager reserves of gold and dollars. But if Britain blocked access to these balances, it might greatly impair the usefulness of the pound as an international currency. White had unsuccessfully attempted to handle the sterling balances within the IMF, but his failure meant that his State Department opponents had to find a new solution to the problem of the balances in order for the pound to play the role they envisioned for it.[67]

Another element of Britain's envisioned role was to be her participation in an international trade organization. The idea for such an organization had originated in British government circles, but American planners had realized that such an organization could play an important part in organizing and policing multilateral trade. It could facilitate trade liberalization, develop a code of behavior for the treatment of international trade and investment, and resolve conflicts among member nations. But the United States needed British cooper-

ation to assure that such an organization would act to discourage state
trading, discriminatory trade practices, and various types of import
restrictions. With British cooperation and support it would presumably
be possible to convince other nations to pursue multilateral policies,
but if the British began equivocating and favoring certain kinds of
controls the task would be almost impossible.[68]

In general, Britain was seen as a kind of bridge between the
United States and the rest of the world. If the United States could
count on British economic, political, and military resources in the
pursuit of U.S. global aims, it was thought that it would then be
infinitely easier to gain the acquiescence of other countries. It was
precisely U.S. dependence on British cooperation in a variety of areas
that made U.S. policy toward Britain so complicated. On the one hand,
if Britain were too strong, if she had substantial currency reserves, it
would be difficult to force her to act according to American wishes. On
the other hand, if Britain were too weak, if her payments position were
desperate, she would be of little help in financing European trade, in
working to eliminate trade and exchange controls, and in a whole
variety of other tasks. The trick, then, was to keep Britain weak and
dependent, but not too weak, and debates that took place within the
United States government over the proper size of British reserves
reflected the subtlety of such an undertaking.[69]

The main reason it was so necessary to maintain financial leverage
over Britain had to do with the contradictions of U.S. commercial
policy. British negotiators on commercial policy who came to Washington during the war made it clear that Britain would be willing to
abandon imperial preference and discriminatory trade practices, if the
United States would agree to major cuts in its tariff level. The British,
in short, would be willing to abandon their preferential trading system
if they could be assured of obtaining access to the huge American
market. While the American negotiators were sympathetic to such a
demand, they were aware that there was little likelihood of Congressional approval for major tariff cuts. Protectionist interests were still
too strong to allow rapid American trade liberalization. The best that
State Department officials could do was advance a strategy of
gradualism; as the U.S. role in international trade expanded, the
power of internationalist interests in Congress would increase, and
further tariff reductions would be made, which would, in turn, expand
U.S. international trade and strengthen the internationalists. However, such a promise of tariff concessions in the future was of little
value to the British, who faced the immediate task of greatly expanding

their exports. But if the U.S. negotiators could not supply the quid pro quo that the British demanded, the Americans could attempt to force the British to make trade .concessions by using leverage in other areas—and that meant financial leverage.[70]

BRITAIN'S OPTIONS

While State Department planners sought to exert the maximum influence on Britain's economic future, the British were debating their own future economic policies. The key issue was the extent to which the British economy would be open to the international economy and its pressures. The cutting edge of openness was the role that sterling would play in the international economy. Would it return to its former position as an international currency, or would it become the currency for only a much diminished Sterling Area? If sterling was to be a major international currency, Britain would have to grant its traders and bankers a large measure of freedom to carry on international transactions. If a less critical role for sterling were envisioned, Britain could maintain a high level of control over the flow of goods and capital in and out of Britain or the Sterling Area. The system of controls inherent in the second option would make it possible for Britain to operate with relatively low reserves of gold and dollars, because the controls could simply be tightened to halt a balance-of-payments deficit. Under the first option, a reimposition of controls would tend to jeopardize confidence in sterling as an international currency, and this would have to be avoided.

As the war was coming to an end, it appeared that the forces in Britain that would tend to favor the second option of a limited role for sterling were considerably stronger than those that preferred a restoration of sterling's international role. The labor movement and the Left had bitter memories from the interwar years of the costs and consequences of maintaining an international currency. Full employment and the social welfare policies favored by the Left would tend to place a strain on the British balance of payments, particularly if the U.S. economy slipped back into recession or depression. The only means, given the aim of full employment, to handle the strain on the payments balance would be extensive international credits, a reduction in the standard of living, or the continuation of extensive controls. Since Keynes had failed in his attempt to obtain assurance of international credit through a clearing union and the reduction of the standard of

living was unacceptable, a continuation of controls was the only remaining option.[71]

Added to the weight of the Left was the sentiment of a significant
section of conservative and business opinion that was oriented toward
the continuation of the British Empire. This group believed that the
only way to preserve the Empire and to protect the economic interests
associated with it was to create a tightly knit sterling bloc. This bloc
would constitute a large protected market for British goods and for the
investment of British capital. Since the defense of this economic area
would absorb the major share of Britain's economic energy, there
would be no need or reason to try to establish a role for sterling outside
of their bloc. Therefore, for reasons strikingly different from those
advocated by the Left, this group came to advocate a system of continuing controls that was inconsistent with an open world economy.[72]

The forces that stood to gain from a prompt lifting of exchange and
trade controls and a return to an international (rather than a regional)
role for sterling were the traditional City interests. The bankers, insurance brokers, and investors located there had historically benefited
from the highest possible levels of international trade, and this led
them to favor multilateral arrangements which would make possible
such high levels of international trade in the postwar period. They
would lose many business opportunities if they were confined to a
narrow sterling area by an extensive system of controls. These City of
London interests could also count on the support of other business
interests that shared an ideological opposition to government controls.
As in the United States, sections of the business community must have
feared that continuing controls on foreign transactions would spill over
into controls on domestic transactions—and thus endanger the autonomy of the business community.[73]

Despite Keynes' conversion to multilateralism, the issue of
Britain's future course remained undecided even after Bretton Woods.
The long transition period that was allowed in the Bretton Woods
Agreement made it possible for Britain to take its time in deciding
whether to pursue a bilateral or a multilateral course.[74] In large part,
Britain's choice seemed to depend on the role that the United States
would play in the world economy. If the United States failed to
liberalize its tariffs and failed to maintain high levels of economic activity, the triumph of forces favoring permanent controls for Britain
would be assured. If, on the other hand, the United States permitted
Britain to achieve her domestic objectives in a multilateral world

economy, the forces in Britain that opposed controls would have a chance to get their way.

NEGOTIATING THE LOAN

The State Department had no intention of allowing the British simply to choose between multilateralism and bilateralism on the basis of the relative strength of the conflicting British interest groups. But the State Department's ability to exercise financial leverage on the British had been blocked during the war by the Treasury's domination of financial foreign policy. However, after Morgenthau's departure and with the approach of Allied victory in Europe, the State Department had its opportunity. Roosevelt had agreed in September 1944 to consult the British before the termination of Lend-Lease and to allow some Lend-Lease aid to be used for British reconstruction. (Ironically, these concessions to the British had apparently been a quid pro quo for British endorsement at that same meeting of the Morgenthau plan for de-industrializing Germany.)[75] It was also expected that Stage II—the period between V-E Day and V-J Day—during which the British would continue to receive Lend-Lease, would last as long as a year. In short, the British assumed that they would be receiving Lend-Lease aid through the middle of 1946. It came as a great shock to Britain, therefore, when Truman abruptly stopped the flow of Lend-Lease aid after the bombings of Hiroshima and Nagasaki brought an early end to the war in the Pacific. The sudden aid cutoff left Britain with inadequate currency reserves, and the new Labour government quickly dispatched Keynes to Washington to negotiate a sizable loan. The State Department could finally proceed to implement the Key Currency Plan.[76]

The Labour government had won a massive, surprise election victory in June 1945. But the long years out of office, the preoccupation of Labour with domestic programs, and the relative unfamiliarity of the Labour ministers with international financial issues placed the government at an initial disadvantage in formulating an international economic policy. Furthermore, the historical legacy of the Labour party pointed it, not in the direction of economic controls, but toward a classical liberal foreign economic policy. In fact, it had been the refusal by MacDonald and Snowden to abandon the gold standard that had led to the fall of the last Labour government in 1931. Even though the Labour party had been swept to victory on the basis of its program for domestic social reform, the party leadership was ill-prepared for the task of formulating an international economic policy that was consistent with its domestic objectives.[77]

The party's lack of preparation and the suddenness of the Lend-Lease cutoff made the new Labour ministers particularly dependent on the permanent staffs of the relevant ministries for the development of policy. However, the career civil servants and the academic economists who joined the ministries during the war were strongly oriented toward orthodox liberal solutions. Furthermore, those civil servants and economists had a theoretician and strategist to lead the struggle for a multilateral foreign economic policy: Lord Keynes. Keynes' understanding of the details of Britain's postwar economic prospects made him indispensable to the government, and his experience in negotiating with the Americans made him a natural choice to negotiate a loan. Moreover, the Labour ministers' difficulties in formulating a clear foreign economic policy of their own gave Keynes a great deal of leeway to formulate his own policies, and he utilized this degree of freedom skillfully. He told the Americans in August 1945 that he would prefer to have the formal loan negotiations take place in Washington rather than in London, so that he would be freer of direct ministerial supervision. At another time, he spoke to the Americans of the need to "educate" the new Labour ministers to the need for multilateralism. And there is no doubt that the relationship between Keynes and the Labour ministers was tense during the long months that he negotiated in Washington. Keynes would beg, badger, and threaten the Labour ministers to accept the terms that he had negotiated with the Americans; the ministers, aware that they were being pushed in a direction in which they did not want to go, would resist for a time but, in the end, agree.[78]

Keynes' ability to push the Labour government toward a liberal economic policy was not completely attributable to his brilliance and cunning. He did have behind him the power of the British financial community and American economic power. The threat of a direct confrontation between the Labour government and international financial interests was always implicit, and Keynes made it explicit in a letter he wrote to Chancellor of the Exchequer Hugh Dalton in October 1945, at a time when the ministers were stubbornly resisting Keynes' demands. "It would be a singular thing," he wrote, "if, the first Labour Government having been brought down by difficulties of external finance, the second should also run into the same deep pit." He went on to argue, "There is no way out remotely compatible with the present domestic policy of the Government except on the basis of substantial American aid."[79]

For the Labour government to stand up to Keynes, it would be necessary to stand up to the United States also, and this was hardly a pleasant prospect. At one point in December, the government came close to breaking off the negotiations. Dalton described his feelings at the time:

> But I was under no illusions as to what would follow if we got no dollar credit. We would go deeper into the dark valley of austerity than at any time during the war. Less food, except for bread and potatoes—less than an Irish peasant's standard of living—in particular less meat and sugar. Little cotton, and therefore, less clothes and less exports. Heavy and growing unemployment in many industries. . . . There would, I had no doubt, be a tremendous patriotic upsurge at the start, supporting our dramatic defiance of America. But it would be a very fleeting "finest hour." Soon, I knew, the tide of public feeling would turn. The Tories would exploit all the inevitable privations. Every shortage would be attributed to the Government's incompetence. Our feet would soon be on the downward slope, leading towards sure defeat at the next election.[80]

While Dalton's scenario is plausible, its validity rests on the assumption that the Labour party's response to the crisis would have been characteristically timid. A more forceful government might well have found a viable long-term alternative to economic reliance on the United States. To be sure, in the short term, intensified austerity was inevitable once Britain cut herself off from American supplies. However, the determined pursuit of national capitalist policies in conjunction with the Sterling Area or Western Europe might well have brought a return to relative prosperity within several years. Of course, such a path would have involved an intense conflict with some of the most powerful banking and business interests in the country. So it was both economic and political timidity that led the Labour government to follow Lord Keynes down the path of American-inspired multilateralism.

Keynes' intention when he went to Washington was to get as large a credit as possible on the most reasonable terms. He had spoken before he left Britain of the possibility of an interest-free loan, but this was probably wishful thinking designed to gain the Labour government's support for the negotiations. His strategy in the negotiations appears to have involved the threat of continuing bilateralism as a lever to assure American generosity. He could always point to the hesitancy of the Labour ministers as a way to force the Americans to produce better terms.[81] For the American negotiators—Fred Vinson, the new Secretary of the Treasury, and William Clayton from State—the size and terms of the loan were almost secondary issues. The American negotiators were willing to be as generous as they could be, within the limits posed by their assessment of the likelihood of Congressional approval. They realized that it would be difficult to get any loan through a Congress which was becoming increasingly impatient with international affairs and progressively more economy-minded. This is one reason they refused Keynes' request for an interest-free loan and forced him to scale his request for $6 billion down to $3.75 billion. But the main concern of the American negotiators was to get specific commitments from the British to begin opening their economy and the Sterling Area. These commitments would be concrete steps toward multilateralism, and each step, in turn, would make it easier to prove the value or benefits of the loan to Congress. The more concrete and far-reaching the commitments, they believed, the easier it would be to get the loan through.[82]

There were three areas in which the American negotiators sought such commitments: the elimination of controls on sterling transactions, the disposition of the sterling balances, and the regulation of commercial policies. The Americans insisted on an early end to the system of dollar pooling, including the elimination of controls on current transactions in dollars throughout the Sterling Area. There was considerable haggling over the deadline by which Britain would have to remove the controls, but it was finally agreed that Britain would restore current account convertibility within one year from the formal beginning of the loan agreement.[83] The British also agreed that at that point they would end all discrimination against dollar imports. Keynes had been under considerable pressure to postpone these commitments as long as possible because the Labour government was aware of their seriousness. However, he was able to force the government into line. Keynes apparently thought that current account convertibility at the end of a year would be viable for Britain, so he was not unhappy with this obligation. The one concession made to the reluctant Labour ministers was the insertion of a clause that allowed for postponement of convertibility—if both sides agreed.[84]

The American negotiators' desire to reach agreement on a settlement of the sterling balances had two origins. First, they must have recognized that current account convertibility was bound to fail unless something was done to block a large portion of the $14 billion of accumulated sterling balances. Second, they feared that the continued existence of the balances might bias Sterling Area countries toward the purchase of British goods. If countries held large quantities of sterling assets, it would make sense to use them to purchase sterling goods, and there were numerous possibilities for bilateral deals. The American preference was to write off a major share of the balances as a contribution to the war effort, and then to fund the remainder. Since the United States had written off Britain's obligations under Lend-Lease, it was only natural to expect such generosity from others.[85]

The problem was that the sterling balances were held mostly by underdeveloped countries such as India, Egypt, and Argentina. The leaders of these countries felt that it was unfair to expect them to act with the same generosity as the wealthy nations. Writing off a portion of the balances would have meant, in effect, subsidizing the standard of living of the British people at the expense of the meager standard of living of their own people. From the British point of view, negotiating some kind of arrangement with these sterling holders was complicated by political factors. Anglo-Indian relations were obviously tense on the eve of Indian independence, and Anglo-Egyptian relations were less than harmonious. Facing Britain was the necessity of maintaining strong bonds with India, Egypt, and other countries to protect British economic interests, a delicate situation. At a time when anti-imperialist and nationalist sentiment was very strong in the underdeveloped world, if Britain unilaterally acted to reduce the sterling balances—renouncing a portion of the debt—or if she took an intransigent negotiating stance, future relationships with India and Egypt might be jeopardized. The importance of the economic interests that Britain sought to protect was great enough to convince the British negotiators to proceed with extreme caution when discussing the sterling balances.[86]

The Americans understood the motives that would lead the British to move cautiously on the balances, but in their eyes the motives were illegitimate. The British were trying to hold on to the remnants of empire instead of facing up to their real responsibility—the restoration of sterling as an international currency. This responsibility as conceived by the United States necessitated a tough, no-nonsense approach to the sterling creditors. In addition, the Americans desired an attenuation of the ties between Britain and the Sterling Area countries, to insure that those markets would be open to U.S. goods. Hence, the Americans demanded, as one of the conditions of the loan, a specific agreement on how Britain would handle the balances. The British reacted with anger to this demand, insisting that the matter was one for the British to decide for themselves. Nevertheless, the British were forced to include in the text of the agreement a statement of their intentions in this matter. The exact percentages of the balances that would be written off, funded, and released were left open to give the British some freedom in negotiating with the sterling creditors. But it was understood that approximately a third of the balances would be written off and 90 percent of the remainder would be funded. Furthermore, the British agreed to carry out these negotiations as rapidly as possible to assure that the return to convertibility would not be jeopardized by massive conversions of the sterling balances. The Americans would have liked being a party in the negotiations with the sterling creditors, and Keynes is said to have favored this as a means of bringing greater pressure on the creditors, but the British government vetoed such an arrangement. The Americans hoped that by the time the sterling creditors were allowed to draw on their sterling, the pound would be convertible on current account, and there would be no incentive for the sterling holders to buy British rather than American goods.[87]

On commercial policy issues, the British were most successful in resisting American pressures. The British position was relatively strong because of the U.S. need for British cooperation in organizing the International Trade Organization and because of the inability of the U.S. negotiators to offer major tariff concessions. Also, commercial policy discussions had been going on since 1943, and the British had had time to develop a much more coherent policy than they had on the sterling balances or on sterling convertibility. Finally, the British managed to resist American pressure to merge commercial policy discussions with the other loan issues, so that it was more difficult for the United States to force commercial concessions in the crisis atmosphere of the loan negotiations.

The American intention was to draw up a set of principles for organizing an International Trade Organization that would commit the British to liberal trade policies. The American negotiators sought to outlaw preferential trading systems and the use of import restrictions. The British insisted that the liberalization of trade be linked to some broad commitment to maintain full employment policies, which would be incorporated into the charter of the new trade organization. The British also demanded that the charter include escape clauses that would allow the use of discriminatory trade practices to protect an economy from balance-of-payments pressures and international deflationary pressures. The Americans resisted any language or policies that would force the United States to accept a commitment to full employment that was stronger than existing American policy. And the American negotiators sought to delineate very narrowly the conditions under which the use of import restrictions were allowed.

Eventually, the differences between the United States and Britain on full employment and import restrictions were papered over by vague formulations that left the issues basically unresolved. The significant concession that the British made was on tariff preference: all tariff reductions would eliminate the margin of preference, and in no case would the margin of preference be increased or new preferences established. This made the system of imperial preference a kind of vestige of the past and eliminated the possibility of making that system a major instrument of economic policy in the future. However, unlike the British concessions incorporated in the Loan Agreement, this concession on imperial preference had to await the creation of the International Trade Organization before it would effectively bind British policy. The commercial policy agreement was not incorporated into the loan agreement, but it was published at the same time so "the American government could claim the 'Proposal' as one of the benefits received in return for the loan to Britain and the writing-off of Lend-Lease."[88] The British government feared domestic trouble if it admitted to being an equal party to the commercial policy agreement, so it was published publicly as an American document: "Proposals for Consideration by an International Conference on Trade and Employment." The British simply indicated that they considered the Proposals to be a sound basis for negotiations on the creation of an international trade organization.[89]

CONCLUSION

At the end of 1945, State Department planners could look with pride at their success in defeating their Treasury rivals and in gaining British acceptance of multilateral principles, despite the existence of a nominally socialist British government. To be sure, there was still much to be done to follow through on the British commitments and to break down British resistance on issues such as import restrictions. But the State Department planners must have felt that they had made a solid first step on the road to reconstructing a multilateral world economy. The next few years would belie that optimism. Every aspect of the British loan would prove problematic. Congressional approval would stimulate a major fight with opponents of U.S. internationalism. The sterling balances would never be funded, the restoration of current account convertibility would be a disastrous failure, and the International Trade Organization would never get off the ground. The struggle to create an open world economy would require new strategies and new expedients.

FOUR. *The Marshall Plan and Rearmament*

In 1946-47, State Department planners and their business internationalist allies faced new dangers and new opponents. The first danger was domestic—that a resurgence of anti-internationalist opinion in the United States and in Congress would make it impossible to mobilize the resources necessary to achieve the objectives of the business internationalists. The second danger was foreign—that the devastation and social turmoil produced by the war was resulting in far stronger resistance abroad to U.S. plans for organizing the international economy than had been anticipated. The weakness of the European economies, the strength of leftist and reformist forces in most European countries, the rise of nationalist and revolutionary forces in the underdeveloped world, and the enhanced international position of the Soviet Union, all served to make the restoration of multilateralism a more difficult task.

The domestic and foreign problems were closely interconnected. The more formidable the task of restoring an open world economy, the greater would be the need for various kinds of economic resources to accomplish U.S. objectives abroad. However, domestic opposition to U.S. internationalism would make it difficult to obtain those resources. And ironically, foreign resistance to American economic ideals served to strengthen the anti-internationalist forces. The strength abroad of socialism, communism, and other "un-American" ideas contributed to a domestic reaction against international involvement. Furthermore, the power of anti-internationalist forces to block measures such as trade liberalization undermined the American claim to international economic leadership. If the United States was unable to act responsibly within its own rules by increasing its imports, Western Europe would be even more reluctant to accept stringent, multilateral rules. American business internationalists struggled fron 1946 on to achieve their goals within the difficult network created by the interaction of their domestic and foreign problems. And they did so with the awareness that failure to create an open world economy would endanger the United States export surplus and increase the risk of an economic downturn in the United States. They were well aware that a severe economic downturn would likely give power to the national economic planners and would virtually assure a devastating and permanent defeat for the idea of an open world economy.

During 1946, State Department officials pursued several lines of policy that had been developed during the war. The British loan was sent to Congress for approval, and other loans with similar conditions were negotiated through the Export-Import Bank. The first meetings of the International Monetary Fund and International Bank provided the opportunity to begin modifying the design and operation of those institutions to make them conform to American global goals. An international meeting was convened to create an International Trade Organization along the lines indicated by the Anglo-American discussions on commercial policy. By late 1946 and early 1947, however, it had become clear that the political-economic situation abroad would require the formulation of new policies to achieve the multilateral goal. Moreover, the problem of gaining domestic support for the effort to achieve the multilateral goal would profoundly affect the character of those new policies.

APPROVING THE BRITISH LOAN

The British loan agreement was approved by both houses of the British Parliament in December 1945. The debate was intense, with voices of the Left and of the Right strongly critical of the terms and the Labour government making only a halfhearted intellectual defense of the agreement. Churchill led the Conservatives in abstaining on the vote. The Labour party saved the agreement by forcing even its most radical members to vote in favor of the agreement, thus assuring its passage. In the House of Lords, Keynes' eloquent defense of the agreement sufficed to prevent the Conservative majority in that body from exercising its anachronistic right to delay approval.[1]

The Truman administration sent the enabling legislation for the loan to Congress in January 1946, confident of prompt approval. Nevertheless, the legislation encountered major resistance that made defeat of the loan agreement a real possibility. The center of opposition to the loan was Senator Robert A. Taft and a group of conservative

Midwestern Republicans. Taft had opposed the Bretton Woods Agreement as well, but at that time his resistance to an internationalist foreign economic policy had little impact. A number of factors served to enhance Taft's influence in the debate on the British loan. 1946 was an election year, the first in many years that would not be dominated by FDR. The attention of the public, with the end of the war, had turned to domestic problems, and many in Congress must have felt that widespread public hostility or indifference to the loan could not be ignored. Public opinion polls in June indicated that 48 percent of those questioned disapproved of the loan, while only 38 percent approved. This negative reaction to the loan was fed by diffuse hostility to different British policies. Conservative anxieties about the Labour government's nationalization of the steel industry, the antagonism toward Britain felt by the American Irish with their historic grievances, Jewish anger over British policies in Palestine, and suspicions toward the British Empire that lingered among diverse groups, all served to heighten distrust of the loan agreement.[2]

The issue of the loan was further complicated by the delicate state of American-Soviet relations. The crucial issue was whether the United States would make a similar loan to its other wartime ally—the Soviet Union—or whether the British loan was the first step toward the consolidation of an Anglo-American alliance against the Soviet Union. The Truman administration continued to talk as though it was keeping open the possibility of a loan to the Russians, in order to minimize opposition to the British loan from those who favored continued good relations with the U.S.S.R. When Congressional leaders who were worried about the British loan's prospects in Congress suggested to the administration that the loan be sold as an anti-Soviet measure, the administration refused to change its rhetoric. Apparently negative public reaction to Churchill's "Iron Curtain" speech had convinced Truman and his advisors that an explicitly anti-Soviet policy might be politically dangerous.[3]

Taft's opposition to the loan stemmed from his skepticism about multilateralism and his financial conservatism. An indication of the latter was his proposal of a much smaller loan—$1.25 billion—to cover Britain's transitional needs. Taft, moreover, insisted that the creation of a multilateral world economy with fully convertible currencies was a delusion. It was not that he preferred the kind of arrangements advocated by the more radical national economic planners, but that he opposed the use of U.S. resources to reshape the world in some ideal image. Taft's political base was largely made up of Midwestern farmers and businessmen who were more concerned with protecting the American market than with opening up European markets to American goods. Taft's sustained opposition to internationalist policies, however, meant that he reflected at times the views of a much broader public, including many who preferred domestic reforms to foreign projects.[4]

Despite the opposition, the loan agreement was approved by Congress in July 1945. The crucial argument was apparently the invocation, by Vandenberg in the Senate and McCormack in the House, of the Soviet menace. Although the administration had resisted this line of argument, the Congressional leadership insisted that the loan was necessary to bolster Britain against possible Soviet threats. While final approval of the loan must have caused relief in the administration, there was little cause for joy. The debate had demonstrated the difficulty of gaining Congressional support for the administration's foreign economic policy. Early in 1946, the National Advisory Council on International Monetary and Financial Problems had discussed the need to ask Congress for another $1-1.5 billion for the Export-Import Bank, but when the British loan ran into trouble it was decided to forgo such a request.[5]

It had been the administration's intention to follow up the British loan with similar loans through the Export-Import Bank to other European countries. Some of these loans were actually negotiated. A French delegation came to Washington in February 1946, requesting a $4 billion credit. Although this sum was out of the question, a $650 million loan was negotiated in exchange for French agreement to participate in a multilateral order and to make some tariff concessions. A larger loan might have been forthcoming if the French had proved more cooperative in their German occupation policies, and a significant motivation of the United States in granting any loan at all appears to have been the desire to strengthen the hand of the non-Communist elements within the French government. But by mid-1946, Congressional distrust of foreign loans meant that the administration's resources for exercising financial leverage were exhausted. The Export-Import Bank had no more funds, and American policy-makers made clear that further loans would have to wait until the International Bank for Reconstruction and Development, the IBRD, started its operations.[6]

THE FIRST MEETING OF THE
BRETTON WOODS INSTITUTIONS

The founding meeting of the International Monetary Fund and the International Bank took place in Savannah, Georgia, in March 1946, while the British loan was still before Congress. Fred Vinson, the Secretary of the Treasury, was determined that the meeting should go smoothly and be a convincing demonstration that American influence was to predominate in these institutions. Keynes came to the meeting with three principal expectations: that Harry Dexter White would be appointed the first managing director of the fund, so as to assure expansionist policies; that the fund would be located in New York City, so as to assure insulation from Washington politics; and that the executive directors of the fund would work only part-time with the fund, so that the principal work of the fund would be done by an internationally oriented staff. On all three of these issues, Keynes would be disappointed, and he left Savannah with considerable bitterness. The experience apparently taxed his strength and he had a major heart attack on the train back from Savannah. He died six weeks later.

It was an easy matter for the Americans to block White from becoming the fund's managing director. The International Bank needed the confidence of Wall Street because it had to borrow money there, so it was only logical for the head of the bank to be an American. But since it would be unseemly for the Americans to direct both of the international institutions, the Americans argued that a European should be managing director of the fund. Since it might well have been possible to find a European with a reputation for financial probity to head the bank, it seems likely that this argument was designed to minimize White's influence over his own creation. In any event, Camille Gutt, a former Belgian Finance Minister, was chosen as the fund's first managing director.[7]

The other two issues centered on the degree of political influence to be exerted by the United States on the fund. Keynes understood that the more the Americans interfered with the fund, the less likely it was that relatively unconditional access to the fund's resources would be maintained. He felt that with the fund in New York, located near United Nations headquarters, and with policy developed by its staff, it would be possible for the fund to develop an internationalist perspective consistent with free access to the fund's resources. The United States insisted that Washington serve as the fund's headquarters and that the executive directors act as full-time participants in the fund's activities specifically to insure that American interests would be upheld within the fund.

During the Savannah meetings, the U.S. negotiators were far less willing to compromise with Keynes than U.S. representatives had been at Bretton Woods and before. A minor concession was made by the United States on the amount that the executive directors would be paid, but otherwise Keynes' arguments were simply swept aside. In fact, Keynes' bitterness about the Savannah meeting seems to have derived as much from anger at American "railroading" of certain measures as by the measures themselves. The situation, however, was that the U.S. vote, when combined with the votes of client regimes in Latin America and elsewhere, was enough to assure American dominance. This dominance was strengthened by the measures adopted at Savannah, and this power was wielded by the United States in the following years to assure that the use of fund resources would conform to the American multilateral design.[8]

THE INTERNATIONAL TRADE ORGANIZATION

The first major event in the history of the International Trade Organization after the British loan negotiations was a meeting in London, in October 1946, of a Preparatory Committee. The Committee had been appointed by the Economic and Social Council of the United Nations to draft a convention to be considered by an International Conference on Trade and Employment. Although there were eighteen nations involved in the London meeting, it turned into another confrontation between the United States and Britain. Again, the major issues were provisions for assuring full employment and those under which the use of quantitative import restrictions would be tolerated. On full employment, American resistance to any foreign meddling with American options forced the British to be satisfied with two mild concessions: a general obligation in the charter for nations to pursue full employment policies, and escape clauses that allowed countries to use direct controls to protect full employment policies when such policies were endangered by international deflation. The United States was far less successful on the issue of quantitative restrictions. The United States had attempted to establish a fixed transitional period that would end at the end of 1949, after which countries would be under strong pressure to eliminate all quantitative restrictions. Not only did the British successfully resist this fixed deadline, but they won a number of escape clauses that allowed quantitative restrictions, and even the discriminatory use of quantitative restrictions under certain conditions.[9]

The outcome of the London meeting was not a good omen for the next round of ITO negotiations, to be held in Geneva in the spring of 1947. The more loopholes incorporated into the ITO Charter at this early stage, the less likely that the Charter would effectively bind countries to multilateral policies. Other countries would probably press for even more exceptions and loopholes than the British, and the lack of solidarity between the United States and Britain would make it difficult to resist their demands. The basic problem behind the ITO negotiations was that the effort to develop a set of rules for international trade was taking place in a context of severe economic turmoil and uncertainty for most of the countries involved. There was always a big gap between the ideal world for which the Charter was intended and the actual world with which governments were struggling in the present.

THE SITUATION IN EUROPE

The actual situation that Western European[10] governments faced during 1946 was an awesome task of economic reconstruction. Economic production had fallen sharply from prewar levels across most of the Continent, and "most countries could expect grain crops in 1946 no better than 60 per cent of pre-war volume." Scarcity of certain goods, manpower shortages, problems of displaced people, and the breakdown of transportation, trading, and communication networks plagued the reconstruction effort. To make matters worse, the winter of 1946-47 was unusually severe, creating shortages of coal—Western Europe's main energy source—that further interrupted the revival of production.[11]

It was the American hope that the process of reconstruction, despite its difficulties, would result in the restoration of liberal capitalist regimes across Europe. Such regimes should open their economies as quickly as possible to market-determined flows of goods and capital. But during the chaotic period of reconstruction in 1946-47, the Western European economies had all evolved elaborate systems of controls over almost all international economic transactions. Some of these controls were simply carried over from wartime, and others were developed specifically for peacetime conditions. The system of controls generally began with exchange controls that made each country's currency inconvertible, so that capital movements were generally illegal. Imports were limited by the government's control of foreign exchange and by restrictions that limited the quantity of certain imports. Quite often the government also directly controlled a substantial share of foreign trade through state trading agencies. Furthermore, as governments attempted to expand foreign trade, they negotiated bilateral trading agreements with other countries. These agreements provided temporary lines of credit of limited magnitude for imports from a participating country on the theory that, over a period of time, trade between the two countries would balance.[12]

While some of these controls could be seen as simply temporary expedients, the proliferation of bilateral trading agreements sharpened American anxieties that controls might well become permanent. And in fact, there were a number of powerful forces pushing Western European countries toward the incorporation of their existing controls within a form of national capitalism that would involve permanent state control over international transactions. The strength of the Left and the labor movement throughout Western Europe, the relative international weakness of the European economies, and the extension of Soviet power into Eastern Europe all served, in somewhat different ways, to push the European countries away from liberal capitalism and toward national capitalism.[13]

THE STRENGTH OF THE LEFT

The strength of the Left in Europe in the immediate postwar period was rooted in a broad, popular desire for social reform after years of the misery of war and depression. The politicians of the Right were often discredited because of the economic disasters of the thirties and the widespread right-wing collaboration with fascism. At the same time, the parties of the Left benefited from the prestige attached to the resistance struggles. Furthermore, the disruptions and dislocations of the war period had ripped people out of old social contexts and increased their availability for political mobilization to achieve social reforms, such as a shift of wealth in favor of the working class and the creation of an economic order that was not prone to cyclical crises. This popular desire for social reform was an important factor in the Labour party's surprise electoral victory in Britain in 1945 and the emergence of the communist parties as the strongest political tendency in Italy and France.[14]

The immediate political-economic consequence of the strength of these popular reformist forces was an intensification of inflationary pressures in most European countries. Inflation was already a serious problem, with shortages of goods and the wartime expansion of the money supply placing strong upward pressure on prices. However, the demands for social reforms and for a redistribution of income in favor of the working class made inflation a more or less conscious strategy of the employers. Increased government spending for social services and significantly higher real wages could only come, in the short term, from a reduction in the share of wealth that went to the capitalist class. Under normal conditions, the capitalist class prevents such an attack on its ability to consume and invest by resisting wage demands and by fighting politically for a limit on state spending and on the taxing of its profits and accumulated wealth. However, in the immediate postwar period, it was difficult for capitalists to exercise power in the traditional ways. To resist wage demands strenuously, for example, would have invited a further radicalization of the working class and raised the specter of revolution. Instead, the employers would concede large wage increases and then compensate by increasing prices. Or if taxes were increased, the employers could pass the cost of the taxes along through higher prices for consumers. In this way, the effort of the working class to increase its share of real wealth could be continually undermined by a rising cost of living.[15]

For most capitalists, this inflationary dynamic represented the lesser of several evils. Continually rising prices created problems, but inflation was preferable to either a potentially disastrous confrontation with the working class or a smaller share of the national product for the industrialists. But one of the major costs of inflation was the impossibility of organizing international trade on a market basis. The rates of inflation were radically different among different European countries and between Europe and the United States. If trade were to proceed on an open basis, with any kind of reasonable exchange rates, all of the high-inflation countries would be deluged by goods from low-inflation countries, and the high-inflation countries would be in serious balance-of-payments trouble. As long as severe inflation plagued these economies, foreign trade would have to be organized through bilateral or state trading procedures in which domestic market prices were irrelevant. And as long as the demands for social reforms and higher wages continued to be pressed strongly, there was little prospect for these countries to stop inflation or to restore liberal capitalism.[16]

It was also possible that controls over foreign transactions might gradually be extended in the direction of controls over the domestic economy. The chaotic situation in European countries in 1946 and 1947 could have been construed as the first stage in the socialist transformation of some of the Western European economies. While most Left parties were pursuing rather cautious policies, it is easy to imagine that European and American businessmen feared that the Labour government in England and the coalition governments in Italy and France that included Communist participation were taking the first steps toward the elimination of private ownership of the means of production. And to the extent to which national capitalism might simply be a way station on the road to socialism, the perception could have been accurate.[17]

THE INTERNATIONAL WEAKNESS
OF EUROPEAN CAPITALISM

The war had done considerable damage to the balance-of-payments position of the European economies. Before the war, Western Europe was able to finance a trade deficit of some $2.1 billion per year with its earnings from invisibles—shipping, banking, and return on foreign investments. By 1947, Europe was running a deficit on these invisibles of $0.6 billion, so that invisible items simply contributed to the overall deficit, rather than reducing it. The reason for this drastic shift in the invisibles account was the liquidation of foreign investments, the accumulation of foreign debts such as sterling balances, and the continuing heavy costs of overseas political and military efforts. France was fighting to hold on to Vietnam, the Netherlands was struggling to maintain its position in Indonesia, and Britain was fighting in Malaya. (The British were also financing the right wing in the Greek civil war, giving aid to Turkey, and bearing part of the costs of the German occupation.)[18] This shift in European finances also disrupted prewar patterns of trade and finance. Europe had traditionally run a trade deficit with the United States, while the United States ran a trade deficit with Asian countries that exported raw materials. The circle was completed when Europe, through visible and invisible trade, earned a surplus in its transactions with Asia that was used to finance Europe's deficit with the United States. In the postwar period Europe had a much larger deficit with the United States, because American importers had substituted Latin American goods for European goods during the war and Europe had vastly increased its dollar imports for relief and reconstruction. In addition, Europe was no longer running a sizable surplus with other parts of the world that could help finance its deficit with the United States.[19]

The breakdown of this traditional multilateral pattern created two strong pressures on the European economies. The first was to reduce their imports from the United States to an amount that could be easily financed. Since American tariffs were still high and European supplies limited, European exports to the United States totaled less than $1 billion a year. Furthermore, there was little flow of private U.S. capital into Europe because of uncertain conditions. Hence, if Europe were not to deplete its currency reserves totally, it would be forced to begin reducing its dollar imports to the $1-billion-a-year level. This could only be done through extensive discrimination against dollar goods, which would amount to Europe's closing itself off from trade with the United States.[20]

The second pressure was to reorganize Europe's trade with its colonies and ex-colonies in the underdeveloped world on a bilateral basis. Because the old triangular pattern no longer worked, it now made sense for the Europeans to organize trade with these areas bilaterally. Under bilateralism, the Europeans would offer manufactured goods and some new capital in exchange for raw materials and agricultural products from these areas. The underdeveloped countries would have to discriminate against dollar goods, but they would gain guaranteed markets for their raw material exports. The advantage of such a bilateral arrangement for the Europeans was that it could protect their export markets in these regions from the competition of American exporters and it would provide the Europeans with the means to purchase important raw materials. These bilateral arrangements might be less advantageous to the underdeveloped countries, who would lose the opportunity to buy U.S. manufactured goods freely with their earnings from raw material exports to the United States. However, many underdeveloped countries had reason to be wary of making their economies dependent on the U.S. economy with its uncertain commitment to the maintenance of high levels of economic activity and high levels of demand for commodity imports. Bilateral arrangements with the European powers had the possible advantages of greater security and more reliable access to capital and, in some cases, were made more attractive by the existence of long historical ties. The perception of the relative advantages or disadvantages of such bilateral arrangements for specific underdeveloped countries varied a great deal, depending on the relative strength of the economies, the outlook of the groups in power, and a variety of other factors.[21]

Whether or not the Europeans would be successful in consolidating such bilateral trading areas, the threat of such an attempt was frightening to the United States. If Europe were to reduce its dollar imports drastically and to reorganize its trade with the underdeveloped world on a bilateral basis, there would be very little of the world left open to free access by American businessmen. Not only would the U.S. export surplus be eliminated, but the possibilities for U.S. firms to expand abroad in the future would be significantly curtailed.[22] There would also be the danger that the United States might be unable to acquire crucial, scarce mineral resources at reasonable prices.

THE POWER OF THE SOVIET UNION

The extension of the power of the Soviet Union into Eastern Europe and the transformation of some of the Eastern European economies along socialist lines placed strong pressure on Western Europe. Part of this pressure was economic; before the war there had been a high level of trade between Eastern and Western Europe. But as the Eastern European countries began organizing their foreign trade permanently along bilateral lines, there was pressure on Western European economies to do the same. It is difficult to organize a significant part of a country's trade on multilateral lines and another significant part on bilateral lines because of the difficulties in coordinating supplies.[23] So the pull of markets in Eastern Europe was another pressure on the Western European economies to resist American pressure for multilateralism.[24]

The pressure was also clearly political. As long as the Soviet Union was the strongest power impinging on Western Europe, there was good reason for the Western European countries to seek to maintain good political and economic relations with the Soviet Union. It must be remembered that in these first few postwar years the Soviet Union enjoyed widespread popular respect for having borne the brunt of the struggle against Hitler. The need to maintain good relations with the Soviets was not seen by the Left-leaning governments in power as a particularly bitter pill to swallow. For U.S. policy-makers and many Europeans, however, the "Finlandization" of Western Europe was a major danger. Not only was there a threat to liberal democracy, but the more the Western European countries accommodated themselves to the Soviet Union, the less likely they would be to reconstruct their economies along the liberal, multilateral lines that the United States saw as so essential.

THE U.S. ECONOMY AND
THE INTERNATIONAL SITUATION

In accordance with most predictions, strong domestic and foreign demand sustained the American economy through the immediate reconversion from war to peace. In fact, the main problem of the American economy was the inflation that resulted, in part, from excess demand. An export surplus of $6.5 billion was achieved in 1946. The surplus was financed by U.S. government aid funneled through the United Nations Relief and Rehabilitation Administration and by foreign countries running down their gold and dollar reserves by some $2 billion. By mid-1947, the export surplus had reached an annual rate of $20 billion a year. However, the financing of the surplus was becoming more and more difficult as foreign reserves neared exhaustion and UNRRA was coming to an end. Without means of financing, foreigners had no choice but to reduce their purchases of U.S. goods. After mid-1947, total U.S. exports began to decrease, and the export surplus sank at even greater speed.[25]

American planners, meeting in a high-level State-Navy-War Coordinating Committee, foresaw in early 1947 that "the world will not be able to continue to buy U.S. exports at the 1946-47 rate beyond another 12-18 months." The lack of available international credit, the planned tapering-off of U.S. aid programs, and the depletion of foreign currency reserves would make a sharp decline in U.S. exports inevitable. The committee warned that "a substantial decline in the U.S. export surplus would have a depressing effect on business activity and employment in the U.S." and they feared that such a decline, if it coincided with an anticipated domestic recession, "might be most serious" in its effects on production, prices, and employment.[26] Nobody was sure when the postwar consumer-demand boom would taper off, but the danger was that the export surplus's stimulating effect on the economy would be lost precisely at the moment that the stimulus was most necessary to cushion the effects of the inevitable downturn in domestic consumer and business spending.[27]

The State-Navy-War Coordinating Committee drew from its analysis the logical conclusion about U.S. prospects: it proposed a major U.S. aid program to finance a continued high level of U.S. exports. This was the embryonic form of the plan that was introduced to the public in Secretary Marshall's famous Harvard speech on June 5, 1947.[28] But the genius of the Marshall Plan was that it was far more than an effort to finance the export surplus for a few more years. It simultaneously attacked all of the forces that were moving Western Europe away from multilateralism: the strength of the European lefts, the relative weakness of the European economies, and the pull from the Soviet Union. But the Marshall Plan became possible only in the worsening international political climate of 1947. Without the intensification of the Cold War, it would have been impossible even to contemplate sending such a massive aid program to Congress.

The stage was set for the Marshall Plan by the enunciation of the Truman Doctrine in March 1947. The British had indicated in February that they would no longer be able to bear the costs of continuing aid to Greece and Turkey. This raised the possibility that the Greek Left would triumph in the civil war and that Greece—a country of strategic importance in the Mediterranean—would move toward alliance with the Soviet Union. The Truman administration responded by asking Congress to vote special aid for Greece and Turkey. Truman made this request, however, in a way designed "to scare the hell out of the country." The left wing of the Democratic party had suffered a major defeat in the Congressional elections of 1946, and the political risk for Truman in invoking the Red Menace had been greatly reduced. So he proceeded to invoke that menace with a vengeance; the speech posed the choice between totalitarianism and freedom, and he asserted that the United States would intervene on the side of freedom wherever necessary. The crisis atmosphere that Truman created resulted in prompt Congressional approval for aid to Greece and Turkey. This success demonstrated that the opponents of American internationalism in the Congress and in the public could be effectively neutralized by the use of anti-Communist rhetoric and the creation of international crises.[29]

The Truman Doctrine was also a signal to conservative forces in Europe that the United States would assist them in the struggle against left-wing forces. It was followed in short order by Dean Acheson's speech of May 8, in which he described the necessity of rebuilding the German and Japanese economies and hinted at massive American aid for the Europeans.[30] In June, Marshall unveiled the aid plan, and negotiations quickly began with the Europeans to give concrete form to the program. While the actual flow of aid could not begin until the spring of 1948 because of the need for Congressional action, emergency aid for Italy, France, and Austria was voted in December 1947. The emergency aid and the prospect of far more extensive aid to come had an immediate effect on the political-economic situation in Europe. In Italy, for example, conservative forces pushed the Communists out of the government and, in anticipation of further American assistance, imposed severely deflationary economic policies in the second half of 1947.[31]

Other events during the course of 1947 both exposed the bankruptcy of the State Department's earlier policy initiatives and affirmed the need for bold new policies such as the Marshall Plan. In the spring of 1947, Geneva was the scene of another meeting on the ITO Charter and of the first sustained negotiations on international tariff reductions. Both events were disappointments for American policy-makers, who had hoped to restore multilateral trade. The British announced at the outset of the trade negotiations their unwillingness to eliminate imperial preference in exchange for the 50 percent tariff reductions which were the maximum that the American negotiators were authorized to offer.[32] Given that the 1946 elections had produced a Congress even more protectionist than earlier Congresses, and that the elimination of imperial preference had been promised to the American public as a quid pro quo for the British loan, the American negotiators were in a very difficult position. Negotiations dragged on for months, but the British refused to budge. In the end, imperial preference was reduced on some goods, but on 70 percent of Britain's exports to the Commonwealth that had carried preferences before the war there was no change. The United States, in turn, reduced tariffs on some goods, often up to the 50 percent limit. In the discussions on the ITO Charter, the British also took a hard line. The result of pressure by the British was the addition of new loopholes in the Charter allowing trade discrimination under various conditions. Other countries also forced through provisions allowing the use of quantitative restrictions by underdeveloped countries for economic development purposes. As these loopholes expanded, the Charter became less and less attractive to American multilateralists.[33]

The other major event of 1947 was the attempted restoration of sterling convertibility. In accordance with the obligations of the British loan, the British moved, on July 15, 1947, to remove the restrictions on the use of sterling earned on current account anywhere in the world. The idea was that foreigners who earned sterling through normal trade channels were free to make use of that sterling in any way, including converting it into dollars at the fixed dollar-sterling exchange rate. Sterling earned on capital account or accumulated in the past was not subject to the same freedom, and the British had negotiated agreements with other governments to enforce continued restrictions on non-current-account sterling. However, these agreements were relatively ineffective, and the convertibility experiment quickly turned into a disaster. Conversion of sterling into dollars took place at a far greater rate than Britain could afford. The British had already used up a good portion of the American loan to cover their dollar deficit from mid-1946 to mid-1947, and the drain of dollars during convertibility threatened to exhaust the loan within a few weeks. The drain increased with each passing week, so that the British were forced to halt the experiment on August 21.[34]

What went wrong was that much non-current-account sterling was converted by sterling holders who saw a unique opportunity to switch out of sterling into a far more reliable currency—the dollar. While it is easy to blame Britain's lax enforcement system for these abuses, the basic problem was that, without confidence, convertibility, even on current account, was an impossibility. And there was little reason for anyone to have much confidence in sterling in mid-1947. For one thing, Britain was still running a substantial balance of payments deficit, and there were also the huge sterling balances that had still not been eliminated as anticipated in the loan agreement. But the basic point was that the international situation in mid-1947 was extremely unstable, and the dollar, despite the United States' own problems with inflation, was a far more secure currency than any other in the world. It was only natural for people in other parts of the world to seize an opportunity to acquire the security of dollar assets, and that is what they did.[35]

The failure of the British to clear up the sterling balances also had done little to increase confidence in the pound. Despite American pressure, the British had been unable or unwilling to negotiate settlements with the largest sterling holders. Keynes, who had recognized the urgency of settling the balances and who had the diplomatic skill to complete the task, had died before he could make a start. After his death the resistance of the sterling holders combined with the pressure of British export interests which feared a weakening of Sterling Area ties sufficed to block action.[36] In short, the Labour government had succumbed on paper to American pressure for multilateralism, but it had still refused to do anything in these first postwar years to close off the bilateral option. This indecisiveness would prove costly over the long term because the sterling balances remained a major cause of the pound's weakness for years thereafter.

Despite the disastrous experience with convertibility and the unsatisfactory results at Geneva, the events of 1947 made clear that the British loan had some beneficial effects for U.S. policy. The loan had solidified an Anglo-American relationship; when Marshall made his speech, Ernest Bevin, the British Foreign Minister, acted quickly to organize the Europeans to receive the aid. In part, with that one loan the British had become addicted to dollar aid, and they were now ready for another "fix." In addition, the first loan had prevented Britain from moving definitively toward bilateralism in the first two postwar years. The fact that Britain had not moved very far toward multilateralism either turned out to be relatively unimportant. In the context of the intensifying Cold War, Britain would play an important role in advancing U.S. political-economic aims.[37]

THE MARSHALL PLAN—
THEORY AND PRACTICE

In response to Marshall's June speech, the Europeans began drawing up a specific request for American aid. The idea was that a coordinated aid plan coming from Western European countries themselves would be more likely to gain Congressional approval.[38] Meeting in the Committee for European Economic Cooperation (later changed to the Organization for European Economic Cooperation), the Europeans drafted a report that called for $29.2 billion of American aid. They also warned that, even after that aid was used up, Europe might still have a substantial dollar deficit. The State Department pressured them to reduce the request to $20 billion, which was far more likely to be approved by Congress. The State Department was also aware that it was necessary to tell Congress that such a massive aid program would solve Europe's economic problems once and for all. Otherwise, there would be no way of answering the argument that Europe was a bottomless pit that would absorb as many dollars as the United States was foolish enough to give away.

The administration sent the legislation establishing the Marshall Plan to Congress in December 1947. Congress was asked to authorize $6.8 billion for the first fifteen months of the program and to approve the authorization of $17 billion for the four years of the program. The request encountered major opposition in Congress; the opponents of American internationalism argued vigorously against this unprecedented giveaway of American resources. Once again, the Truman administration sought to manipulate Congressional and public opinion by exaggerating the immediate threat from the Soviet Union. The task of the administration was simplified by events in Czechoslovakia in February 1948 that brought the Communists to power in that country. The "fall" of Czechoslovakia provided the background for a major war scare that was fueled by Truman's speech before both houses of Congress on March 17. In his speech, Truman warned of the grave danger from the Soviets and called for Congress to enact not only the Marshall Plan legislation, but also a program of universal military training. By the end of March, Washington was filled with rumors of an imminent outbreak of war. In this crisis atmosphere, the Marshall Plan legislation was finally approved by Congress. But despite the war scare, which cooled dramatically after the legislation had been approved, Congress did force some changes in the structure of the Marshall Plan. First, the administration of Marshall aid was taken away from the State Department. An independent agency—the Economic Cooperation Administration—was set up to administer the aid and, to minimize partisan opposition, it was to be headed by a Republican businessman. Second, Congress refused to authorize more than one year of aid at a time, so as to maintain maximum control over the program. The administration would face the threat each year of drastic cutbacks in the amount requested, especially if Congress felt that the Plan was not accomplishing its goals.[39]

The Marshall Plan made it possible for the United States to respond simultaneously to a whole range of interrelated problems. It provided a means of financing a large export surplus and influencing Western Europe's economic course. The actual economic aid that was given made it possible for the Western European countries to afford some steps toward multilateralism while easing the pressure on internal resources.[40] Standards of living could be maintained because the United States subsidized consumption, and this helped ease the threat from the Left.[41] The European Recovery Program also provided a counterweight to the pull of Eastern European trade on Western

Europe.[42] At the same time, the Marshall Plan won an enormous propaganda victory for American foreign policy; it created a pool of political capital that the United States could use to implement far less popular policies. The most important of these unpopular policies was the restoration of German industrial strength. The restoration of Germany had long been a central tenet of State Department policy, but opposition in the United States and particularly in Europe had made progress in this direction extremely difficult. However, under the humanitarian cover of the Marshall Plan, German industrial reconstruction became far more legitimate. Similarly, the Marshall Plan gave the United States the opportunity to support the colonial wars of the European powers against extreme nationalist movements in areas such as Malaya and Indochina. The United States needed European military and political strength to help police Third World areas to prevent the spread of communism. And as long as the Western European countries were moving toward multilateralism, the United States would be willing to recognize their special interests in certain colonial areas.[43] Yet the Marshall Plan had to be much more than a simple giveaway of dollars if it was to accomplish the goal of restoring Western Europe to full participation in a multilateral world economy. During the plan's four-year life, it would have to improve Western Europe's competitiveness in international trade to the point where Western Europe would be able to earn enough dollars through private transactions in the post-Marshall Plan period to balance its trade on a multilateral basis. In short, Europe's dollar position had to improve enough that the forces pulling toward bilateralism or closure could be resisted once the flow of aid stopped in 1952. This required a transformation of the European economy that would end the inflation and significantly increase industrial productivity. The price of European goods had to be pushed down to the point where Europe could compete successfully in an open world economy, and the supply of goods for export had to be dramatically increased.[44]

The necessity of improving Western Europe's dollar receipts gave the Marshall Plan its paradoxical quality. To assure markets for American exports to Western Europe, the United States had to make that area more capable of competing with the United States. To preserve the U.S. export surplus, it was necessary to expand Western Europe's exports to the United States. The explanation of the paradox is simple. If Western Europe continued to experience extreme difficulty in earning dollars (other than aid dollars), it was likely to impose permanent and stringent controls on dollar imports and strict exchange controls with dollar areas. These would have the effect of cutting Western Europe off from the United States. To prevent this, the Marshall Plan had to show the Western European countries that they could compete successfully, albeit as junior partners, in a U.S.-dominated, multilateral world economy. In short, the Marshall Plan had to improve Western Europe's capacity to earn dollars both through increased exports and by an expanded inflow of U.S. investment, and this required fundamental changes in the organization of Western Europe's economies. Once the task was completed, the export surplus would continue to exist, but it would be based on a higher level of exports and imports and it would be financed by private investment flows.

The full story of the American effort to transform Western Europe in the Marshall Plan years has not yet been told. It includes sordid incidents such as the active involvement of the U.S. intelligence apparatus in efforts to split the European labor movements and complex political machinations that brought conservative governments to power in France, Italy, and Germany. In these years, American influence extended deep into the fabric of European society; American intervention had a great deal to do with decisions as to who was advanced into crucial positions of leadership in government, business, and the labor movement. For our purposes, however, it is sufficient to look at the main dimensions of Marshall Plan economic policy.[45]

The three key economic goals of the Marshall Plan—the restoration of multilateralism, price stability, and the recovery of production—were closely interconnected, but the means to achieve the goals were sometimes contradictory, and progress toward the different goals was uneven. The achievement of multilateralism was dependent on price stability, since an end to inflation would make price levels realistic enough for open trade. The agreements between the United States and the recipient countries included pledges to restore multilateralism, but as with earlier pledges these accomplished little by themselves. Under Marshall Plan auspices, the first Intra-European Payments Agreement went into effect in October 1948. Its purpose was to make possible intra-European trade that was not balanced bilaterally. There had been extensive debate about the degree of multilateralism to be incorporated in the Payments Agreement mechanisms, with the British strongly opposing a high level of multilateralism. Despite American pressure, the British view prevailed. The result was that the Payments Agreement did little more than provide additional credits for trade organized on a bilateral basis. There was little opportunity for transferring credits earned in trade with one country to make purchases from another country.[46]

Progress in achieving price stability was more tangible in the first years of the Marshall Plan. The Plan's structures gave the United States a good deal of leverage to shape the domestic economic policies of the recipient countries, and this leverage was multiplied when U.S. goals coincided with those of important interest groups in the recipient countries. The main components of U.S. leverage were the counterpart funds and the power to determine the distribution of aid among the countries. The counterpart funds resulted from provisions requiring the recipient countries to put into a special account an amount of their own currency equivalent to the dollar value of aid they received. Five percent of these funds were available for the use of the United States; this was designed to cover the administrative expenses of the aid missions. The remainder could be used in any way agreed on by the recipient government and the Marshall Plan administration. The money in the counterpart accounts was taken out of circulation, and this in itself had a mildly disinflationary effect on the economy. However, by blocking the use of the funds until adequate progress had been made in the fight against inflation, the ECA would exert stronger disinflationary pressure. Similarly, when the decisions were made as to how the dollar aid would be divided, countries that had done little to slow inflation risked penalization.[47]

In countries where the Left was particularly strong, reversing the inflationary patterns was not easy. Businessmen and politicians were hesitant to take the risks of holding the line on wages and government spending. But U.S. policy often found allies in the banking community, where opposition to inflation was a deeply held conviction. With this kind of support, drastic deflations were carried out between 1947 and 1949 in Italy, France, Germany, and other countries. These deflations resulted in dramatically high levels of unemployment, which in turn made it possible to resist wage demands directly.[48] The danger of social turmoil was minimized by American efforts to weaken the Left forces. The basic U.S. tactic was to split the working class movement along communist/anti-communist lines. CIA operatives, American labor representatives, and Cold War rhetoric were used to persuade non-communist trade unionists to cooperate with economic policies that were disastrous for the working class. Of course, the rigidity, the orientation toward the Soviet Union, and the strategic miscalculations of the various communist parties made it easier to accomplish this task. But as a consequence of U.S. efforts to split the labor movements, it became possible to label as "Communist wreckers" many of those struggling to defend the working class's economic position and to keep alive the dream of significant social reform.[49]

Defeating the Left also contributed to the recovery of industrial production. High levels of industrial investment were possible only if consumption and expenditures for social services were kept down. This required defeating the demands of labor and the Left for higher standards of living and expanded social services.[50] Productivity drives, organized by the Marshall Plan, attempted to alter working conditions and to speed up the pace of production. These drives depended on the cooperation of non-communist trade unionists who were persuaded to accept the American model of labor-management collaboration to achieve higher productivity.[51]

High levels of new investment and efforts to increase labor productivity were crucial to the restoration of European competitiveness. New investment was facilitated by the counterpart funds, which were often used for infrastructural investments in public utilities, transportation, and communications. In addition, special project grants made dollars available for American-approved investments, which were often financed by a combination of dollars and local funds.[52] However, investment was the main area in which Marshall Plan goals were contradictory. The deflations that were designed to contribute to price stability interfered with high levels of investment.[53] The deflationary policies often relied on credit restrictions, which made it difficult to borrow to finance new investments. Furthermore, the economic slowdown decreased profits and made it difficult for firms to finance investment internally. The deflation also decreased consumer demand, which often discouraged additional investment.

On the other hand, if the level of investment was pushed too high, it would tend to have inflationary effects. The result was that there was continuous conflict between different interest groups over the proper mix between investments and price stability. The Marshall Plan administration's strategy for dealing with this tension was to encourage a high degree of planning of investment decisions at the national and the regional levels. The idea was that, if each investment dollar was used in the most efficient way possible, an optimal trade-off between investment and inflation could be attained. This meant avoiding redundant investment by having different countries specialize in certain goods. Yet the Marshall Plan administrators' support for planning was limited by their opposition to planning mechanisms that would involve extensive coercion of capitalist firms or that could lead toward national capitalist policies. In France, the Monnet Plan was strongly supported by the ECA, and it clearly represented the kind of coordination of investment decisions without coercion that ECA policy-makers wanted to see in other recipient countries.[54] However, plans to coordinate investment across national lines had few results because countries were not willing to forgo the development of key industries, and even the level of national coordination achieved in France was not replicated elsewhere.[55]

THE CRISIS OF THE MARSHALL PLAN

The failure to coordinate investment decisions at the national or regional levels reflected the limits of the Marshall Plan. As an improvised policy, it had succeeded brilliantly in changing the drift of European developments. It provided a temporary solution to the dollar problem, halted the movement toward economic closure, and transformed the European political climate. Yet despite its successes in weakening the Left and in slowing inflation, the accomplishment of its long-term goals remained elusive. To make Western Europe's economy self-supporting in dollars in an open world economy required reversing structural changes in the pattern of world trade. But in attempting major structural changes in Europe, the Marshall Plan reached the limits of its effectiveness. It could not in the course of a few years fundamentally alter the practices of European businessmen or develop efficient planning mechanisms or attain a high level of economic coordination across national lines. In short, the task was simply too large and the likelihood remained that, in 1952, Western Europe would still have no way of earning an adequate quantity of dollars to cover its dollar trade deficit. The United States would be faced with the same dangers—the loss of the export surplus and the progressive insulation of the European economy—that had led to the implementation of the Marshall Plan in 1947.[56]

The logical response would have been to extend the Marshall Plan for another three or four years or however long it took to assure that Europe would be able to earn enough dollars through trade with third countries and through U.S. private investment to cover its trade deficit with the United States. This option was not available, however, because of Congressional suspicion toward the Marshall Plan. The most that the Truman administration could hope for was to get approval for the appropriations for all four years without disastrous cutbacks. Even this required a constant sales program that emphasized the Plan's great accomplishments. The idea of going back to Congress in 1951 or 1952 and asking for another $10 billion or $15 billion was unthinkable.

During the course of 1949, American policy-makers grappled with this overarching problem: how could they assure that the progress made under the Marshall Plan would not be reversed when that program came to an end? Simultaneously, they were forced to confront a number of more immediate but closely related problems that also threatened major American policy objectives. These subsidiary problems were an American recession, a new British currency crisis, and a crisis of political cooperation among the nations of Western Europe.

The American recession began in late 1948 and continued through most of 1949. It is generally described as an inventory recession, because there was a major disinvestment in business inventories. However, the recession may also be seen as resulting from the decline of business investment after the first quarter of 1948. For example, purchases of producers' equipment—capital goods—declined some $6 billion between the first quarter of 1948 and the last quarter of 1949. This decline in investment reflected concern on the part of the business community that, despite high levels of demand in 1948, there was little justification for expanding capacity further.

One possible explanation for this investment caution was the record of U.S. exports. Exports had reached their peak in the second quarter of 1947, and then had begun to decline. The flow of Marshall Plan aid had, as intended, a positive effect in maintaining export flows: the decline in total exports was stopped during 1948. However, exports again began to fall in the second half of 1949—declining by $3.6 billion on an annual basis. The fluctuations in total exports and the increasing percentage of exports that were financed by temporary aid flows meant that export demand did not appear strong or stable enough to justify new additions to industrial capacity.[57]

Whether this was a key element in the investment slowdown or not, it is certain that a further drop in exports would have deepened an already serious recession. Unemployment averaged 5.9 percent in 1949 and reached a peak of 7.6 percent in February 1950. The high levels of unemployment provoked concern in the labor movement and caused the business press to speculate that rising productivity might result in expanding production combined with continuous increases in unemployment.[58] Furthermore, the anxieties generated by the recession were far more serious than the economic statistics alone might suggest. Since this was the first postwar recession, there was little reason to assume that recovery would occur automatically. It was just as plausible to see the economic downturn, even if it halted temporarily, as the first step toward a return of the Great Depression.[59]

One of the major consequences of the American recession was a worsening of the position of the pound sterling. The recession slowed American imports from Britain and, even more important, reduced U.S. demand for Sterling Area raw materials. The consequent drop in Sterling Area dollar earnings was significant enough to precipitate the second major postwar sterling crisis. The position of the pound had remained precarious after the failure of convertibility in the summer of 1947. The reimposition of exchange controls had not solved Britain's problems but had merely contained them. The flow of Marshall Plan aid had been important in allowing the British to muddle through in 1948 and early 1949, but it had done little to solve Britain's major problems.

The most significant of Britain's difficulties was the sterling balances. Bilateral agreements had finally been reached with most of the major holders, but these agreements provided a fairly high ceiling for annual use of the balances. The consequence was that a not insignificant portion—perhaps 20 percent—of British exports went to the holders of the balances rather than to markets where dollars or other hard currencies could be earned.[60] In addition, the size of the foreign balances meant that, even with an efficient control mechanism, there were bound to be some illicit conversions of pounds into dollars when the pound appeared weak. The system of pooling Sterling Area dollar receipts generally tended to counteract the negative effects of the sterling balances. By continuing the regional role of sterling, Britain was in a position to control the dollar receipts of the whole Sterling Area, and this, in turn, strengthened the position of the pound. However, when the Sterling Area's dollar receipts dropped, as they did in response to the U.S. recession, the cushioning effect disappeared, and the full weakness of Britain's position became evident.[61]

In the second quarter of 1949, Britain's deficit with the dollar area reached $660 million, twice the size of Marshall Plan dollar aid.[62] The British responded by attempting to cut imports and trying to acquire additional dollar aid. The Commonwealth Finance Ministers Conference in July 1949 agreed to a common effort to reduce dollar expenditures by 25 percent from 1948 levels; and in the same month Stafford Cripps, the Chancellor of the Exchequer, was reported to desire a major new U.S. loan to stabilize the pound. Given Congressional sensibilities, the likelihood of such a loan was remote, and the British pursued the more likely course of increasing their request for Marshall Plan aid. This increased British request heightened the already acute decision-making crisis within the OEEC.[63]

The United States had given the OEEC the task of planning the distribution of Marshall Plan aid among the various recipient nations. In 1949, the task was complicated by the reduction by Congress of the total available funds and by ECA's insistence that $150 million from the 1949-50 appropriation be used to promote a rapid liberalization of intra-European trade through the creation of a new European payments mechanism. Given the profound differences in Western Europe over the proper pace and scope of liberalization, the American demand intensified the tensions within the OEEC over a new payments arrangement and over the distribution of aid in general. Tensions were heightened further when the British submitted a memorandum to the OEEC that substantially raised their estimates of Britain's expected dollar deficit and resulting aid needs. The result was a major crisis within the OEEC that threatened a breakdown of European cooperation within this U.S.-designed structure. At the last minute, through extraordinary means, a formula for distributing the aid was devised by the OEEC, but it involved ignoring the U.S. demand to set aside the $150 million. The ECA responded by relieving the OEEC of the task of distributing the aid money. One can imagine that the U.S. action, coming after the enormous difficulties that the OEEC had in reaching any agreement, generated a high level of skepticism about continued European-American cooperation.[64]

These interlocking crises created the context for U.S. policy in 1949-50. Their seriousness was such that the fears about what might happen when the Marshall Plan came to an end in 1952 took on an added urgency, because it began to appear that these dreaded events might occur even sooner. *Business Week,* in the second half of 1949 and early 1950, spoke with anxiety of the dollar and non-dollar areas becoming closed to each other, of Britain moving toward the restoration of a closed sterling bloc, of a new business downturn in the second half of 1950, and of another sterling crisis coming in 1950. Meanwhile, the OEEC officials threatened to increase European discrimination against dollar goods, unless the United States drastically reduced its tariffs and agreed to raise the price of gold.[65] In short, in this period all of the major goals of American foreign economic policy seemed in jeopardy, and the health of the U.S. domestic economy was also problematic. The crisis provoked a number of responses from the United States government, as different agencies devised strategies to cope with the mounting dangers. Strategies of two agencies—the Treasury Department and the ECA—were given limited trials, but they were then supplanted by the more radical policy of the State Department.

THE TREASURY PLAN

The Treasury plan was essentially a continuation of the traditional multilateralism that had been advanced by the State Department in 1945-46. Full currency convertibility abroad would make possible a large U.S. export surplus that would be financed by a flow of U.S. private capital into Europe and other regions. The Treasury's means to this end was a major realignment of currency values through a devaluation of all of the major European currencies. Devaluations would make possible greater European sales in the United States and other markets, and would be followed shortly by full currency convertibility, which would lay the basis for expanded U.S. private investment in Europe. In short, the realignment of exchange rates was the central means by which Europe would develop the capacity to earn dollars on a sufficient scale in the post-Marshall Plan period.[66]

The need for European devaluations to counter the impact of the wartime and postwar inflations had been discussed in American circles for some time. However, in the period from 1945 to 1948, it was generally acknowledged that, until European production recovered, it made little sense to tinker with exchange rates. Devaluations have their desired effect through a market mechanism; by lowering the value of its currency, a country can make its exports cheaper and, at the lower prices, increased foreign demand will lead to a significant improvement in the quantity of goods exported. Essentially, an increase in the volume of exports will make a positive contribution to total export receipts, despite the fact that receipts per unit will decline. This desired effect, however, is not always achieved. If the volume of exports remains constant after devaluation (because foreign demand is not sensitive to price differences or because extra production for export is not possible), the effect of devaluation on a country's export receipts will be perverse; they will decline. This was the danger that American policy-makers pointed to in the immediate postwar period. Much of international trade at that point was relatively insensitive to price differentials, and European production was still at low levels, while domestic demand was high, so a devaluation might simply lower the standard of living in Europe without improving Europe's trade position. Furthermore, lowering the standard of living, which could be achieved only by making imports from outside Europe significantly more expensive, would intensify the class struggle and add to the problem of inflation.[67]

By 1949, the Treasury position was that, regardless of the merits of this argument in the past, the time was now ripe or overripe for a realignment of exchange rates. European production had recovered enough to make possible significant increases in the volume of goods available for export. Treasury felt that even if the continued use of exchange controls and bilateral trade agreements made the flow of international trade relatively impervious to price changes, it was still appropriate to use a technique—such as devaluation—that relied on market mechanisms. The Treasury's reasoning was that realistic exchange rates had become a precondition for clearing away the structures of state trading, bilateral trading, and exchange controls that interfered with a market-determined flow of international trade. Once devaluation had re-established realistic exchange rates, the road would be open to a full multilateralization of international trade. If this path were not followed and present exchange rates were allowed to continue, progress toward multilateralism would be postponed indefinitely.

With increasing urgency through the first half of 1949, the Treasury Department placed pressures on the European governments, particularly Britain, for devaluation. This pressure was exerted directly and also indirectly through the International Monetary Fund. According to its Articles of Agreement, the fund had no authority to question a member nation's exchange rates; its role was rather to participate in consultations initiated by member nations. Nevertheless, the United States successfully pushed the fund to initiate informal consultations with member governments on exchange rates. In addition, a U.S.-proposed Ad Hoc Committee of the fund issued a report calling for immediate action to readjust exchange rates. The Ad Hoc Committee was a device by which the United States could press its case on the Europeans while staying within the rules of the fund.[68]

The end of the Treasury Department's campaign came with the

sharpening of the sterling crisis in August and September 1949. Ironically, the crisis was precipitated by the American recession that had sharply reduced British and Sterling Area dollar receipts. However, the occasion of a major run against sterling gave the Treasury Department the leverage to force the devaluations which it had for some time seen as essential but which had so far been resisted by the Europeans. At times during the crisis, Treasury tactics were so aggressive that the State Department became anxious about a deterioration in Anglo-American relations.[69] The politics of the period are complex and difficult to discern, but it seems clear that the British were anxious to obtain a new dollar loan as a quid pro quo for agreement to devalue. The idea of a $1 billion or $2 billion stabilization loan for Britain was leaked to the press, but the difficulty of gaining the approval of a suspicious Congress again led to abandonment of the proposal.[70] In the end, the British were forced to devalue without benefit of a loan. They were granted the right, however, to discriminate systematically against U.S. imports. This concession to British needs conflicted with Treasury's commitment to multilateralism, but it was granted at the urging of the Marshall Plan administration.[71]

The British devaluation came on September 18, and it set off the expected chain of European devaluations. The magnitude of the British devaluation (30.5 percent) took many by surprise and created mumblings on the Continent about the possibility of a trade war. The huge British devaluation was prompted by the desire to gain advantage over European competitors who were also expected to devalue, but by smaller amounts. The drastic devaluation was also motivated by a desire to establish a parity that would definitively end speculative pressure against the pound. The thinness of British reserves and the unavailability of an American loan made it important to avoid a renewed sterling crisis. The tactic worked and, although some European countries—Norway, Denmark, and the Netherlands—devalued as radically as Britain, others, including France and Belgium, did not.[72]

The Treasury Department gained the currency realignment it had hoped for, but the victory was hollow. The realignment had been accompanied by increases in trade discrimination, and the restoration of multilateralism was no closer. Treasury pressure on Britain to reestablish sterling convertibility was blocked by the State Department and the ECA because these agencies recognized immediate sterling convertibility to be impractical.[73] Worse yet, from the Treasury perspective, the devaluations were followed in short order by a drift in

U.S. policy toward increased support for European economic integration, including toleration of discrimination against dollar goods. The Treasury Department lacked the muscle to force European governments or the American administration itself to adhere to the Treasury's orthodox path to a multilateral world economy, and little wonder, since the Department's plans were basically unrealistic. The likely result of a restoration of European currency convertibility in 1949-50 and an abandonment of trade restrictions would have been a series of balance-of-payments crises, exchange depreciations, and ultimately a rapid retreat from multilateralism.

THE EUROPEAN COOPERATION ADMINISTRATION PLAN

The position of the ECA was stated in a speech by Paul Hoffman, Marshall Plan administrator, on October 31, 1949, at which time he called in the strongest terms for European economic integration. From the start, the Marshall Plan had represented a shift away from the rigid multilateralism of Hull, in that the Plan recognized regional economic realities. However, in its earlier years, the main content of that regionalism was an emphasis on the development of political and economic cooperation among the governments of the region. With Hoffman's speech, the emphasis turned to integration, by which Hoffman meant "the formation of a single large market within which quantitative restrictions on the movement of goods, monetary barriers to the flow of payments, and eventually, all tariffs are permanently swept away."[74] The difference between cooperation and integration was that the latter implied the unleashing of market forces, while the former relied on political decision-making.

The theory behind this emphasis on economic integration was simple; the creation of a European-wide market would make it possible for European industry to modernize and increase its international competitiveness. A greatly expanded market would make possible the economies of scale and the technological advances that had been the major advantages of American industry. In addition, the lowering of national barriers to trade would allow the fresh wind of competition to clear away the stale air of cartels, informal agreements, and other devices used to protect European firms from intense competitive pressure. Heightened competition would inspire more aggressive business practices, including more determined efforts to increase production and lower prices. The problem of lagging European exports could be

solved by creating conditions under which European capitalists themselves, under the pressure of the market, would be forced to improve
the competitiveness of their products. This would make it possible for
Europeans to increase their sales in the U.S. market, and it would put
U.S.-European trade on a more reciprocal basis. Furthermore, the
creation of a Europe-wide market would stimulate the flow of U.S.
investments into Europe. In sum, as with the Treasury's emphasis on
currency realignment, the ECA's emphasis on European economic
integration was to be a means to achieve the original vision of a large
U.S. export surplus, based on a large flow of trade between the United
States and Europe and financed by private U.S. investment flows.[75]

The creation of a European Payments Union was one of the central mechanisms by which European economic integration was to be
effected. Plans for an EPU had been circulating since 1947, but strong
official support was not forthcoming until late 1949 and early 1950.[76]
The EPU's purpose was to revive intra-European trade by creating a
multilateral payments mechanism within Europe. At base, the EPU
would be a clearing union that would encourage intra-European trade
by allowing countries to use their trade surpluses with one country to
purchase goods from another country. The union would also provide
credit so that countries would no longer be forced to keep their trade
with the rest of Europe restricted to achieve continuous balance. The
theory behind the union was the same as that of European integration.
The only way that the European countries could realistically be expected to progress toward equal participation in an open world
economy was by stages. First, the Europeans must be weaned from
their systems of controls and bilateral trade by multilateralizing trade
on a regional basis. During this first stage, discrimination and controls
would still operate toward the rest of the world, especially on dollar
trade and payments. However, the increased openness on the regional
level would force European industry to increase its competitiveness,
making possible a gradual dismantling of the remaining controls. In the
second stage, there would be an end to trade discrimination and currency controls; full convertibility would be restored. In other words,
the EPU was the key element in what was seen as a gradual evolutionary process that would take Europe from bilateralism to full
multilateralism.[77]

The Marshall Plan administration put strong pressure on the
countries of Europe to agree to the creation of the EPU in the last
months of 1949 and in the first half of 1950. The strongest resistance

came from the British, who had multiple reasons to resist the plan. They had consistently resisted U.S. pressure for multilateralizing European trade because of the pound's extreme vulnerability; they preferred the security of organizing trade with Europe through bilateral channels; and they feared that, within the EPU arrangements, European governments would have the opportunity to convert their already existing sterling balances into dollars, further weakening the pound's position. Furthermore, British participation in the EPU raised the larger problem of Britain's relation to European integration. The British were unwilling to give up their global role for the sake of progress toward European economic integration, and they feared that the EPU could not be reconciled to the continuation of Britain's obligations to the Sterling Area. Finally, those in Britain who looked forward to a restoration of sterling's prewar international role were profoundly suspicious of the EPU because it substituted an intergovernmental credit mechanism for the historic credit-providing role of British bankers. Nevertheless, a combination of arm-twisting and strategic concessions on the part of the United States won British acquiescence to the EPU, and the Agreement establishing the Union was signed on September 19, 1950.[78]

At the same time that the British were resisting the EPU, the U.S. Treasury Department was offering a continuing critique of the logic behind the EPU. The Treasury critique was based on the conviction that one could not trust an evolutionary process to eliminate a system of controls. They reasoned that, behind any system of trade and exchange controls, new economic interests would develop whose existence would be dependent on the controls. These new interests (and the longer the controls lasted, the more numerous and powerful they would be) would constitute a lobbying force opposed to the dismantling of controls. The Treasury men were traditionalists who believed that the way to eliminate controls is to eliminate them, and that temporizing only insures their continued existence. But the Treasury position was not simply that the EPU would do little to actually liberalize trade and payments; rather, the EPU would facilitate a development that had long been feared: Europe would become a high inflation area, largely insulated from trade with the United States. The availability of credit within the EPU would provide countries with a means to resist the discipline of the international economy and to avoid taking disinflationary actions. The continued existence of controls on trade with the dollar area would make it possible for European price levels to continue rising in relation to U.S. prices, and there would be no reason or mechanism to reverse the process.[79]

The Treasury Department was unsuccessful in turning U.S. policy away from the EPU, but despite this failure the Treasury critique made sense. While Treasury's own solutions were inadequate, Treasury officials were able to see the limitations of opposing policy directions. The limitation of the emphasis on European integration was that it failed to resolve the problem of what would happen when the Marshall Plan ended. Progress toward European integration, even with the EPU implemented, was likely to be painfully slow, and the consequent modernization of industry would not occur overnight. In short, the increasing competitiveness of European industry was not likely to materialize until well after 1952. If U.S. aid were actually ended in 1952, and Europe were left with few resources with which to earn dollars, the EPU could well become the institutional base for turning Europe into a monetary area that was insulated from the dollar area by a system of permanent controls. In short, Europe could adopt national capitalism on a regional basis.

In fact, the ECA gave token recognition to the validity of this objection by speaking of the need to continue the Marshall Plan past 1952.[80] But given the state of Congressional opinion, this proposal was whistling in the dark. The reality was that the line of policy advocated by the ECA had certain attractive elements, but in itself the ECA emphasis on European integration did not provide a solution to the overlapping difficulties that faced U.S. foreign economic policy. The ECA plan did nothing to assure that European regionalism would not evolve in opposition to the United States once Marshall Aid ended. This problem was understood by State Department planners, and they proceeded to formulate policies that would allow European regionalism to develop in a context that guaranteed permanent links between European and American capitalism.

STATE DEPARTMENT PLANS

Two different plans developed in the State Department in this period. The first is interesting not because it had a major effect on policy but because its unconventionality indicates the seriousness with which the crisis of 1949 was viewed. This first plan was developed by George Kennan of the State Department's Policy Planning Staff. Kennan believed in a variation of the key currency theory that saw the problems of the British economy as central to European recovery and to the achievement of U.S. global aims. Since options in which the United States aided Britain directly were ruled out by Congressional opposition, Kennan was forced to devise more extreme measures when the pound was suffering its second major postwar crisis in 1949. His answer was an economic merger of the United States, Great Britain, and Canada. The precise mechanism by which this would work was not clear, but the idea was that the merger would make it possible for the United States to underwrite the pound and many of Britain's international activities.[81]

At the time Kennan put forward this idea, others outside the administration were advocating an Atlantic Union of Democracies that would create a free-trade area that included Western Europe, Britain, the United States, and Canada. William Clayton, no longer in the government, was a major supporter of the Atlantic Union idea. Both Kennan's and Clayton's ideas were attempts to solve the problem presented by Western Europe by absorbing it into the United States. Kennan did not go as far as Clayton, probably because he believed that, if Britain were absorbed into the United States, that would be sufficient to assure close economic cooperation between the United States and Western Europe. Both ideas were efforts to confound American anti-internationalists by persuading them that these foreign areas were really a part of the American nation and hence worthy of continuing economic support. However, there is little evidence that anyone was fooled, and these ideas of economic union were never implemented.[82]

The other line of State Department thinking, although far more successful in shaping American policy, was no less radical in its willingness to break with established policies and practices. This approach centered around Secretary of State Acheson and Paul Nitze, who replaced Kennan as head of the Policy Planning Staff in late 1949. There is evidence that, through 1949, these men were dissatisfied with the plans put forward by the ECA and the Treasury Department. They saw neither European integration nor currency realignments as adequate to maintain a significant export surplus or to continue American-European economic ties after the end of the Marshall Plan.[83] The new line of policy they proposed—massive U.S. and European rearmament—provided a brilliant solution to the major problems of U.S. economic policy. Domestic rearmament would provide a new means to sustain demand so that the economy would no longer be dependent on maintaining an export surplus. Military aid to Europe would provide a means to continue providing aid to Europe after the expiration of the Marshall Plan. And the close integration of European and American military forces would provide a means to prevent Europe as an economic region from closing itself off from the United States.

The evolution of the rearmament policy can be traced from the fall of 1949. In the wake of U.S. intelligence reports in September that indicated that the Soviet Union had exploded an atomic device, and the shock to the United States of the "fall of China" in October, a high level re-evaluation of U.S. foreign policy was initiated. One crucial decision that required consideration was whether to attempt production of a hydrogen bomb. The feasibility of a fusion bomb was uncertain, and the project would be quite expensive.[84] Nevertheless, the Soviet atomic explosion, coming four years ahead of U.S. estimates, made the H-bomb project appear irresistible. Some of those who favored a go-ahead on the H-bomb, however, believed that the decision should be made only in the context of a major reconsideration of the U.S. defense posture.[85]

This reconsideration was required because of the commitment by the Truman administration to a rigid ceiling on the defense budget. James Forrestal, the first Secretary of Defense, had fought a losing battle within the Truman administration for abandoning the ceiling in the budget for fiscal 1950. Forrestal believed, with others, that the ceiling imposed by Truman made attainment of an appropriate level of military preparedness impossible. Forrestal's arguments ran against the orthodoxy of the period, an orthodoxy that in retrospect appears strange but prophetic. This was the concept that precisely what the Soviet Union desired was for the United States to increase its defense budget until it finally spent its way into national bankruptcy. This view derived its strength from traditional business ideology, which opposed expanded government expenditures and higher tax levels. But it was also supported by serious concern over inflationary conditions within the U.S. economy during much of 1948. In addition, the Truman administration's willingness to accept this orthodoxy during the debate over the 1950 budget is probably attributable in part to fears for the second year of Marshall Plan aid. One of the original arguments used to gain Congressional support for the Marshall Plan had been that the plan was an alternative to the increased defense budgets that would be necessary if the United States failed to come to the aid of Western

Europe. If the administration proposed significant increases in the defense budget, the economy-conscious Congress was likely to limit the size of the defense increase and significantly cut back the appropriation for the second year of the Marshall Plan.

Forrestal's successor as Secretary of Defense, Louis Johnson, did not share the former's views about the need to expand the military. On the contrary, Johnson, a lawyer who had been rewarded with the Defense position for his services in Truman's 1948 campaign, was a budget-cutter determined to lower defense spending further. It has been suggested that Johnson's political ambitions did not stop with the Defense Department, and this might explain the fervor of his campaign for economy in defense. Whatever his motives, he had enough support from Truman and from the business community to hold the line of the budget ceiling and to resist pressures from the Joint Chiefs of Staff.[86]

Forrestal's defeat and Johnson's successes made things difficult for those who favored new military measures. For example, if it was decided to go ahead with H-bomb production while retaining the current ceiling, other areas of defense would have to be cut back. Even if one did not take seriously the threat of the Soviet army invading Western Europe, it was apparent that further military cutbacks might well interfere with U.S. global aims. There were enough trouble spots in the world where strong revolutionary movements existed to suggest the possibility that the United States might become militarily engaged. The commitment of the Truman Doctrine was to defend "freedom" wherever it was threatened, and in the world of 1949 that might well require military intervention.

While considerations of military preparedness played a role in the initiation of the policy review, the evolution of the rearmament policy indicates that military needs were not the only reason for the new policy. Discussions of the H-bomb decision led to the initiation of a "Broad appraisal of the nation's foreign commitments, capabilities, and the existing strategic situation" within the National Security Council. This appraisal was directed by Paul Nitze and dominated by State Department representatives. The group deliberated from early January 1950 until March of that year, and the result of these discussions was a document entitled "NSC-68." Although this document has not yet been published, we know that it drew a picture of a global confrontation between the United States and the Soviet Union and called for an enormous increase in American defense spending and a concerted effort to rearm Western Europe as well.[87] Accounts of the deliberations on "NSC-68" indicate that the Defense Department representatives on the committee initially resisted proposals that would exceed the existing $13.5 billion ceiling on defense spending. Under pressure from the State Department representatives, the Defense representatives gradually raised their sights to the level of $17-18 billion. However, this still did not satisfy State's representatives, who favored a figure of $35-50 billion. The conservatism of the Defense Department representatives reflected their awareness of the opposition to increased defense budgets by the Secretary of Defense, the Bureau of the Budget, and the Congress. Nevertheless, the size of the difference between Defense and State figures suggests that military considerations were only one part of the State Department's support for massive rearmament.[88]

The rhetoric associated with "NSC-68" indicates some of the other motives behind the new policy. This rhetoric is summarized in the phrase "negotiation from strength," which meant that only when the West had overwhelming military superiority could it afford to work out a modus vivendi with the Soviet Union.[89] The suggestion is that, if negotiations with the Soviet Union to settle the issues of divided Europe had begun in 1949-50, the West would find itself in a weak position. This reflected the United States' perception that the Soviet "peace campaigns" had become a serious threat. There was mounting pressure at this time for negotiations with the Soviet Union to resolve the European situation. The United States feared that with the relative weakness of most of the Western European regimes and with the economic pull of Eastern European markets, negotiations would result in a settlement far too favorable to the Soviet Union. The crucial issues were the future of Germany and the possibilities for East-West trade. The United States realized that a negotiated settlement would almost by definition interdict the U.S. desire to incorporate West Germany in an anti-Soviet alliance. Furthermore, if West Germany were neutralized or tied to Eastern Europe by strong trading bonds, the economic pull on the other Western European powers by Germany and the East would tend to weaken their ties to Washington. In short, the U.S. goal of a multilateral world economy, which was dependent upon a revived and economically liberal Western Europe, was endangered by the possibility of accommodation with the Soviet Union in 1949-50. Rearmament provided a useful means to intensify the polarization of Europe, and the idea of negotiation from strength gave the United States a justification for avoiding a settlement that would endanger its goals.

As with the Marshall Plan, the rearmament policy was multi-faceted. It provided a solution to a whole set of interlocking problems. While the rhetoric of "NSC-68" focused entirely on the military and political-strategic issues, the policy was also a response to pressing economic problems.[90] A tripling of defense spending would pull the economy out of the doldrums and solve the problem of stagnating levels of employment. It would also save those industries, such as machine tools and aircraft production, that had fallen into deep depression during the postwar period. Most important, military spending would put a floor under the economy, so that every downturn in business investment or in export demand would not threaten the return of depression conditions. In short, the rearmament policy involved an acceptance of Keynesian theory, but not with the radical implications of national economic planning. Military Keynesianism was consistent with maximum continued freedom for domestic capitalists, and it eliminated the danger of a disruptive economic crisis.

Internationally, rearmament would advance American economic goals by creating a context in which European regionalism would not be a danger. Military aid to Europe after the Marshall Plan would eliminate any pressure for Europe to cut itself off, because there would be a continuing source of dollar aid.[91] This would also make it possible to finance the exports of certain industries that would still be dependent on foreign markets even after rearmament. Finally, European rearmament under American leadership would make Europe dependent on American military hardware. This dependence could then be used to prevent Europe from drifting away from the United States.[92]

But the rearmament policy, for all its advantages, still required popular and Congressional approval. This was no easy matter because of continuing opposition to high levels of government spending and resistance to American internationalist policies. Furthermore, the Truman administration's manipulation of international crises to push legislation through Congress had become so commonplace as to lose much of its effectiveness as a tactic.[93] Having accepted "NSC-68" as official policy in the spring of 1950, the administration had three choices. It could wait for a more propitious moment to begin pushing for rearmament; it could adopt a policy of increasing the defense budget gradually over a period of years; or it could again resort to the manipulation of international crises to convince Congress and the public that massive rearmament was absolutely necessary. This dilemma was quickly solved when the outbreak of the Korean War created a political context in which the administration gained a free hand for the pursuit of its rearmament plans.

In the context of the Korean War crisis, expenditures on national security programs quickly increased from $13 billion in 1950 to $22.3 billion in 1951, to $44 billion in 1952, and then to $50.4 billion in 1953. Only a part of this dramatic increase in military spending went to pay for the war effort in Korea; $4.5 billion of the $10.5 billion asked for in the first supplemental appropriation for the Korean War was actually designated for long-term rearmament.[94] And the percentage for non-Korean War purposes increased in subsequent appropriations. With this rapid increase in military spending, the major problem of the American economy was once again inflation. Instead of overcapacity and unemployment, there were strong demand pressures on existing resources. The Truman administration responded to this problem with a major program to expand industrial capacity so that the Korean War effort and rearmament would not mean a sharp reduction in civilian consumption. The Defense Production Act provided extensive tax incentives for business to engage in new investments, and under the program many millions were invested in expanding the economy's industrial base.[95]

It is ironic that the rearmament policy, which was in part a response to surplus capacity in the economy, led to an even greater expansion of industrial capacity. However, the rearmament policy was not simply intended to absorb the economy's surplus resources. On the scale envisioned in "NSC-68," military spending would make possible a dramatic expansion of total production so that real wages and consumption would be able to increase steadily even as a major portion of the economy's resources were put into military production. In short, military spending would act to stimulate dynamic growth in the economy to assure an ever-growing economic pie.[96] The problem with this strategy, as the Eisenhower administration learned, was that, with expanded industrial capacity, reductions in the level of military spending led to recession. Only by increasing the total level of military spending could the dynamism of the economy be maintained. However, in the long term, these increases in military spending would sap the economy's strength.

FIVE. *Toward European Convertibility*

At the beginning of the 1950s, despite several years of Marshall Plan aid, little progress had been made toward the achievement of a multilateral world order. The dollar gap was still a major problem, most European trade continued to be organized along bilateral lines, and no major European currency was yet convertible. By the end of the decade the picture was very different: the dollar gap had been replaced by a dollar glut, all major European currencies were convertible, and most of the structure of bilateralism and quantitative restrictions had been dismantled. In short, by the end of the 1950s, the Western European countries had opted for liberal economic policies. The American success in restoring a multilateral world economy during the 1950s can largely be attributed to the interrelated policies of rearmament and support for European regionalism. These policies were instrumental in guiding European reconstruction along lines consistent with American goals. Nevertheless, rearmament and support for European regionalism were policies that would have substantial long-term costs for the United States. The very means used to restore a multilateral world economy distorted that world eonomy in fundamental ways. The consequences of these distortions would be the chronic crises of the international monetary system in the 1960s.

THE LIQUIDITY PROBLEM—
TOO MUCH OR TOO LITTLE

The central problem for American foreign economic policy through most of the 1950s revolved around the seemingly technical issue of regulation of the supply of international liquidity.[1] In the aftermath of the Marshall Plan's early years, the leaders of most Western European countries were willing to adapt themselves to the American goal of a multilateral world economy, provided that the domestic costs of this adaptation would not be too great. In other words, the Europeans would gradually remove controls over trade and payments if this did not require further sharp cuts in domestic levels of employment and real income. The removal of controls could be facilitated by an ample supply of international liquidity that could insulate countries from the more painful adjustments of employment and income. However, if international liquidity were too scarce, countries would be unwilling to risk the removal of controls. Instead, they would be likely to organize trade along bilateral lines and form regional blocs that were closed off from the United States in order to avoid the discipline of a multilateral system. But if international liquidity were too abundant, there would be too little pressure on countries to hold inflation in check, and the lack of domestic monetary discipline would become an obstacle to an open world economy by making the relaxation of controls impossible. The trick, then, was to maintain the supply of international liquidity at such a level that countries exercising a reasonable degree of monetary discipline could move toward eliminating exchange controls. To find this optimal level of international liquidity was not easy, especially because different economies had very different international liquidity needs.

But even if an optimal level of international liquidity could be computed, the other problem was that U.S. policy-makers did not have a free hand to determine how much liquidity would flow into the world economy. There was continuing strong pressure by foreign countries for plans that would dramatically increase the supply of international liquidity. And domestic opposition to American internationalism served to keep the United States from easily setting its contribution to international liquidity at the optimal level. The strength of American protectionist forces made it impossible for the United States to increase the number of dollars earned abroad simply by increasing its imports. And opposition to American internationalism made it impossible for the United States to continue programs such as the Marshall Plan that put dollars directly into foreign hands. American policy-makers dealt with this dilemma by fighting, on one front, to block proposals for uncontrolled international liquidity creation and, on another front, to increase the flow into foreign hands of liquidity subject to American control.

The struggle against uncontrolled liquidity creation had begun with U.S. resistance to Keynes' ambitious credit-union scheme and the withdrawal of White's early radical plans. It continued after Bretton Woods with the American effort to make the conditions for drawing on the International Monetary Fund far more stringent than those outlined in the Articles of Agreement that White and Keynes had devised. The fund was scheduled to begin permitting use of its resources in March 1947, and almost immediately thereafter the American campaign to limit the use of those resources achieved its first major success. The Articles of the fund provided that a country was entitled to draw on the fund if "the member desiring to purchase the currency represents that it is presently needed for making in that currency payments which are consistent with the provisions of the Agreement." In May 1947, the United States pushed through the following interpretation of that seemingly unambiguous provision:

The word "represents" in Article V, Section 3(a)(i), means "declares." . . . But the Fund may, for good reasons, challenge the correctness of this declaration, on the grounds that the currency is not "presently needed" or because the currency is not needed for payment "in that currency," or because the payments will not be "consistent with the provisions of this Agreement." If the Fund concludes that a particular declaration is not correct, the Fund may postpone or reject the request, or accept it subject to conditions . . .[2]

Through this and other "interpretations," the American representatives on the fund succeeded in greatly expanding the fund's ability to block access to its resources. There was opposition to this alteration of the fund, especially from the French, but the Americans had the votes to get their way.

The next step in the American campaign to transform the fund was the demand that the fund block drawings by recipients of Marshall Plan aid during the four years of that program. The justification for this demand was that drawings from the fund by Marshall aid recipients would be redundant, but cutting off other sources of liquidity to Western European countries clearly had the effect of increasing the leverage of the Marshall Plan administrators. The demand was accepted, despite some protests by European members of the fund. These protests, one would imagine, were muted by the fear that the more vociferous protestants might be punished by the reduction of Marshall Plan aid to them. At any rate, this decision served to give the United States a longer period of time in which to tighten the fund's rules. For four years, most countries that would attempt to draw on fund resources would be underdeveloped countries, and it would be far easier to establish strict precedents with them than with the more independent European countries. During these four years, the United States pushed for strict provisions governing the repayment of fund drawings and for a procedure that would tie drawings to a specific program of action by the drawing members. The United States wanted to make the fund operate according to traditional international banking procedures that required the borrower to insure its capacity to repay by embarking on a program of deflation. While the United States did not succeed on all of these points right away, drawing on the fund became increasingly difficult. Total drawings from the fund fell from $467.7 million in 1947 to zero in 1950. Total drawings did not exceed the 1947 level again until 1956.[3]

The effort to transform the International Monetary Fund did not exhaust the U.S. fight against additions to international liquidity that the United States did not control. The United States, for example, opposed proposals by South Africa and others for increasing the dollar value of gold. It had been argued after the war that, while all other commodities had increased their dollar price dramatically since 1934, gold remained frozen at the same price, $35 an ounce. This was a particular hardship for Britain, since the gold that was produced within the Sterling Area had sharply dropped in its purchasing power relative to goods. Even though the United States owned most of the world's gold reserves, it opposed this proposal adamantly because of the fear that an increase in the dollar value of gold reserves would stimulate inflation. The U.S. theory was that, if governments found their reserves dramatically increased overnight, they would use the gain to finance additional imports, placing strong upward pressure on international prices. Or they would simply be much too lax about protecting their reserves in the event of a balance-of-payments deficit. Proposals to raise the gold price, always with strong South African support, were advanced on different occasions during the 1950s, but the American response was consistently negative.[4]

Another movement for increased international liquidity emerged within the United Nations, and it received an equally cool reception from U.S. policy-makers. Two studies were commissioned by the United Nations' Economic and Social Committee to propose international measures that could be taken to prevent spreading deflation. Like much thinking of the time, the studies were conditioned by fears of a slowdown in the American economy and the danger that that would set off another world depression. The first report, prepared by a committee of economists in 1949, contained a proposal that countries suffering from economic slowdowns would recompense other countries for the reserves that those countries lost through the decline in import demand in the deflationary country. In short, it was a proposal for countercyclical flows of international reserves to assure international full employment. The proposal was rejected by the IMF, under U.S. pressure, on the grounds that the fund "could not consider full employment more important than a freely operating multilateral trading system" and that the proposal was technically deficient.[5] The second report, by a different group of experts, was published in 1951; it called simply for a liberalization and expansion of the IMF's resources. This, too, was rejected by the IMF with the arguments that the fund's primary responsibility was not anti-deflationary, that the fund's resources were too limited for the job of preventing a world depression, and that there was little prospect for expanding the fund's resources. The experts' report did, however, stimulate some grumbling among countries such as France which argued that the suggestions for liberalizing IMF resources would be entirely unnecessary if the Fund's original articles were correctly interpreted.[6]

The second report prompted a study by the IMF's staff of the adequacy of the current level of international reserves and of the resources available through the fund itself. The conclusion of the report was that international reserves and the fund's resources were generally inadequate. This came as little surprise, because in 1949-50 the fund's staff had already recommended doubling the fund's quotas. In each case, the fund's directors, and in particular the American director, rejected the findings and opposed any attempts to increase the fund's resources.[7] In the early 1950s there was a certain logic to this American position, in that drawings on the fund were almost nonexistent, a result of the stringent conditions on drawings that the United States had pushed through. But starting in 1956, the size of drawings began increasing dramatically. Drawings averaged $73.2 million a year from 1950 to 1955, and then jumped to $692.6 million in 1956 and $977.1 million in 1957. The increased use of the fund's resources stimulated new demands for an increase in quotas, but the United States opposed an expansion of the fund's resources through 1958.[8]

The American policy of limiting access to IMF resources and blocking other proposals for increasing international liquidity had a number of advantages for the United States. It assured that the fund would work to reinforce the traditional discipline of the gold standard. It also increased the leverage of various U.S. aid programs, since there were no other ready sources of international liquidity. Finally, maintaining an international liquidity shortage increased the desirability of U.S. private investment dollars; countries were more likely to encourage such investments and provide a hospitable climate for U.S. businessmen when liquidity was in short supply. However, the United States had to be careful that liquidity did not become too scarce or foreign countries would simply refuse to play by multilateral rules.

From the standpoint of U.S. policy-makers, the ideal solution to the liquidity shortage would be an expansion of U.S. private investment abroad. New York would play the role that London had played in the nineteenth century: making credit available to foreign countries to ease their payments difficulties. The problem was that U.S. private investment failed to reach high enough levels in the ten years after World War II. The central reason for this was the absence of stable monetary conditions abroad. As long as foreign countries had severe inflation problems and continued to use exchange controls, private investors were reluctant to send money abroad.[9] This was a classic vicious circle: if liquidity was too short, countries could not afford to remove exchange controls. But if they did not remove exchange controls, there would be very small flows of international private investment, and liquidity would remain scarce. U.S. policy was designed to resolve this dilemma in such a way that New York would finally be able to play the role of international financial center.

One means of resolving the dilemma was to provide incentives for U.S. foreign investment. Various tax subsidies, insurance schemes, and exchange guarantees were used during this period as incentives to increase the flow of capital abroad.[10] However, the flow of private capital still had to be supplemented with public funds, at least until foreign conditions improved enough to make possible the removal of exchange controls. Public funds had been provided during the 1940s by the British loan, by Export-Import loans, and finally by the Marshall Plan. By the end of the 1940s, it was becoming increasingly difficult to get Congressional approval for these continued aid programs, but the U.S. rearmament policy provided a means of continuing to pump dollars into foreign hands as long as the liquidity shortage continued.

REARMAMENT AND FOREIGN ECONOMIC POLICY

The rearmament policy increased the flow of dollars abroad in a number of different ways. After the Korean War had begun, the Marshall Plan was reorganized as the Mutual Security Administration. This transformation was presumably designed to ease Congressional approval of the final year of Marshall aid. The new label made the plan more attractive in the heightened Cold War climate and minimized the danger of major Congressional cutbacks. In addition, a major program of military aid to Western Europe was launched. The Truman administration had first proposed military aid for Europe in the fiscal

1950 budget. But this was before the Korean War and the massive domestic rearmament program, and the appropriation encountered serious opposition in Congress. The bill finally passed Congress in late 1949, but the requested $1.45 billion appropriation was cut back to an even $1 billion. However, in the very different political climate created by the Korean War, the administration quickly gained Congressional approval for over $5 billion of military aid to NATO nations.[11] This kind of military aid continued at relatively high levels through the end of the 1950s.

Not all of this direct military aid was useful in overcoming Europe's dollar shortage, because a part of it was used to finance Europe's purchases of American military equipment, purchases that often would not have been made without the aid funds. However, some military aid dollars were used to finance the expansion of Europe's industrial base, which was seen as necessary for an expansion of Western Europe's contribution to NATO. And other military aid dollars were used for off-shore procurement—the purchase by Country A of goods from Country B with dollars supplied by the United States. This meant, for example, that Britain could obtain dollars by selling small arms to France, even though France would have been unable to make these purchases with hard currency. Furthermore, even some of the grants of military equipment were useful for balance-of-payments purposes. France was fighting in Vietnam during the early 1950s and would have had to purchase much of the equipment that was given to it by the United States.[12]

In addition to the dollars that flowed out through military aid, there was an enormous increase in U.S. defense spending abroad. The stationing of large numbers of U.S. troops in Europe greatly increased the number of dollars earned by the European countries. The prosecution of the Korean War and the establishment of a network of military bases around the world also increased the flow of dollars into foreign hands. Even when these dollars flowed into Asian countries, they were often used to purchase goods in Europe and served to lessen the European liquidity shortage. The outflow of dollars for direct military expenditures in the U.S. balance of payments increased from $576 million in 1949 to $2.615 billion in 1953. Significantly, this item continued to rise even after the Korean War, finally reaching a peak of $3.435 billion in 1958.[13]

What the United States gained internationally from the rearmament policy was not limited to the easing of Europe's liquidity problems. Rearmament was also a means of solidifying Western Europe's

ties to the United States. The United States envisioned a highly integrated Western defense effort that would make Western Europe dependent on American military hardware. The combination of Western
Europe's dependence on the United States for conventional armaments and its dependence on the U.S. nuclear deterrent would ensure
continued close cooperation on economic and political issues. Furthermore, the stationing of a large number of American troops in Western Europe served as a counterweight to the pull of the Soviet Union
on Western Europe. These factors were of particular importance in
shaping the political and economic development of West Germany.[14]

West Germany had long been seen by American policy-makers as
critical to the reconstruction of Western European capitalism along
liberal lines. Germany's great industrial strength could restore the
vitality of European capitalism and improve Europe's international
trade and payments position. By the 1950s the danger was that West
Germany would be seduced by the Soviet Union into accepting political neutralism in exchange for German reunification and access to
Eastern European markets. This development would place Germany's
formidable economic strength outside the NATO alliance and would
put powerful pressure on the rest of Western Europe to accept political
neutralism and economic integration into an all-European trading system that would be built on bilateral and state trading principles.
American fears about West Germany's future were realistic in the light
of the complexities of German domestic politics in this period. The
Adenauer government's commitment to the Western alliance was not
particularly popular in Germany, and the possibility existed that either
the government would fall or it would be forced to abandon its strongly
pro-Western policies.[15]

A number of factors underlay the precariousness of the Adenauer
government and its policies. First, the Western occupation of Germany had created a political order that was fundamentally artificial.
The occupation had repressed the workers' councils formed by the German working class immediately after the war, and it had imposed a
government that had little relation to the actual social and political
forces in the country.[16] This meant that there was more than the usual
possibility of a major political upheaval. Second, the major opposition
party, the Social Democrats (SPD), bitterly opposed the foreign policy
orientation of the Adenauer government in the late 1940s and early
1950s. The Social Democrats set the goal of German reunification
ahead of closer ties with Western Europe. Reunification would help

the Social Democrats politically by restoring areas in the East that traditionally had been strongholds of support for them. But the Social Democrats were also profoundly distrustful of closer economic ties with Western Europe. The liberal free-market economic policies of the Christian Democrats in France, Italy, and Germany were seen to be inconsistent with the socialist economic measures favored by the Social Democrats. With their economic radicalism and their militant nationalism, the Social Democrats could count on significant support within the West German electorate. Finally, the Social Democrats' preoccupation with reunification was paralleled in sectors of the business community that had strong historic ties to East Germany and to Eastern European markets. While these business groups differed sharply with SPD politics, they did constitute another significant interest group that was opposed to Adenauer's exclusive Western orientation.[17]

The strategy of the United States and of the Adenauer government was to link West Germany with the rest of Western Europe by powerful economic ties. The theory was that a major segment of the German business community had a strong interest in maintaining close economic ties to Western Europe, and that would provide a firm base of political support for Adenauer's policies. However, the slow progress in the first two years of the Marshall Plan toward European economic cooperation created doubts that West Germany could be linked to the rest of Western Europe strongly enough or rapidly enough by economic ties alone. The American response was to propose German rearmament, so that economic ties could be reinforced by close military ties among West Germany, the rest of Western Europe, and the United States. German rearmament, under American sponsorship, was seen as a means of preventing any future drift by Germany toward political neutralism.[18]

The United States began openly pushing for German rearmament in 1950, but the U.S. initiative encountered immediate and strong resistance from France. The French were hardly willing to see their historic enemy become a military threat once again. But when the French realized that the United States might push forward with German rearmament without French agreement, they proposed a plan for the creation of a Western European army that would include German divisions and would have a supranational command. After some modification, the plan gained American support, because it did provide a means to integrate Germany militarily with the rest of Western

Europe. This proposal for the creation of a European Defense Community with a military force that included twelve German divisions would dominate Western European politics through 1954.

Part of the enthusiasm of American policy-makers for the EDC can be traced to the fact that the twelve divisions to be provided by Germany would greatly strengthen Europe's own defense. This was of crucial importance for persuading a reluctant Congress that Europe deserved U.S. military support because the Europeans were making real sacrifices to defend themselves. For the Adenauer government, the advantages of the EDC lay in the concessions that the United States would grant in exchange for German participation. While rearmament was likely to be unpopular within Germany, the United States would restore most of Germany's sovereignty and grant Germany an equal role in Europe as a reward for German cooperation. These crucial political concessions would bolster Adenauer's political position. He would be able to steal the nationalist thunder of the Social Democrats by demonstrating that his policies had succeeded in restoring Germany to her rightful place in the world.[19]

This complex web of motives explains John Foster Dulles' distress in 1954, when it appeared that the EDC treaty might go down to defeat in the French Parliament. Even though France had originally proposed the plan, support for German rearmament was simply too dangerous for any of the fragmented political parties of the French Fourth Republic to take responsibility for the EDC's passage through Parliament. Dulles talked of an "agonizing reappraisal" of American policy toward Europe if the EDC treaty were not approved, and it was clear that he was threatening American withdrawal from Europe. While his threat was idle, Dulles was deeply worried that the defeat of the EDC could bring down the Adenauer government and open the way for a very different West German foreign policy. This did not happen, and instead the British jumped into the breach after the French Parliament defeated the EDC. The British put forward a new plan that preserved West German participation in the European defense effort, on terms that were reassuring to the French. In October 1954, agreement was reached on a plan that restored close to full sovereignty to West Germany in exchange for German participation in NATO and in a newly created Western European Union. The Western European Union was the Brussels Treaty Organization—Britain, France, and Benelux—with the addition of Italy and West Germany. German force levels were to be the same as they had been under the

EDC, and the whole deal was cemented by the British commitment to maintain her forces on the Continent in perpetuity. While the WEU lacked the supranational elements of the EDC, it did successfully integrate West Germany into the Atlantic Alliance.[20]

THE COSTS OF THE REARMAMENT POLICY

The rearmament policy was not without costs, and in some ways it interfered with the achievement of a multilateral world economy. One important consequence of domestic rearmament was a weakening of the forces in the United States that favored trade liberalization. The strong domestic demand generated by much higher levels of military spending made exports relatively less important for the economy. Firms that had exported large quantities of capital goods, for example, during the late 1940s now found very strong domestic demand for their products. As fewer firms were oriented toward exports for their immediate survival, the concern with trade liberalization as a means of protecting and expanding those overseas markets diminished. This was reflected in increasing Congressional opposition to tariff reform, with each subsequent extension of the Reciprocal Trade Agreement Act further limiting presidential powers to liberalize trade. And the executive branch was reluctant to use its political clout to push trade liberalization, when far more immediate international projects might be endangered. As a consequence, the United States dragged its feet through much of the 1950s in international trade negotiations, opposing the principle of across-the-board tariff reductions which was widely seen as a necessary step to push trade liberalization forward. The Truman administration abandoned the ITO charter in 1950, and another attempt to create an international trade organization in the mid-1950s received little support from the Eisenhower administration. As a consequence, American and foreign tariffs remained relatively high during the 1950s.[21]

The international aspects of the rearmament policy also involved serious costs. Congressional resistance to U.S. military involvement in Europe forced the Truman administration to pursue policies that interfered with the process of economic recovery and reconstruction in France and Britain. After the Korean War began, there was little debate within the United States over the necessity for domestic rearmament, but a debate did begin in late 1950 over the international dimensions of the policy. This was the so-called Great Debate over the future of U.S. policy toward Europe. The Truman administration saw the commitment of U.S. troops to Europe and massive military aid to Western Europe as a means to achieve the restoration of liberal capitalism in Western Europe. To push these policies through Congress, the Truman administration used the familiar technique of emphasizing the threat of the Red Army. But by stressing the direct military threat from the Soviet Union, the Truman administration played into the hands of its anti-internationalist opponents. Men like Herbert Hoover and Robert Taft could, in all sincerity, argue that it might be more efficient to concentrate on building Fortress America to defend the United States from the Soviet threat. They suggested that Western Europe was essentially indefensible and that the resources used to defend Europe could much more effectively be used to build up defenses in the Western Hemisphere. Joseph Kennedy, for example, argued: "Had we the defenses in Iceland today that one-hundredth of the money spent in Berlin could have built we would have purchased safety with our money rather than additional danger."[22]

To counter this argument, the Truman administration stressed the importance of Western Europe's industrial capacity, pointing out that if the Russians captured Western Europe's industry they would have clear economic superiority over the United States. But the administration was forced to go beyond this position. Administration spokesmen had to argue that the United States should contribute to Western Europe's defense because Western Europe itself was already making a major contribution to its own defense. Reluctant Congressmen, it seemed, were willing, like the Almighty, to help those who helped themselves. The problem with this was that the administration was then forced to prove that the Western European countries were, in fact, making a significant effort at rearmament. General Eisenhower, speaking for the administration, reassured both Houses of Congress in early February 1951 that he had found on his most recent trip to Europe, "a rejuvenation, a growth of determination, a spirit to resist, a spirit again to try to live the lives of free men, to hold their heads up in the world, to do their part, and to take the risk."[23] Eisenhower's rhetoric notwithstanding, the reality was that France and Britain were extremely reluctant to interrupt the process of economic rebuilding by making a major rearmament effort.

It was therefore necessary to use a considerable amount of arm-twisting to convince France and Britain to begin their showcase rearmament efforts. The major element of American leverage was the threat that the United States would abandon its economic and military activities in Europe. The Truman administration could simply point to the strength of anti-internationalist forces in Congress to drive this threat home. While there was little immediate military threat to France and Britain at this point, their political and economic dependence on the United States was enough to make the threat of U.S. withdrawal from Europe frightening. Both the British and French governments formulated ambitious rearmament plans in early 1951. The British put forward a three-year plan that called for military spending at twice the previously anticipated levels. And the French proposed a similarly ambitious program. But these plans would prove costly both politically and economically.[24]

The rearmament program of the British Labour government led to the resignation of several ministers of the Bevanite left as a protest against new revenue measures designed to help pay for the defense effort. It is likely that the anger of the Labour party's left wing at the government's willingness to trade off social welfare for armaments was a factor in the electoral defeat that brought the Conservatives to power in late 1951. More importantly from the U.S. point of view, the British rearmament effort contributed to a new sterling crisis in 1951-52. Rearmament led to a diversion of production from exports to arms and a rapid increase in raw materials imports. The new Conservative government was forced to tighten credit and impose new import restrictions to protect the balance of payments. Similarly, in France the rearmament stimulated sharp political protests and an economic crisis. The increased government spending contributed to powerful inflationary pressure, speculation against the franc mounted, and the French monetary reserves dropped sharply. The government attempted to solve the problem by tightening credit and cutting other government expenditures, but this proved insufficient. The French were forced to abandon their efforts at trade liberalization and impose new quotas on imports.

The interruption in progress toward the elimination of controls in Western Europe was only temporary. Both Britain and France sharply reduced rearmament plans from the 1951 levels as American pressure eased.[25] But there is evidence that permanent damage was done to the British economy by the high levels of defense spending in the 1951-53 period. Britain lost foreign markets for a range of capital goods to West German competition during the period in which Britain was preoccupied with increasing military production. This gain in markets was a boon to the West German economy, but Britain was never able to recapture those markets.[26] This contributed to a weakening of Britain's foreign-trade position that was a cause of the recurrent sterling crises of the 1950s and 1960s.[27]

There is good reason to believe that the American rearmament effort also had a negative effect on the American economy's health. While there was no real alternative to military Keynesianism for maintaining aggregate demand other than some type of national capitalism, the rearmament policy contributed to stagnation in civilian sectors of the American economy. Military spending at levels of $40 billion or $50 billion a year diverted capital and crucial resources away from the civilian sector of the economy. Scientific and engineering talent was siphoned into the military sector, limiting the resources available for technical innovations in the civilian sector. At the same time, because rearmament had weakened the forces favoring liberalization of American tariffs, the continuing high tariff levels meant that U.S. civilian firms were often under minimal competitive pressure from imports. Hence there was sometimes little incentive for the civilian firms to pursue technical innovations, and when they did seek to capture foreign markets, especially in the second half of the 1950s, continuing high tariffs abroad discouraged American exports. Instead of modernizing their domestic plants to increase production for foreign markets, American firms began establishing branch plants abroad to penetrate foreign markets. Hence, the combination of military spending and high tariffs meant that a large segment of the American industrial plant was far less efficient and modern than it could have been. And this would have a definite effect on the U.S. trade balance as foreign trade competition intensified.[28]

SUPPORT FOR EUROPEAN REGIONALISM

U.S. support for European regionalism was designed to achieve the same ends as the rearmament policy. European regionalism provided badly needed liquidity to Western Europe and it served to tie West Germany to the rest of Western Europe. The Americans hoped that European regionalism in the context of Atlantic military coordination would serve to bind the Western European economies permanently to the United States. But the danger of European regionalism for the United States was that it could provide a long-term alternative to multilateral economic policies for the Western Europeans. Discrimination against dollar goods could become permanent, the Western European currencies could remain inconvertible into dollars, and Western Europe could be closed off to U.S. investment.[29] The response to this danger that the United States gradually evolved was to throw its support behind the development of a highly integrated "little European" region, while opposing the evolution of a "greater European" region.

The strong U.S. push for European regionalism began with Hoffman's speech in October 1949. The concrete policies that the United States supported were the creation of a European Payments Union and a program for intra-European trade liberalization. The EPU was essentially a device for creating liquidity to finance trade within Europe and between Europe and the Sterling Area. As long as the pound sterling was subject to strict exchange controls and the dollar remained scarce, some means had to be found to finance this trade, as an alternative to bilateral agreements. From the U.S. point of view, multilateral clearing, even if confined to a region, was preferable to bilateral arrangements. And since the United States provided the basic capital needed to make the EPU work and had a large say in its operations, U.S. policy-makers were relatively confident that the EPU would work to smooth the way toward global multilateralism.[30] This involved making sure that the EPU did not function in the same way as the clearing union that Keynes had proposed during the war, that is, by encouraging countries running a deficit within the clearing union to deflate while pressuring surplus countries to inflate. If the stronger European countries inflated their economies to eliminate their surplus position within the EPU, their capacity to compete with U.S. goods would be impaired and multilateralism would not be advanced. So the United States had to work to make sure that the EPU placed all the pressure for adjustment on deficit countries.

Another aspect of U.S. efforts to advance Western European regionalism was pressuring the Organization for European Economic Cooperation to establish a schedule for the removal of quantitative restrictions on intra-European trade. The OEEC agreed in November 1949 to reduce existing quotas by 50 percent, and in January 1950 agreed to even further quota reductions after the start of the EPU. This program of intra-European trade liberalization involved increased discrimination against dollar goods, because restrictions were being removed for European goods but retained for American goods. The theory on which the Economic Cooperation Administration acted in pushing this policy was again that a revival of trade and competition within Europe would contribute to the reduction of inflation and to the increasing of efficiency so that the European countries could then afford to compete directly against the United States. In short, the reduction of intra-European trade restrictions would make possible the eventual reduction of restrictions against dollar goods.[31]

Because of the existence of the European Payments Union, any plan that liberalized trade within a European region was essentially liquidity saving. Intra-European trade liberalization (either through removal of controls or lowering of tariffs) increased the likelihood that countries within Western Europe would purchase goods from European suppliers so that the transactions would be financed through the EPU rather than with scarce hard currency. However, the nature of the region within which European trade would be liberalized became a critical issue. Both the EPU and the intra-European trade liberalization program pointed toward a Western European economic region that included all the recipients of Marshall Plan aid, but the United States quickly began retreating from this conception of European regionalism. In 1950 the United States began pressing for a Little-European region, throwing its support behind the proposal for a European Coal and Steel Community. The ECSC was to be a supranational agency that would control the coal and steel resources of member nations. It was primarily a means of solidifying Franco-German relations by resolving the historic conflict over the Saar and by limiting Germany's capacity to make war. Italy and the Benelux countries were the only other nations that joined with France and Germany in setting up the ECSC. But the architects of the ECSC saw it as a first step toward the development of a European common market with supranational government. And in supporting the ECSC, the United States was throwing its weight behind the idea of an integrated political and economic region of those six countries.[32]

The Little-Europe conception appealed to American policymakers for a number of reasons. First, the idea of a common market in which goods and capital were completely free to cross internal boundaries was consistent with liberal economic principles. It was difficult to imagine that a group of countries would organize their economic transactions with each other on such liberal terms and then engage in the use of import restrictions and other illiberal devices in their trade with other countries. Second, the development of a high level of economic and political integration would serve to bind West Germany firmly to the West. A common market would provide West Germany with the Western markets that it needed, and the process of political integration would reinforce economic and military bonds.[33] Finally, a small, tightly integrated region might well result in some loss of markets to the United States, but the loss of markets would be smaller than that caused by a much larger region that encompassed all of Western Europe.[34]

The strong U.S. support through the 1950s for the development of Little Europe also had much to do with the political and ideological agreement between American policy-makers and the architects of Little-European unity. The Christian Democratic politicians in Italy, France, Belgium, West Germany, and the Netherlands who strongly supported European unity generally shared official American views on economic, political, and military issues. They were, in general, committed to financial discipline, economic liberalism, militant anti-Communism, and a united Atlantic military effort. This agreement was reinforced in some cases by close personal ties that dated back many years. For example, John Foster Dulles and Jean Monnet, the chief architect of European unity, had been friends since the Versailles Peace Conference after World War I. These personal ties increased U.S. confidence that this Little-European region would not develop in antagonism to U.S. economic interests.[35]

Had the British chosen to join, the American ties to Little Europe would have been even closer, and the British would also have helped assure that Little Europe developed along liberal lines. Yet the British resisted U.S. pressures to join in efforts for European unity because of the continuing British commitment to a global role. The United States realized that if Britain attempted to join Little Europe while holding on to the Sterling Area ties, the result would have been a much looser European economic federation than the United States desired. Such a loose federation might not have effectively bound West Germany to Western Europe, and it might well have involved even greater discrimination against American goods. Rather than see the idea of a tightly knit Little Europe destroyed, the United States reluctantly decided to support the Europe of the Six without the British.[36]

The American orientation toward the Europe of the Six was not fully consolidated until the British refused to join in the creation of the

Coal and Steel Community. Thereafter, the United States championed
the projects of the Six without reservations. The European Coal and
Steel Community and the European Defense Community were both
proposed in 1950, the French playing a crucial role in developing both
proposals. The two projects shared several aspects in common: they
were organized around the Six, they provided a solution to the problem of the German role in Europe, they created supranational institutions to govern the new organization, and they were strongly supported by the United States. Although the EDC was held up by a
prolonged debate, the Coal and Steel Community actually began operations in September 1952, amid general expectations that rapid progress was being made toward uniting the Six.

In fact, in 1953 a concrete proposal was developed for a European
Political Community. The idea of the EPC was that it would link the
supranational institutions of the ECSC and of the soon-to-be-approved
EDC into one federal structure that would be the basis for an eventual
supranational government for the Six. In short, a proliferation of agencies would be avoided by going directly to the creation of a central
government structure that could then organize the various functional
communities. But even before the EDC treaty went down to defeat,
the second thoughts of the European governments about their willingness to surrender sovereignty led to the tabling of the EPC.[37]

But as is now familiar, the defeat of the European idea was only
temporary. Shortly after the defeat of the EDC in 1954, Jean Monnet
abandoned his job as high commissioner of the ECSC to work for
further steps toward the unity of the Six. As a result of Monnet's
efforts, representatives of the Six met at Messina in June 1955 and
agreed to study proposals for the creation of a common market and a
common atomic energy program. This began the process that culminated in the signing of the Treaty of Rome, in March 1957, that created
the European Economic Community and the European Atomic
Energy Community. Throughout this difficult process, American diplomatic support was a resource that the architects of Little Europe
were able to draw upon.[38] This was particularly important when the
British, in 1957 and 1958, attempted to head off the division of Europe
into EEC and non-EEC nations by proposing that Little Europe be
surrounded by a larger European free-trade area. At this point, U.S.
opposition to the idea of a Greater-European economic region was
crucial in blocking the British proposal.

U.S. opposition to a Greater-European economic region had faced an earlier test at a meeting of the General Agreement on Tariffs and Trade in 1954.[39] Belgium had argued then that Western Europe as a region should be able to continue discriminating against dollar goods as long as Western Europe was making progress toward regional trade liberalization. The Belgian position was strongly supported by the French, who argued against the appropriateness of a multilateral world economy in light of increased governmental regulation of economies. The French view at this point was that the only real alternative to national autarchy was the freeing of trade on a regional basis, which required stopping far short of full multilateralism. The United States strongly opposed the French and Belgian positions and effectively blocked the rule change that Belgium had proposed. The U.S. stance made it clear that movement toward a greater European region would risk a confrontation with American power.[40]

There were two consequences of this confrontation. First, it was made clear to France and Belgium and others that the only way to make further progress in liberalizing Western European trade while retaining discrimination against dollar goods was to develop a common market, which was allowed under GATT rules. And because such a common market would appeal to only a relatively small number of Western European countries, this meant building Little Europe. Significantly, the Messina meeting occurred shortly after this confrontation with GATT. Second, rapid progress was made toward removing restrictions on dollar imports into Western Europe during the rest of the decade. By 1960, very little remained of the imposing structure of restrictions against dollar imports that had existed in 1950. However, the effect of removing dollar-import restrictions was often muted because high tariff levels remained to slow the influx of dollar goods. Hence, toward the end of the 1950s tariff liberalization replaced the removal of import restrictions as the key trade issue.[41]

The British proposal in 1957 for a West European free-trade area called for the removal of all tariff walls within Western Europe. Each nation, and the EEC nations acting as one, would be free to set whatever tariffs on non-European trade they desired. The Treaty of Rome had called for a common external tariff for the EEC which would be a rough average of the existing tariffs of the Six. The EEC plan would involve some increased discrimination against dollar goods, since German goods, for example, would enter France tariff-free, while U.S. goods still faced a stiff tariff. However, the British proposal would have meant much more general discrimination against dollar goods. Under the British plan, British or Norwegian goods would also enter France tariff-free, while U.S. goods would be subject to a tariff. Similarly, the British plan would open the non-EEC countries to the free entrance of other Western European goods, while retaining tariffs on U.S. goods.[42]

The French adamantly opposed the British plan because they perceived it as a threat to the Treaty of Rome. The French, through laborious negotiations with the other countries of the Six, had created an economic structure in which they felt that they could safely remove some of their tariffs. One of the crucial concessions that the French had gained was agreement that the EEC would develop a common agricultural policy. This would assure that France would have the opportunity to gain in agricultural trade what she might lose in industrial trade. Other concessions involved harmonizing social welfare and wage policies, which the French insisted on because they felt that their more progressive policies put them at a disadvantage in international trade. The French opposed the British plan because they were not willing to liberalize trade without the safeguards of the Treaty of Rome. Moreover, the French feared that the Germans, who had reluctantly agreed to some of the French conditions at Rome, might ignore French protests and go along with the British proposals. This would destroy the EEC before its birth. In fact, the Erhard faction of the German Christian Democrats favored the British proposal because it created a greater open market for German industrial goods than the EEC, with fewer limitations on Germany's economic freedom.[43]

The British did not gain German support, however, because De Gaulle, who came to power in France in 1958, reached an understanding with Adenauer. The substance of the understanding was that Adenauer would hold the Erhard forces in check and support the French position against Britain. In exchange, De Gaulle agreed to give West Germany the strongest diplomatic support in its struggle to hold onto West Berlin and to resist Soviet pressure for some kind of concessions on the German question.[44] This agreement had American blessing because the United States remained convinced that the EEC was a better means to bind West Germany to Western Europe than the far looser free-trade area. As the negotiations over the British proposal dragged on into 1959, U.S. support for the French position was strengthened by two other factors. 1958 marked the first year in which the U.S. balance-of-payments deficit led to a run on the American gold stock, and this run continued into 1959. U.S. policy began to switch from efforts to pump more dollars into foreign hands to efforts to strengthen the U.S. payments position. This made the United States even more sensitive to the potentially serious trade discrimination that would result from a West European-wide free-trade area. Finally, as a kind of icing on the cake, the French, backed by the EEC commission, developed the argument that further European trade liberalization should come on a fully multilateral basis. This was in response to British demands that the EEC should do something to minimize the discriminatory effect of the EEC's internal tariff reductions on other West European countries. The French appeal to the principle of global trade liberalization was music to the ears of U.S. policy-makers because it created the image of the EEC as a force for worldwide tariff reductions. This was a far cry from the autarchic regionalism that some had feared.[45]

The French position was not completely rhetorical. In March 1960, the EEC commission proposed a speed-up in the schedule for reducing internal tariffs and harmonizing external tariffs, and it simultaneously offered a 20 percent reduction in the level of the EEC's external tariff.[46] This helped to minimize the immediate trade-diverting effects of the first steps toward creating a common market. It was an indication of good faith in the direction of global tariff liberalization, but it still indicated little about the future development of the common market. There was still the possibility that the EEC could move in political or economic directions that were hostile to American policy. The fact that Britain, the United States' closest European ally, was outside the EEC, served to reduce U.S. leverage over the EEC's development. However, U.S. policy-makers remained confident that the close political and military bonds between the United States and the EEC would continue to prove leverage enough to influence the EEC in a liberal, multilateral direction.[47]

THE ROAD TO CONVERTIBILITY

Whatever ambiguities existed at the end of the 1950s about the future trade policies of the EEC, it was clear by that time that the United States had achieved the goal of restoring Western European currency convertibility. Fears that the European Payments Union would become the basis for a closed payments region were completely dispelled in December 1958, when the EPU was dissolved and all the major West European countries made their currencies convertible. This was the culmination of a long process, but the key point was that the Western European economies had become strong enough to earn all the dollars they needed to cover their transactions with the United States. This, in turn, was largely a result of the rapid and dynamic economic growth and recovery in Western Europe during the 1950s. However, the rate at which the various Western European economies recovered differed, and this created a problem in the timing of the move to restore convertibility. The moment at which the step would be taken was the subject of long debate.

West Germany was one of the countries most eager to dissolve the EPU mechanism and move to full convertibility. The severe 1948 currency reform, the relative quiescence of the German working class, Erhard's free-market economic policies, and strong demand for German industrial goods during the period of Korean War rearmament had combined to restore the international competitiveness of the West German economy. West Germany became a chronic creditor within the European Payments Union by 1952-53 because of its positive balance of trade with the other European countries. This created a problem for the West Germans because they could not use their positive balance with Europe to cover the deficit with the dollar area. Deficit countries were required to settle only a portion of their deficit in gold or dollars, so that surplus countries accumulated large credits with the payments union. This acted as an obstacle to an expansion of West German exports to the rest of Europe since West Germany would pile up credits instead of earning hard currency. In other words, the EPU was structured to discourage countries from achieving an extreme debtor or an extreme creditor position, and this acted as a restraint on the ability of West German capitalists to sell their goods in Western Europe and in the Sterling Area.[48]

The West Germans understood, however, that it would be dangerous for them to move toward currency convertibility unilaterally and force an early end to the EPU. The risk was that the German mark would become as scarce as the U.S. dollar; other countries would be unable to earn the marks they needed to pay for their imports of German goods, so they would be forced to discriminate against German goods. Instead, the Germans pressed for a hardening of the EPU's settlement mechanism. In mid-1954, it was agreed that all EPU balances would be settled by 50 percent gold or dollars and 50 percent credit. In August 1955, the hard-currency share was increased to 75 percent.[49] These changes made it easier for the Germans to earn dollars and gold to settle their accounts with the rest of the world, and it made it easier for Germany to export to other EPU countries because the Germans would accumulate credit more slowly. The West Germans also eased many of the exchange restrictions on the mark. This had the effect of making it easier for foreigners to earn marks and thus reduce the possibility of a mark shortage. But the Germans had to wait for other countries, particularly Britain, before moving all the way to convertibility.

Britain's position on convertibility during the 1950s was highly complex. On the one hand, there were still powerful interests in Britain that wanted a restoration of sterling convertibility so that London could be restored as an international financial center. On the other hand, the British balance of payments was weak and Britain's currency reserves were at low levels. Britain had not experienced the dynamic industrial growth of West Germany; her trade balance remained weak, and she had heavy balance-of-payments outflow on military and capital accounts. The issue was complicated further by the continued existence of the Sterling Area and the dollar-pooling mechanism. While the Sterling Area arrangements appeared to strengthen the pound, they actually had the effect of undermining Britain's international economic position.

The continued existence of the Sterling Area had two main benefits for the British economy. First, the Sterling Area and the remnants of imperial preference gave British goods privileged access to a large overseas market. Second, the British colonies earned a significant surplus in their trade with the Dollar Area which the British were able to use to finance their dollar deficit and the dollar deficits of the independent Sterling Area countries.[50] But the Sterling Area arrangements also had severe disadvantages. The privileged access to overseas markets protected British industrialists from the need to modernize and become more competitive, so British industry often stagnated in comparison with the rest of Western Europe's industry.[51] Furthermore, a quid pro quo for maintaining the Sterling Area was free access for Sterling Area countries to the British capital markets. The resulting outflow of British capital to the Sterling Area was a real burden on the British economy, particularly since that capital was badly needed at home.[52] Finally, Britain had to maintain a far-flung military apparatus to provide security for the Sterling Area, including the colonies. The foreign-exchange cost of this effort was a major reason for the weakness of the British balance of payments.[53]

In retrospect, it is clear that the costs of these new arrangements for the vitality of the British economy were great. At the time, however, the strength of the interests that benefited from the continued existence of the Sterling Area prevented any serious re-evaluation of British policy. And the financial interests in the City of London which were primarily concerned with sterling's role in financing international trade probably feared that an end to sterling's reserve role would undermine sterling's potential usefulness as an international transaction currency.[54] As a consequence, British policy during the 1950s was oriented toward preserving the Sterling Area and restoring sterling convertibility. However, the chronic payments crises and the memory of the 1947 debacle forced the British to move with caution.

In 1952 and 1953, the Conservative government toyed with the idea of making sterling convertible on a floating basis. The idea was that a float would place less pressure on Britain's slim currency reserves but, even so, this plan for convertibility was dependent on gaining another American loan to bolster the pound. The United States, however, was unsympathetic to the idea of a float and made it clear that no loan would be forthcoming. The idea of a float was dropped, but the British continued to demand an American quid pro quo for British movement to convertibility. In September 1954, at the IMF annual meetings, the British made U.S. trade liberalization and credits a condition for British convertibility, with a similar negative reaction from the United States. But even while action on convertibility was postponed, the British government did dismantle some of the economic controls that interfered with international economic transactions. The international commodity markets, including the London gold market, that had historically operated in London were reopened, and the area outside Britain in which sterling was transferrable was broadened. The British also pressed the other EPU nations to allow multilateral arbitrage transactions in each other's currencies by authorized banks.[55]

These and other liberalizing moves brought Europe to a kind of de facto convertibility, since mechanisms now existed for moving from one currency to another through various forms of commodity arbitrage. This de facto convertibility intensified the pressures to make

European-wide convertibility official, since techniques existed for circumventing many of the remaining controls. By 1955 the British balance payments had strengthened, so that official convertibility seemed very close. The countries of the OEEC negotiated a European Monetary Agreement that would replace the EPU when general convertibility was established. The negotiations were difficult, because the British insisted on conditions that were not generally popular. However, even though agreement was finally reached on the provisions of a European Monetary Agreement, 1955 slipped by without a decision to move toward official convertibility. 1956 brought the Suez crisis and a dramatic worsening of the British balance of payments; and the third postwar American recession put additional strong pressure on the British and French payments balances in 1957. Convertibility was delayed until late 1958, when it came in the context of a major French financial crisis.[56]

France had a severe balance-of-payments problem through most of the 1950s. Although the French economy, in contrast to Britain's, had high levels of new investment and economic growth, the Indochina and the Algerian wars placed strains on the French balance of payments. The combination of a militant working class and foreign adventures also meant that there was a continuing problem of inflation that weakened France's international trade position. This inflation problem was one of the main reasons why the French had fought so hard to surround the European Common Market with a high external tariff and to include provisions in the Treaty of Rome that could be used to protect the French economy from an influx of foreign goods. But the severity of France's balance-of-payments difficulties in 1958 gave rise to widespread fears that France would be unable to live up to its obligations under the Treaty of Rome to begin tariff liberalizations on January 1, 1959. In early 1958, the French were forced to borrow $655 million from the United States, the IMF, and the EPU to cover their balance-of-payments deficit.[57]

In June 1958, when France appeared to be on the brink of civil war over the future of Algeria, De Gaulle returned to power. He came as the saviour delivering France from the political turmoil and chaos of the Fourth Republic. After easing the immediate political crisis and establishing a new constitution, De Gaulle turned his attention to the economic crisis. He sought advice from upholders of traditional financial wisdom, and they put together a program of economic reforms designed to squeeze inflation out of the French economy. The package included a massive devaluation of 17.55 percent which was backed up by a program of severe domestic deflation. Many social welfare benefits, subsidies, and pensions were cut back sharply. As a consequence of the package of reforms, total consumer income fell by some 95 billion francs, while the cost of retail goods rose some 265 billion francs; in short, the standard of living of the average French citizen was successfully reduced. Such an extreme program of imposed austerity was possible only because of De Gaulle's extraordinary stature at that point. The parties of the Left were confused and disoriented, and they were unable to mount a campaign of resistance against the austerity program.[58]

The French reforms and the devaluation in December made it possible for France to fulfill its obligations to liberalize Common Market trade at the beginning of 1959. But the shift in financial policy also made the French more receptive to the idea of a restoration of currency convertibility. While the French had earlier clung to the relative safety of the EPU, they were now willing to risk convertibility. The initiative came from Britain, and the other major European countries quickly agreed, so that in late December 1958 all the major European currencies were made freely convertible on current account for nonresidents.[59] Almost simultaneously, the International Monetary Fund announced that its quotas would be increased to expand the fund's lending power. This happened because the United States had finally agreed to an increase in the fund's resources, apparently as Britain's reward for finally restoring convertibility.[60]

CONCLUSION

The restoration of European convertibility was the culmination of the American struggle to re-establish liberal capitalism in Western Europe and to return international trade and payments to a multilateral basis. The struggle had been longer and harder than State Department planners had anticipated during World War II, and a series of new policies and new expedients had been required to achieve the goal. The struggle had also been costly, not only in terms of the billions of U.S. dollars sent overseas for aid, but in its effects on the structure of the world economy. While multilateralism had been restored, it was flawed in a number of ways. First, 1958, the year in which convertibility was restored, was also the first year in which there was a sizable drain on the U.S. gold stock. For a while this was seen as a temporary or cyclical phenomenon, but over time it became clear that the U.S. balance-of-payments deficit was related to the very means by which the United States had worked to restore convertibility. Second, international trade was still impaired by relatively high tariff levels. The resistance of forces in the United States to general tariff liberalization had led Europe, in turn, to retain many of its tariffs, and the European Common Market was to be surrounded by a significant tariff wall. Third, the very existence of the Common Market represented an exception to a purely multilateral world order. The potential still existed for that Common Market to evolve toward a closed economic bloc. Finally, the international institutions that were designed to regulate this multilateral world were underdeveloped. The defeat of the ambitious Keynes and White plans meant that the role of managing the international monetary system fell once again to a national power—the United States. And the absence of strong international bodies meant that future economic relations among Western Europe, the EEC in particular, and the United States would develop outside a formal structure or set of rules.

The U.S. gold drain was an indication that U.S. policies had succeeded too well in pumping dollars into foreign hands. During most of the 1950s, the United States ran a balance-of-payments deficit of $1 billion a year. The foreign countries that earned those dollars used them to build up their currency reserves to adequate levels. By the late 1950s, however, some countries' reserves were large enough so that they could begin to concern themselves with the composition of their reserves. Historically, the countries at the center of the capitalist world economy tended to hold most of their reserves in gold rather than in other currencies. They had done this because of the prestige and independence associated with holding reserves predominantly in gold.[61] So, for the same reasons, Western European countries in the second half of the 1950s began converting into gold the new dollars that they earned. This would not have been a major problem except that the size of the U.S. deficit jumped upward in 1958 and remained at a level of $3 billion or $4 billion a year thereafter. The result was that the conversion of dollars into gold began to have a major impact on the U.S. reserves of gold.[62]

The increase in the size of the U.S. deficit occurred in part because of U.S. measures to make more dollars available overseas. In the early 1950s, efforts had been made to encourage U.S. private investment abroad. But private-capital flows remained too small to ease the dollar shortage, and the dollar gap was filled by dollars pumped abroad for military and political aid and for the upkeep of U.S. troops stationed at military bases around the world. In short, the extension of U.S. political and military power on a global basis during the first half of the 1950s made sense in terms of the balance of payments because foreign countries badly needed the liquidity that was provided by these government expenditures. But by the second half of the 1950s, more stable conditions abroad stimulated a revival of U.S. private foreign investment that was encouraged by the incentives established earlier. However, when the private sector was finally ready to provide foreign liquidity needs, the worldwide military and political apparatus could simply not be dismantled. So the United States continued to pump dollars abroad on both capital and government account, and the result was a larger deficit.

The deficit increased also because of a deterioration in the U.S. trade balance. This deterioration was almost inevitable because the extraordinary preeminence of the United States in international trade was bound to fade somewhat as the Western European and Japanese economies recovered from the war. However, continuing high tariff levels and the impact of American military Keynesianism shaped the U.S. response to this increasing international competition. To a significant extent, American firms responded to the new conditions not by modernizing their domestic plants to make their exports more competitive, but by establishing branch plants abroad. These branch plants made it possible for U.S. firms to circumvent European tariffs and to take advantage of tariff liberalization within Europe. The consequence of this was that the capital outflow for direct investment continued to increase, while the U.S. trade balance in many manufactured goods worsened. Because capital was sent abroad rather than used to modernize domestic facilities, the ability of domestic production in certain goods to compete internationally declined.

Furthermore, the high external tariff around the European Common Market was an indication that the U.S. gamble in supporting Little Europe might not pay off in the end. Little Europe might still evolve in such a way as to close itself off from the United States in certain ways, or it might attempt to challenge U.S. international hegemony in economics or politics. U.S. policy-makers believed that Europe's military integration with the United States in the Atlantic Alliance would serve to preclude any such development, as would the bonds of common understanding between the U.S. leaders and the architects of the EEC. However, the United States would have to attempt to influence the EEC's evolution through direct diplomacy because of the weakness of the international economic institutions that might have exercised some influence on the EEC's direction. The IMF had been badly compromised as an international institution because of its domination by the United States, and the defeat of the ITO had left GATT a shadow organization with little power. In short, the United States had failed to create international institutions that could effectively govern the international economy.[63]

Furthermore, the weakness of the international economic institutions meant that there was no adequate or appropriate forum in which the problems created by the U.S. balance-of-payments deficit could be discussed. The international organizations were also too weak to deal with the problem of short-term speculative capital flows that became much more serious once convertibility was restored. Both White and Keynes had anticipated continuing controls over such flows as the only way of avoiding the chaos that such capital flows had created in the 1920s and 1930s. However, the United States had established a world economy that was open to these short-term capital flows without creating an institutional mechanism to control them. The problem of speculative capital flows was one illustration of the strains in the international monetary order at the end of the 1950s. A multilateral world economy had been restored, but it lacked an adequate organizational infrastructure. This meant that the smooth working of the world economy was extremely dependent on the exercise of responsible economic leadership by the United States. The next decade would show that the United States was unable to provide that leadership.

PART II: *The Unmaking of an International Economic Order*

SIX. *The Roots of the U.S. Deficit*

The U.S. balance-of-payments position was the dominant issue of international monetary politics from 1958 to 1973. Yet throughout much of this period, debate raged within academic and policy circles over the proper way to interpret the U.S. payments position. The debate reflected two important realities. The first is that balance-of-payments accounting is a matter of choosing among different conventions, each of which makes a number of somewhat arbitrary assumptions; in short, there is no "objective" technique for analyzing a country's international payments position. The second is that the determination that a particular country is running a chronic payments deficit or surplus has very serious international political implications. The paradox is that an interpretation of a country's international payments position that is inevitably somewhat arbitrary has serious consequences because the interpretation affects the actual behavior of nations and of international agencies. The paradox can be resolved, however, when it is recognized that much of the debate about proper interpretation of the balance of payments is really an argument about the appropriate ways for nations to organize their international economic transactions.[1] In other words, the assertion that a particular country is in balance-of-payments deficit is a shorthand statement that that country has organized its international economic transactions poorly, and there is an implicit conception of what that country's payments position should look like.

This subjective dimension of balance-of-payments analysis creates problems in interpreting the history of the period from 1958 to 1974. On the one hand, a grasp of the U.S. payments position is absolutely critical for an understanding of the international monetary politics in that period. On the other hand, any particular technique of balance-of-payments analysis prejudges the issue, because it rests on assumptions that are subject to dispute. To untangle this problem, it is important to examine systematically the changes in the various items of the U.S. balance of payments across the entire period from 1950 to 1974.[2]

TABLE 1

GOVERNMENT TRANSACTIONS (IN $MILLIONS)

	Direct Military Expend- itures (1)	Sales of Military Goods (2)	Loans and Grants (3)	Govern- ment- Financed Exports (4)	Repayment of Loans (5)	Other Govern- ment Trans- actions (6)	Balance on Govern- ment Account (7)
1950	− 576	n.s.s.*	−4285	2571	295	− 119	−2114
1	− 1270	n.s.s.	−3496	2098	305	+ 278	−2080
2	−2054	n.s.s.	−2809	1685	429	− 217	−2966
3	−2615	192	−2542	1525	487	− 110	−3063
4	−2642	182	−2061	1237	507	+ 12	−2765
5	−2901	200	−2627	1576	416	− 69	−3405
6	−2949	161	−2841	1705	479	− 198	−3643
7	−3216	375	−3233	1940	659	− 204	−3679
8	−3435	300	−3131	1879	544	− 131	−3974
9	−3107	302	−3040	1824	1054	− 69	−3036
60	−3087	335	−3414	2046	642	− 142	−3620
1	−2998	402	−4044	2396	1279	− 347	−3312
2	−3105	656	−4289	2503	1288	− 111	−3058
3	−2961	657	−4568	2882	989	+ 136	−2865
4	−2880	747	−4289	3032	720	− 212	−2882
5	−2952	830	−4287	2952	874	− 542	−3125
6	−3764	829	−4688	3152	1234	− 565	−3802
7	−4378	1152	−5234	3523	1005	− 669	−4601
8	−4535	1392	−5369	3346	1386	− 640	−4420
9	−4856	1528	−5049	3094	1200	− 373	−4456
70	−4855	1501	−5047	3110	1722	−1423	−4992
1	−4819	1926	−6042	3322	2115	−2389	−5887
2	−4784	1163	−5827	2972	2086	−2660	−7050
3	−4658	2342	−7178	3371	2596	−3011	−6538
4	−5103	2914	−9905	3894	4853	−3771	−7088

*n.s.s.—not shown separately.

The data comes from *Survey of Current Business,* October 1972 and June 1975. Column 4 data is derived from *SCB* Table on Government Expenditures. Figures for 1950-59 are estimated based on the assumption that 60% of the grants and loans was spent on U.S. commodities. Note that aid-financed exports include those financed by the Agency for International Development and its predecessor agencies, P.L. 480, and the Export-Import Bank. Government-assisted agricultural exports are not included among the government-financed exports. This means that the figure is only a rough approximation of the dollar value of exports that might not have been sold without government financing. The miscellaneous items included under Column 6 are interest payments on U.S. government assets and liabilities, sales and purchases of services by the government, government pensions, and changes in U.S. government nonliquid liabilities to other than official reserve agencies.

GOVERNMENT ACCOUNT

The impact of the federal government on the U.S. balance of payments can be seen by grouping together the major governmental balance-of-payments items (Table 1). These include overseas military expenditures, sales of military goods, aid-financed exports of U.S. goods, aid money spent abroad, and repayments and interest payments on earlier governmental loans. Throughout the whole period, this account has been in deficit, but the size and significance of that deficit has changed substantially. In the 1940s and 1950s, the deficit on government account was a crucial means for financing the surplus on the private trade account and for expanding the supply of international liquidity. The positive financial side effects of these government deficits facilitated the rapid expansion of American military and political commitments around the world. However, by the late 1950s this relationship began to change. Other items in the balance of payments, particularly private capital flows, became more negative, thus increasing the size of the overall deficit. At the same time, many European nations began to feel that their reserves had finally reached levels that put them no longer in need of additional international liquidity. While these governments had earlier been willing and eager to accumulate dollars in their reserves, they began in the late 1950s to convert their excess dollars for gold, resulting in a major run on the U.S. gold stock.

But if the government account deficit was no longer functional for the balance of payments as a whole, the expenditures were still important for achieving American global aims. The U.S. troops stationed in Europe were an essential element in the Atlantic Alliance, and they could not be withdrawn simply because the Europeans no longer had a pressing need for the dollars spent to maintain the American military presence. Similarly, aid programs and military bases in other parts of the world were of crucial importance to the struggle against social revolution in the underdeveloped world, a struggle that was intensified in the wake of the Cuban revolution. The government responded to the dilemma by introducing a variety of economy measures designed to reduce the direct balance-of-payments costs of its foreign military and aid programs without sacrificing important policy goals. While these economy measures succeeded in reducing the government account deficit by a billion dollars between 1961 and 1964, the intensification of the Vietnam War quickly obliterated the effects of the economy campaigns. And even after de-escalation in Vietnam, the government account deficit continued at higher levels than in the early 1960s.[3]

The military part of the government account deficit (Columns 1 and 2 of Table 1) increased steadily through the 1950s. In fact, the outflow for direct military expenditures jumped from $576 million in 1950 to $2.6 billion in 1953, dramatic evidence of the impact of rearmament and the Korean War. But the outflow continued to increase after the end of the Korean War, reaching a peak in 1958. Economy measures offset agreements by which other governments compensated the United States for the cost of maintaining troops abroad,[4] and increased foreign military sales resulted in a $1 billion reduction in the outflow between 1958 and 1964. However, the demands of the Vietnam War quickly eliminated that saving and the outflow continued rising through 1970, despite significantly higher sales of military goods abroad. It is probable that this data underestimates the direct balance-of-payments costs of the Vietnam War, although it is impossible to tell by how much. In recent years, a further increase in the level of foreign military sales has helped stabilize the government account.[5]

The aid part of the account (Columns 3, 4, and 5 of Table 1) has fluctuated around a deficit of 700 million dollars.[6] The deficit became greater in the early 1960s, probably reflecting the ambitious programs of the Alliance for Progress, but then it was cut down at the same time that controls on private capital movements were imposed. The increased use, through most of the 1960s, of loans rather than grants for aid to underdeveloped countries has meant an increased inflow of dollars for repayment of earlier loans. But quite obviously the increased burden of repayment is difficult to carry for most underdeveloped countries, unless they can continue to get new loans from other sources. Significantly, in 1974 U.S. grants and credits for the purpose of financing the repayment of earlier loans were more than $3 billion greater than they had been in earlier years. Yet the substitution of loans for grants and the tying of aid to purchases in the United States has prevented the various aid programs from contributing to an increased balance-of-payments drain for the United States.

The other items in the government account—income on U.S. government assets abroad, sales and purchases of miscellaneous services, pensions, interest on U.S. government liabilities to foreigners, and changes in U.S. government nonliquid liabilities to foreigners—had relatively little impact on the balance of payments for many years. However, interest on U.S. government liabilities did turn strongly negative beginning in the mid-1960s. As foreign dollar-holdings increased during the 1960s, a good portion of those holdings were invested in various kinds of U.S. government securities. Interest payments on these obligations moved from $489 million in 1965 to $1.8 billion in 1971 and $4.3 billion in 1974.

PRIVATE MERCHANDISE TRADE

The trade account—exclusive of exports financed by government aid—has historically been one of the strongest items in the U.S. balance of payments (Table 2). The substantial trade surplus that existed in the interwar period continued into the post-World War II period. During the years of postwar reconstruction, the size of the commercial export surplus was limited by the dollar shortage abroad. The substantial export surplus that the United States ran in those years was the product of massive quantities of government-financed exports through the Marshall Plan and other programs. As foreign economies recovered, however, the commercially financed export surplus increased. It reached a high point in 1956-57. There was a sharp downturn in 1958 and 1959, and then another period of strength from 1960 to 1964. This was followed by a sustained drop that pushed the U.S. commercial trade balance into deficit by 1968.

Because the trade account includes such diverse elements as agricultural goods, raw materials, finished consumer goods, and capital goods, fluctuations in the overall balance can reflect a wide range of different influences. For example, the improvement in the balance in 1956-57 and the subsequent decline in 1958-59 can be traced, in part, to shifts in trade in raw materials produced by the closing of the Suez Canal. When the trade account is divided up into different commodity groups, it is possible to see the emergence of clear patterns. The most striking is that the balance of trade on consumer manufactured goods (excluding automotive products) declined steadily from 1951 to 1971. In contrast, the balance on capital goods—machines and tools used in the production of other goods—improved steadily over the same period. The balance on automotive goods also declined, but the pattern is different from that of consumer goods. The balance on automotive goods declined starting in 1957, with a period of recovery in the early 1960s followed by a sharp decline in the second half of the 1960s.

TABLE 2
TRADE (IN $ MILLIONS)

	Trade Balance Exclusive of Government-Financed Exports (1)	Trade Balance with Government-Financed Exports (2)	Balance on Consumer Goods except Auto (3)	Balance on Automotive Vehicles (4)	Balance on Capital Goods (5)	Balance on Foods, Feeds, and Beverages (6)	Balance on Industrial Supplies and Materials (7)
1950	−1449	1122	310	723	2033	−1160	− 1135
1	+ 969	3067	445	1180	2356	− 654	− 762
2	+ 926	2611	352	968	2585	− 955	− 984
3	− 88	1437	329	945	2705	−1444	− 1630
4	+1339	2576	310	1019	2699	−1604	− 285
5	+1321	2897	143	1191	2817	− 889	− 778
6	+3048	4752	113	1250	3470	− 383	− 291
7	+4331	6271	126	1010	4087	− 525	+ 1074
8	+1583	3462	119	568	4292	− 882	− 508
9	− 676	1148	− 261	343	4026	− 574	− 2197
60	+2846	4892	− 505	633	4949	− 116	+ 37
1	+3175	5571	− 448	805	5217	87	− 9
2	+2018	4521	− 821	780	5685	256	− 1441
3	+2342	5224	− 831	882	5781	529	− 1052
4	+3769	6801	− 943	962	6424	934	− 378
5	+1999	4951	−1506	990	6581	982	− 2107
6	+ 665	3817	−1877	444	6756	990	− 2549
7	+ 277	3800	−2102	150	7531	412	− 1885
8	−2711	− 635	−3041	− 842	8291	− 458	− 3155
9	−2487	+ 607	−4040	−1400	9129	− 551	− 2384
70	− 507	+2603	−4834	−2242	10555	− 315	− 1324
1	−5590	−2268	−5714	−3521	10992	− 312	− 4274
2	−9381	−6409	−7863	−4208	11118	224	− 6342
3	−2416	+ 955	−8480	−4543	13928	5962	− 6947
4	−9422	−5528	−8484	−3798	20616	7889	−20875

Column 1 is derived by subtracting Column 4 in Table 1 from the total balance of trade, Column 2, Table 2. Data is from *SCB*, June 1975, and U.S. Department of Commerce, Office of Business Economics, *United States Exports and Imports Classified by OBE End-Use Commodity Categories 1923-1968*. Note that Columns 2 to 7 include government-financed exports. Columns 3 to 7 do not include all categories of exports and imports. Finally, Column 6 does not include all of the items normally included in the agricultural trade balance because it excludes a variety of nonedible agricultural products.

Together, the decline on consumer goods and on automotive goods exceeds the gains on capital goods trade.

The long-term decline in the consumer goods account can be traced to a variety of factors. One of the most important was the revival of competition from European and Japanese capitalists, once the period of postwar reconstruction had been completed. Capitalists in these countries had the "advantage of backwardness." They began production, quite often, with the most modern technology because the prewar industrial plant had been destroyed. They also had the advantage of a work force with much lower wage levels. Furthermore, the desire to catch up inspired aggressive managerial policies, which often contrasted with the far more conservative management of established American firms. It was to be expected that this competitive challenge would be concentrated at first in consumer goods because their production generally requires less initial investment and less scientific sophistication than capital goods production.[7]

But the revival of competition alone does not explain the worsening of the U.S. trade balance in consumer goods. The United States had the resources—capital, skilled labor, technological sophistication, and entrepreneurial competence—to meet the competitive challenge directly and successfully. But, for a number of reasons, the resources were not used in that way. Because during much of the 1950s ample production facilities already existed for many consumer goods, and because the domestic market was relatively protected by tariffs from foreign competition, there was little reason for domestic producers to modernize their production of these goods. And when firms decided to increase sales in foreign markets, they did so, especially after 1955, by building branch plants abroad. The decision to sell to a foreign market through branch plants rather than through exports often meant that capital was diverted from the expansion and modernization of domestic facilities.

Businessmen base their decision to supply a market through a branch plant rather than through exports on a variety of factors. Size of market, transportation costs, labor costs, and the political-social climate of the host country are all factors. There is also a fairly typical pattern that leads from export sales organized by a foreign representative to the establishment of a foreign sales office and finally to the building of a plant. This pattern long predated the 1950s.[8] However, two particular factors seem to have played a special role in the decision by American businessmen to pursue the direct investment path from the mid-1950s on. The first is the organization of federal taxes, which create a tax incentive for direct foreign investment.[9] The second is the level of tariffs in the postwar world. Because American tariff liberalization efforts were basically blocked by domestic protectionists, little progress was made in forcing a reduction in foreign, particularly European, tariffs before the second half of the 1960s. The existence of high tariff walls and the emergence of trading blocs behind those walls—the Sterling Area, the EEC, and the EFTA—increased the incentive for branch-planting strategy by American firms. The creation of the Common Market, in particular, was a stimulus to U.S. direct investment, because plants built behind the EEC's common external tariff could take advantage of a huge internal market.[10]

The rearmament decision of 1950 also had a significant impact on the consumer goods industries. The creation of a huge military-industrial complex drained scientific and technical talent away from civilian sectors of the economy. The cost of this talent was bid up to levels beyond the reach of civilian firms by cost-plus contracting, and the entire definition of engineering skills came to be shaped by problems of military and space-exploration technology. While the total technological resources of Europe and Japan were far more limited than those of the United States, a far larger share of those resources were devoted to consumer goods production than in the United States. And where there were technological spin-offs from the military research effort, these usually did not make a direct contribution to the strength of the civilian consumer goods sector.[11]

However, it is these spin-offs that have been an important part of the strength of the capital goods trade account. Jet planes, computers, and other advanced electronic equipment are among the high technology items that have bolstered the U.S. international trade position. In fact, it is possible to take a sanguine view of the declining U.S. competitiveness in a variety of consumer goods on the grounds that the United States should specialize instead in high technology products, particularly capital goods. But there are a number of problems in this line of argument. The limited size of the market for the most sophisticated items points to the difficulties of balancing a deficit on consumer goods with a surplus on capital goods. Consumer goods such as household appliances can conceivably be placed in every home, but only a limited number of generators can be sold in a particular country. Moreover, some of the sophisticated items are of sufficient strategic importance—aircraft, computers, atomic energy equipment—to give other countries a strong incentive to make an effort, with governmental assistance, to decrease their dependence on U.S. imports for these items.

Furthermore, the strength of U.S. capital goods exports can sometimes be traced more to political factors than to superior U.S. competitiveness. The data cited in Columns 2-7 of Table 2 includes government financed exports, and these make up a much larger share of capital goods than of consumer goods.[12] In addition, U.S. political influence has clearly been important in winning many large capital goods contracts for U.S. firms. Revelations of widespread foreign bribery by officials of American firms suggests that these contracts are often awarded on less than objective, competitive criteria. Finally, evidence exists that the U.S. lead in high technology goods is shrinking; the time it takes for other countries to duplicate an American innovation becomes shorter with each passing year.[13] The export of U.S. technology through branch planting and through the leasing of techniques to foreign producers has speeded this process, and other countries have also expanded their research efforts and now have the capital to finance efforts that they could not contemplate ten or fifteen years ago.[14]

Trade in raw materials, including fuels, and basic industrial goods, including chemicals, shifted less dramatically in the period up to 1971. The U.S. position in fuels, lubricants, and other industrial materials worsened fairly steadily starting in the early 1950s. The worsening accelerated in the second half of the 1960s with increased imports of oil and steel. The deterioration in this account was countered by large sales of coal and lumber, especially to the Japanese, in the second half of the 1960s, and the balance on chemicals improved slightly but steadily from the 1950s on, reflecting the high level of technical innovation in sectors of that industry.

After 1971 this segment of the trade balance turned dramatically negative as a result of the oil-price increases by the Organization of Petroleum Exporting Countries. The price of oil imports jumped from $3.3 billion in 1971 to $4.3 billion in 1972, $8.0 billion in 1973, and $25.9 billion in 1974. Some of the negative balance-of-payments impact of the oil-price rise was offset by improvements in the exports of raw materials and chemicals because the international economic boom of 1973-74 pushed up demand and prices for these commodities. Another substantial share of the increased petroleum bill was offset by another oil-related item that shows up elsewhere in the balance-of-payments account. Repatriated profits on U.S. foreign investments jumped $8 billion between 1972 and 1974, largely because of the vastly increased profits of the U.S. oil companies. Nevertheless, the phenomenal increase in the cost of importing petroleum places an enormous strain on the U.S. balance of payments.

This strain has been kept to a minimum by another phenomenal shift in U.S. trade. As Column 6 in Table 2 indicates, the agricultural trade balance followed an irregular course in the period from 1951 to 1971. The irregularity reflects shifts in foreign demand in response to changing crop conditions, fluctuations in the ability of underdeveloped countries to pay for agricultural imports, and changing policies on agricultural imports in the developed countries. Efforts to take advantage of the efficiency and productiveness of American agriculture to improve the U.S. trade balance had repeatedly run up against the reluctance of the developed countries to allow increased agricultural imports. But after 1971, U.S. efforts to expand agricultural exports succeeded beyond the wildest dreams of American policy-makers. A fortuitous combination of events—the devaluation of the dollar, poor harvests elsewhere in the world, and Western Europe's expanded need for food grains to satisfy a growing appetite for meat—served to push the dollar value of U.S. agricultural exports up from $7.8 billion in 1971 to $22 billion in 1974.

SERVICES, TOURISM, AND
PRIVATE REMITTANCES

This account (Table 3) includes services such as banking, shipping, and insurance; tourism; and remittances by private citizens. It worsened steadily, but slowly, from the early 1950s on. While the service account has been positive, the balance on travel and transportation has been consistently and increasingly negative. It is significant, however, that the travel deficit has grown rather slowly. This is, in part, a result of deliberate government policy. Aware that the popularity of foreign travel with large sectors of the U.S. public could lead to a major balance-of-payments drain, the government has taken a number of steps to limit the potential outflow. These actions include "see America first" campaigns, limits on the dollar value of duty-free goods that Americans are allowed to bring back from abroad, and efforts to encourage foreign tourism in the United States. Because the encouragement of foreign tourism coincided with European and Japanese prosperity, it was possible to increase U.S. tourist receipts relatively rapidly, enough to prevent a rapid increase in the tourism deficit.

TABLE 3

SERVICES AND TOURISM TRANSACTIONS (IN $ MILLIONS)

	Balance on Travel and Transportation (1)	Balance on Other Services (2)	Private Remittances (3)	Total (4)
1950	− 120	124	− 454	− 450
1	+ 298	104	− 409	− 7
2	+ 83	112	− 443	− 248
3	− 238	91	− 503	− 650
4	− 269	72	− 504	− 701
5	− 297	51	− 456	− 702
6	− 361	160	− 555	− 756
7	− 189	216	− 570	− 543
8	− 633	219	− 563	− 977
9	− 821	220	− 599	−1200
60	− 964	217	− 414	−1161
1	− 978	250	− 424	−1152
2	−1150	304	− 467	−1313
3	−1312	378	− 563	−1497
4	−1149	402	− 602	−1349
5	−1283	559	− 664	−1388
6	−1333	624	− 640	−1349
7	−1751	716	− 862	−1897
8	−1548	728	− 817	−1637
9	−1763	819	− 921	−1865
70	−2023	965	−1050	−2108
1	−2315	1126	−1058	−2247
2	−3024	1277	−1034	−2781
3	−2862	1381	−1210	−2691
4	−4692	1585	−1029	−4136

SCB, October 1972 and June 1975. Column 1 is not an accurate balance of tourism; for that see *SCB*, July 1972. Column 2 includes fees and royalties from unaffiliated foreigners.

TABLE 4
DIRECT INVESTMENT (IN $ MILLIONS)

	Direct Investment Outflow (1)	Earnings on Direct Investment (2)	Foreign Direct Investment in U.S. (3)	Earnings on Foreign Direct Investments (4)	Total (5)
1950	− 621	1540	80	− 182	817
1	− 508	1764	90	− 208	1138
2	− 852	1711	132	− 207	784
3	− 735	1747	158	− 218	952
4	− 667	2053	124	− 200	1310
5	− 823	2285	197	− 210	1449
6	−1951	2609	232	− 216	674
7	−2442	2695	155	− 224	184
8	−1181	2563	98	− 245	1235
9	−1372	2771	238	− 250	1387
60	−1674	2945	141	− 255	1157
1	−1598	3430	73	− 237	1668
2	−1654	3844	132	− 242	2080
3	−1976	4019	− 5	− 284	1754
4	−2328	4687	− 5	− 269	2085
5	−3468	5162	+ 57	− 367	1384
6	−3625	4629	+ 86	− 436	654
7	−3072	5201	+ 258	− 443	1944
8	−2880	5581	+ 319	− 468	2552
9	−3190	6352	+ 832	− 518	3476
70	−4281	6750	+1030	− 552	2947
1	−4738	7910	− 175	− 739	2258
2	−3530	8531	+ 380	− 842	4539
3	−4968	11354	+2656	−1164	7878
4	−7268	20703	+2224	−1190	14469

SCB, October 1972 and June 1975. Columns 2 and 4 include fees and royalties earned by affiliated foreigners.

DIRECT INVESTMENT

The direct investment account (Table 4) includes both outflow and return on U.S. direct investment and inflow and return of profits on foreign direct investment in the United States. In almost all postwar years this account has been positive because the return of profits on earlier investments has been larger than both the outflow for new investment and the net payment on foreign direct investments. The account has improved more or less steadily, with a brief downturn in 1956-57, and rapid improvement after 1966. The 1956-57 downturn was largely accounted for by a temporary jump in petroleum investments abroad. The improvement in the second half of the 1960s was a product of government-imposed controls, at first voluntary, later mandatory, specifically designed to strengthen the balance of payments by reducing the outflow of funds for direct investment.

In the 1970s, there has been increased fluctuation in the items of this account. The level of foreign direct investment in the United States jumped to the level of $2 billion a year in 1973 and 1974, reflecting the use of foreign oil revenues for direct investment. However, in 1974, the repatriation of earnings on foreign direct investment rose by almost $5 billion from the previously stable level. This extraordinary shift is probably accounted for by the efforts in that year by Western Europe and Japan to finance their own huge petroleum deficits. While OPEC countries were increasing their direct investments in the United States, traditional direct investors were forced to repatriate profits that they otherwise would have reinvested to expand their American subsidiaries. Yet while European and Japanese multinationals were curtailing their expansion in the United States, American multinationals were accelerating their foreign expansion. The federal government's controls on foreign direct investment were lifted in January 1974, making possible a $2 billion rise in the outflow of direct investment funds by U.S. firms between 1973 and 1974. This was more than offset by the rise in repatriated profits by the oil companies.

The direct investment account has been the subject of controversy concerning the impact of U.S. direct investment on the overall payments balance. The controversy was fueled by the imposition of government controls on the level of direct investment outflows. These controls were not intended to slow, and did not have the effect of slowing, the growth of U.S. multinational enterprises. American firms continued to expand their investments abroad, but they did so by increasing the quantity of their borrowing abroad. Capital exported from the United States became less important in financing foreign expansion as compared to the reinvestment of profits and the borrowing of capital abroad.[15] Nevertheless, the multinationals were dissatisfied with government controls because the cost of borrowing abroad was often greater than that for U.S. capital, and they were limited in their use of domestic profits to finance foreign expansion. Over and over again, the spokesmen of the multinationals argued that the strength of the direct investment account proved the irrationality of limiting the outflow of direct investment capital. They argued that, since new investments result in later profits, stopping the outflow of capital now will dry up the future flow of profits. The more sophisticated cited the nineteenth-century British example of a mature creditor economy that was able to finance a significant trade deficit because the returns on earlier investments were so much larger than the outflow of new investments. In this view, a premature halt to the outflow of capital would make it impossible for the United States to reap the benefits of a mature creditor economy later.[16]

An analysis of the actual flow by industries indicates that there were some problems with the anticontrol arguments. The strength of the return flow of profits has been based largely on the enormous profits earned by the oil industry, particularly in its Middle Eastern operations. Between 1950 and 1964, direct U.S. investment by the petroleum companies in Asia, Africa, and Latin America totaled $3.1 billion. The return over the same period from those areas totaled $15.2 billion. This net gain of $12.1 billion compares with a $3.2 billion gain for all manufacturing direct investment during the same period.[17] In the period from 1965 to 1971, of the total balance-of-payments gain from all direct investments (including royalties and fees) of $21.9 billion, $16.5 billion was accounted for by the Middle East and Latin America. This pattern was still true even in a period in which the government had intervened to improve the direct investment balance with the industrial countries. (For the 1968-71 period, when foreign direct investment controls were mandatory, the Middle East and Latin America accounted for $10.6 billion out of a total $15.6 billion.) This relationship existed despite the fact that, in 1970, 60.5 percent of the total book value of U.S. foreign investment was located in Canada and Western Europe.[18] In short, U.S. direct investments in Latin America and the Middle East have been profitable out of proportion to their size.

The matter is more complex than simply comparing the annual outflow for all direct investment with the annual total return flow of profits. The return flow reflects the whole previous history of U.S. foreign direct investment, including fabulously profitable raw material investments, many of which long predated World War II. In fact, when one looks at the account for manufacturing direct investment alone, only in the years of mandatory controls is there a significant positive balance-of-payments effect, and this is still small. That does not mean that U.S. manufacturing direct investments are not profitable (although they are clearly less profitable than investments in Middle Eastern oil), but that the expansion of existing facilities and new investments eats up the profits on earlier investments. Since much of the enormous increase in direct investment over the past twenty years has been in manufacturing ($28.4 billion out of a total increase in book value of $66.3 billion from 1950 to 1970 was accounted for by manufacturing),[19] the validity of the mature creditor model depends on the idea that the huge stock of U.S. manufacturing direct investment will some day generate a flow of profits that far exceeds requirements for expansion or new investment. But since the total annual expenditure for new plant and equipment by U.S. firms abroad has been growing steadily and at a faster rate than domestic manufacturing investment,[20] that day seems very far off.

The other major controversy about direct investment centers on its impact on the trade balance. Beginning in the 1960s, sectors of the American labor movement became concerned over the export of American jobs through branch-planting abroad. Since this was happening at a time when the balance-of-payments deficit was a major problem and the balance of trade was deteriorating rapidly, some trade union leaders put forward a critique of the multinationals that emphasized their damage to domestic employment and to the balance of trade. They argued that the export of American technology, through branch-planting and licensing agreements, made it easier for foreign capitalists to compete with American-produced goods. In addition, they suggested that imports into the United States from American-owned factories abroad were a major factor in the worsening trade balance.[21] The multinationals and their defenders responded to these charges with a number of counterarguments. They insisted that the great bulk of foreign direct investments was necessary to avoid losing markets to foreign competitors. If American firms could compete successfully by branch-planting, at least that would aid the U.S. balance of payments through the return flow of profits. Furthermore, they argued that American firms abroad aided U.S. exports by buying U.S. capital goods and by facilitating and encouraging the sale abroad of U.S.-made products.[22]

Weighing the relative merits of these arguments presents serious problems. It is, of course, impossible to measure the quantity of U.S. exports that have been displaced by branch-planting or by the leasing of technology to foreign producers. It is equally difficult to calculate what percentage of U.S. export business would have been lost had it not been for the presence of U.S. manufacturing firms abroad. However, a number of points can be made. First, it would seem that those exports that are facilitated by the presence of U.S. branch plants a-broad could have been sold anyway by sufficiently aggressive foreign marketing. (Total export sales to U.S. overseas affiliates in 1966 were $7.8 billion, of which 9 percent were capital goods, 40 percent were items for further processing, and 51 percent were goods destined for immediate resale or lease.)[23] Second, to the extent that branch-planting has been an alternative to the development of more modern and more technologically sophisticated domestic production facilities, it has done severe damage to the trade balance. The argument that firms must move abroad to meet foreign competition because of high domestic costs always assumes existing technologies of production. And having the option of moving abroad might well have discouraged manufacturers from the riskier course of investing in technical innovations. Finally, recent investments by foreign firms in U.S. production facilities to produce items such as television sets and steel products suggests that either U.S. firms could have successfully competed internationally with U.S. production facilities or that their profit expectations have been unreasonably high.[24]

OTHER LONG-TERM CAPITAL FLOWS

The flows of private, non-direct investment, long-term capital into and out of the U.S. (Table 5) are subject to a variety of determinants, the analysis of which lies beyond the scope of this study. However, shifts in these flows have had a significant impact on the U.S. payments balance at a number of points. The tendency for the outflow of long-term capital to increase in the period after 1957 was brought to a halt by the imposition of government controls beginning in 1964. The controls included an Interest Equalization Tax designed to discourage foreign

TABLE 5

LONG-TERM CAPITAL FLOWS (IN $MILLIONS)

	Outflow of Long-Term Capital (1)	Inflow of Long-Term Capital (2)	Balance on Long-Term Capital (3)
1950	− 495	− 12	− 517
1	− 437	+ 115	− 322
2	− 214	+ 33	− 181
3	+ 185	+ 79	+ 264
4	− 320	+ 149	− 171
5	− 241	+ 193	− 48
6	− 603	+ 363	− 240
7	− 859	+ 235	− 624
8	−1444	− 17	−1461
9	− 926	+ 472	− 454
60	− 856	+ 289	− 567
1	−1025	+ 369	− 656
2	−1227	+ 142	−1085
3	−1718	+ 322	−1396
4	−2143	− 34	−2177
5	−1079	− 87	−1166
6	− 515	+1277	+ 762
7	−1354	+1259	− 95
8	−1451	+5201	+3750
9	−1676	+3991	+2315
70	−1509	+3325	+1816
1	−1893	+2423	+ 530
2	−2168	+5250	+3082
3	−2125	+4614	+2489
4	−3550	+ 157	−3393

SCB, October 1972 and June 1975. The data on long-term capital flows for the 1950-59 period is not complete.

TABLE 6

MISCELLANEOUS BALANCE-OF-PAYMENT FLOWS (IN $MILLIONS)

	Balance on all Private Non-Direct Investment Interest Flows (1)	Short-Term Capital Outflows (2)	Short Term Capital Inflows (3)	Errors and Omissions (4)	Changes in U.S. Gold Holdings (5)
1950	+ 24	—	—	− 124	+1743
1	+ 13	—	—	+ 354	− 53
2	+ 31	—	—	+ 497	− 379
3	+ 37	—	—	+ 220	+1161
4	+ 46	—	—	+ 60	+ 298
5	+ 42	—	—	+ 371	+ 41
6	+ 61	—	—	+ 390	− 306
7	+ 113	—	—	+1012	− 798
8	+ 98	—	—	+ 361	+2275
9	+ 137	—	—	+ 260	+1075
60	+ 135	− 1349	+ 217	−1060	+1703
1	+ 258	− 1556	+ 1259	−1032	+ 857
2	+ 318	− 546	+ 103	−1165	+ 890
3	+ 321	− 786	+ 597	− 406	+ 461
4	+ 454	− 2147	+ 1667	− 954	+ 125
5	+ 479	+ 754	+ 280	− 506	+1665
6	+ 448	− 414	+ 2680	+ 575	+ 571
7	+ 399	− 1228	+ 1971	− 189	+1170
8	+ 178	− 1087	+ 4569	+ 446	+1173
9	− 931	− 569	+ 8744	−1492	− 967
70	− 920	− 1132	− 5338	− 476	+ 787
1	+ 297	− 3429	− 6706	−9698	+ 866
2	+ 479	− 3010	+ 4943	−1884	+ 547
3	+ 302	− 7020	+ 5125	−2436	0
4	+1107	−20902	+18622	+4834	0

SCB, October 1972 and June 1975. Data on short-term capital flows, Columns 2 and 3, is not available for 1950-59. Note that a positive entry in Column 5 indicates a reduction in U.S. gold holdings, while a negative entry means an increase in gold holdings.

bond offerings in the United States and the Federal Reserve Bank's Voluntary Credit Restriction Program that encouraged banks to limit their foreign lending operations.[25] It seems clear that these controls did prevent a worsening of this account, and after the removal of the controls in January 1974 much larger outflows became possible, such as an outflow in excess of $2 billion in the first quarter of 1975 alone. The inflow of long-term capital has been extremely volatile, but the large inflows between 1968 and 1973 clearly helped bolster the U.S. payments position. The sudden drop in 1974 was also a consequence of the energy crisis, when oil-consuming nations were forced to liquidate some of their investments in the United States to pay the increased price for petroleum.

OTHER BALANCE-OF-PAYMENTS FLOWS

1. Interest payments (Table 6, Column 1)

This includes all interest flows except those that are part of the government and direct investment accounts. As Column 1 indicates, this item has had little net impact on the overall balance because the inflow and outflow of interest payments have generally moved in the same direction.

2. Changes in the flow of short-term capital (Table 6, Columns 3 and 4)

The changes in U.S. short-term claims and liabilities are itemized separately because these two items are treated differently in some of the balance-of-payments conventions. The changes in liabilities, the net inflow of short-term capital from abroad, is often thought of as one of the flows that helps to finance a U.S. deficit. However, when confidence in the dollar was weak in 1970-71, despite the deficit there was a sharp reduction of foreign short-term lending to the United States. Once again, the sharp shift in 1974 is a product of the energy crisis; it is a result of short-term investments by the OPEC countries.

3. Errors and omissions (Table 6, Column 5)

The errors and omissions item has sometimes been quite large. It is generally suspected that it is largely comprised of unrecorded capital outflows. The strongly negative figures in 1971 and 1973 coincide with speculative assaults on the dollar.

THE OVERALL BALANCE OF PAYMENTS
AND THE DEFICIT

Because of the inadequacy of the data for the pre-1960 period, there is only one balance-of-payments measure that allows a reasonably accurate measure of the movement of the payments balance across the entire period from 1950 to 1974. This is the Gross Liquidity Balance presented in Column 5 of Table 7. In this measure, changes in official reserves and changes in liquid liabilities to private and official foreigners are considered the balancing items. In other words, all of the items except for these balancing items are added up and, if the sum is negative, the balance of payments is in deficit. For the sake of comparison, another measure, the Basic Balance, (Column 6) is included for the years from 1960 to 1974. The Basic Balance counts all short-term capital flows as balancing items; it simply presents the sum of all current and long-term capital transactions. To get a sense of their contribution to the overall payments position, some of the major balance-of-payments accounts that we have discussed are also listed in Table 7.

Table 7 indicates that, though the gross liquidity deficit fluctuated around $1-5 billion through most of the period under discussion, there were shifts in the composition of the deficit. These shifts helped lay the basis for the dramatic worsening in the size of the deficit in 1971-72. While the government account deficit grew gradually and steadily, the balance of trade shifted dramatically. From an annual surplus averaging $2.5 to 3 billion between 1958 and 1964, the trade balance moved to an annual average deficit of the same magnitude in the period 1968-71. This shift was counterbalanced by the shifts in the direct and non-direct capital accounts. The imposition of controls, first on non-direct capital outflows and later on direct investment outflows, led to a sharp improvement in the impact of these items on the overall balance. In short, the forced improvement on the long-term capital items prevented the worsening of the trade balance from dramatically increasing the payments deficit, but the capital controls could do no more than postpone disaster.

THE PERSISTENCE OF THE DEFICIT

While the specific composition of the deficit changed over the 1950-70 period, the fact that the deficit persisted, despite serious efforts to eliminate it, suggests that the deficit was a reflection of contradictions

TABLE 7

OVERALL PAYMENTS BALANCE (IN $MILLIONS)

	Government Balance (1, col. 7) (1)	Commercial Trade Balance (2, col. 1) (2)	Direct Investment Balance (4, col. 5) (3)	Long-Term Capital Balance (5, col. 3) (4)	Gross Liquidity Balance (5)	Basic Balance (6)
1950	−2114	−1449	+ 817	− 517	− 3489	—
1	−2085	+ 969	+ 1138	− 322	− 8	—
2	−2966	+ 926	+ 784	− 181	− 1206	—
3	−3063	− 88	+ 952	+ 264	− 2184	—
4	−2765	+1339	+ 1310	− 171	− 1541	—
5	−3405	+1321	+ 1449	− 48	− 1242	—
6	−3643	+3048	+ 674	− 240	− 923	—
7	−3679	+4331	+ 184	− 624	+ 621	—
8	−3974	+1583	+ 1235	−1461	− 3348	—
9	−3036	− 676	+ 1387	− 454	− 3648	—
60	−3620	+2846	+ 1157	− 567	− 3711	− 1211
1	−3312	+3175	+ 1668	− 656	− 2432	− 20
2	−3058	+2018	+ 2080	−1085	− 2865	− 1043
3	−2865	+2342	+ 1754	−1396	− 2554	− 1339
4	−2882	+3769	+ 2085	−2177	− 3088	− 100
5	−3125	+1999	+ 1384	−1166	− 1421	− 1817
6	−3802	+ 665	+ 654	+ 762	− 2165	− 2621
7	−4601	+ 277	+ 1944	− 95	− 4890	− 3973
8	−4420	−2711	+ 2552	+3750	− 2169	− 2287
9	−4456	−2487	+ 3476	+2315	− 5919	− 3949
70	−4992	− 507	+ 2947	+1816	− 4466	− 3760
1	−5887	−5590	+ 2258	+ 530	−23779	−10637
2	−7050	−9381	+ 4539	+3082	−15786	−11113
3	−6538	−2416	+ 7878	+2489	− 9602	− 977
4	−7088	−9422	+14469	−3393	−25156	−10927

Columns 1-4 are taken from the preceding tables. The basic balance, Column 6, is unavailable before 1960 because of the inadequacy of the data on long-term capital flows for that period. *SCB*, October 1972 and June 1975.

in the U.S. role in the world economy. The fact that all of the standard balance-of-payments adjustment techniques were inappropriate for solving the problem of the U.S. deficit highlights the special nature of that deficit. The two most fundamental adjustment techniques—deflation and devaluation—are both designed to strengthen the balance of payments by improving the trade account, but the United States actually had a trade surplus during much of the period of the deficit. Deflation or devaluation could have restored balance to the U.S. payments position only by giving the United States a trade surplus large enough to offset the deficit on government account. However, other countries were understandably reluctant to see the United States run that kind of trade surplus, especially when they had the competitive capacity to prevent it. In other words, had a U.S. devaluation in the early 1960s improved the U.S. international trade position, it is likely that other countries would have devalued correspondingly to regain their earlier competitive position and to reverse any improvement in the U.S. trade balance. Furthermore, a U.S. deflation to achieve the same results would have been unthinkable because of the dire domestic consequences, and any serious deflationary efforts by the United States would also have slowed down the rest of the world economy. Worldwide deflation would have diminished the U.S. trade gain and led to intense international pressure on the United States to reflate.

Capital controls as a cure for the deficit conflicted with the American obligation to keep its capital markets open to foreign borrowers. The United States had succeeded in reconstructing an international monetary order along classical lines, with New York playing the role that London had played before World War I. One obligation of this role was to provide capital to other countries for a variety of purposes, but especially to help them cushion balance-of-payments disequilibria through private borrowing. In this sense, those who argued that the United States had special responsibilities as the world's banker[26] were right; cutting off that flow of capital was potentially dangerous to the orderly working of the world economy. These considerations did not apply to controls on foreign direct investment outflows, but it would have been extremely difficult to control one without the other. For one thing, American multinationals would have devised ways of financing foreign investment by drawing on uncontrolled American capital sources. And if U.S. multinationals simply increased their own borrowing abroad, that would very likely divert foreign borrowers to the U.S.

market. In short, other long-term capital flows would probably have increased by about the same amount that direct investment outflows were reduced.

Actually, when the United States did resort to capital controls, the disruptive impact on foreign borrowers was minimized by the rapid evolution of the Eurodollar market, although other problems ensued. The Eurodollar market, made possible by the large quantity of dollars held in foreign hands because of the U.S. deficit, is a capital market in which these dollar claims in foreign hands are loaned and borrowed. A variety of loans that might earlier have been made in New York could be made in London in Eurodollars, including loans to cover balance-of-payments disequilibria. Because of the U.S. controls, the already existing Eurodollar market expanded greatly and became the dominant international capital market, making London once again the center of international finance. However, this time London was dealing in an alien currency and the British authorities exercised little control over the Eurodollar market. In fact, the central weakness of this new international capital market has been the absence of strong regulation and supervision to control the banks in the market and to provide a lender of last resort should a crisis develop. In other words, the U.S. capital controls added immeasurably to the fragility of the world economy by elevating the shaky Eurodollar market to the role of dominant international capital market.[27]

The point is that the use by the United States of the standard balance-of-payments adjustment mechanisms did and could do little to ease the deficit, while doing much to weaken the international monetary order. This is a classic contradiction: the continuation of the deficit threatened to destroy the international monetary order, but all of the potential remedies for the deficit tended to produce the same result. In other words, a solution that eliminated the U.S. deficit in a way that was acceptable to other countries would have required a fundamental reorganization of the world economy along lines that conflicted with the basic goals of U.S. policy-makers.

A structural solution to the deficit would have required a fundamental shift in the American military stance and in the American orientation toward overseas political and economic expansion. A serious reduction in U.S. overseas military expenditures, including the elimination of much of the global network of military bases, would have eliminated a big piece of the U.S. deficit. A reduction in military expenditures at home, had it been undertaken early enough, could have halted the deterioration in the U.S. trade balance. Had a sizable portion of the scientific and engineering talent devoted to military and space efforts been released to the civilian sector and used productively, the chances are great that the U.S. trade balance in civilian goods would have strengthened dramatically. Similarly, if U.S. firms had competed internationally through exports from technologically intensive, high-productivity U.S. factories, rather than branch-planting abroad, the trade balance would have been strengthened further. Finally, without the expansion of U.S. firms abroad, much of the aid expenditures designed to make foreign countries safe for U.S. investment could have been dispensed with, eliminating another source of the deficit.

But such a scenario would have been unrealistic because the basic intent of U.S. foreign economic policy has been to facilitate the overseas expansion of U.S. business.[28] The exercise of American political and military power on a global basis has been designed to gain foreign acceptance of an international monetary order that institutionalizes an open world economy, giving maximum opportunities to American businessmen. It would be absurd for the United States to abandon its global ambitions simply to live within the rules of an international monetary order that was shaped for the purpose of achieving these ambitions. So it is hardly surprising that the United States continued to pursue its global ambitions despite the increasing strains on the international monetary order. The fundamental contradiction was that the United States had created an international monetary order that worked only when American political and economic dominance in the capitalist world was absolute. That absolute dominance disappeared as a result of the reconstruction of Western Europe and Japan, on the one hand, and the accumulated domestic costs of the global extension of U.S. power, on the other. With the fading of the absolute dominance, the international monetary order began to crumble. The U.S. deficit was simply the most dramatic symptom of the terminal disease that plagued the postwar international monetary order.

SEVEN. *Managing the U.S. Deficit*

American policy-makers were slow to recognize that the U.S. balance-of-payments deficit was a reflection of more basic contradictions in the world economy. They continued to see the deficit as a relatively superficial problem for some time after the drain on the U.S. gold stock first became an issue in 1958. These policy-makers assumed that the deficit could be solved simply by pressuring the Western European nations to modify their economic behavior because the American policy-makers thought of American international dominance as undiminished. However, it gradually dawned on U.S. officials that the nations of Western Europe had become less malleable to U.S. designs as their economies had strengthened. When the Western Europeans failed to cooperate on U.S. terms, the deficit was finally seen as a consequence of real political-economic conflicts. But it was still some time before American decision-makers were able to take the critical final step of deciding that, if the deficit was caused by the pursuit of U.S. global aims, other countries were simply going to have to learn to live with it.

The development of U.S. policy toward the deficit in the period from 1958 to 1975 can be divided into three periods, corresponding to stages in the understanding of the problem. The first was the period of naive Atlanticism, from 1958 to 1963, when the United States attempted to eliminate the deficit by revitalizing the Atlantic Alliance. The second was the period of semisophisticated delay from 1964 to 1968, when the steady escalation of the Vietnam War and the resulting expansion of the deficit forced the United States to devise a complex strategy to prevent an international monetary crisis that would be disastrous for the U.S. international position. This was followed by the period of the worldly abuse of power from 1968 to 1975, when the United States, with increasing self-consciousness, pursued its global self-interest with little regard for the international "rules of the game."

Through all three periods, there is a continuing dialectic between developments in the foreign exchange and gold markets and the policies of the governments and central banks of the major capitalist countries. Speculative purchases or sales of currencies or gold are usually set off either by anticipation of government policies—devaluations, interest-rate changes, capital controls—or by the absence of government policies to overcome balance-of-payments disequilibria. But the intensity of speculative pressures often has little to do with a specific stimulus, and speculation, once under way, can feed on itself. The structure of the international monetary order after the start of European convertibility in 1958 meant that governments were generally required to respond to speculation by supporting the established price of their own currency.[1] When speculation was intense against a particular currency, the active cooperation of other governments was needed to maintain the established price.[2] If this assistance was not forthcoming or not adequate, the government whose currency was under attack might be forced to take unilateral action—devaluation or capital controls—which might have the effect of turning the speculative pressure on to other currencies. Again, this would pose for another government the choice of international cooperation or unilateral action. Any apparent weakness in the structure of international cooperation tended to stimulate speculation by increasing the likelihood that a particular government would respond to a disequilibrium with either a devaluation or capital controls.[3] But as speculation intensifies, it places further strains on the fabric of international cooperation as the demands for assistance placed on other governments increase. Hence, there was always the fear that the intensification of speculation would interact dynamically with an unraveling of international cooperation to produce a real crisis, one which would plunge the world economy into depression as in the 1930s.

For the United States the danger took the specific form of a run on the U.S. gold stock. The United States had the obligation to maintain the price of gold at $35 an ounce for both private and official purchasers. This meant that foreign central banks could turn in their dollars for U.S. gold and that the United States had to supply enough gold for sale in the European gold markets to prevent the gold price from rising above $35 an ounce. Lack of confidence in the dollar could lead to stepped-up official gold purchases as well as private, speculative gold purchases, and the resulting reduction in U.S. gold reserves would further undermine confidence in the dollar. In the early period, when experience with speculative crises was limited, there was considerable anxiety that a run on the U.S. gold stock might be set in motion fairly easily. This would force unilateral U.S. action that could, in turn, lead to an international economic collapse. Each new speculative crisis was seen to have the potential of tripping the fuse of the ultimate crisis. However, as experience with these speculative crises accumulated, it became clear that the system had a good deal of resilience and that the common interest in avoiding economic disasters would prevent speculative crises from getting out of hand. After a point, the speculative crises began to lose their ability to terrify. The more aggressive balance-of-payments policies of the United States in the period from 1968 to 1975 had their roots in U.S. policy-makers' relative familiarity with international monetary crises.

PHASE 1—NAIVE ATLANTICISM

Despite what now seems like an exaggerated fear of speculative crises, it is nevertheless accurate to describe the period from 1958 to 1963 as one of relative optimism abou the U.S. balance-of-payments position. The optimism was indicated by the belief, generally held in U.S. policy circles, that the U.S. deficit could be solved by fairly minor adjustments, most of which involved shifts in the relationship between the United States and its European allies. Throughout this period, efforts to eliminate the U.S. deficit coincided with, and were often inseparable from, efforts to maintain and strengthen the Atlantic Alliance. However, optimism about the U.S. deficit faded as it became clear that the strains within the Atlantic Alliance were serious and could not be solved by cosmetic adjustments. The differences within the Alliance blocked the minor adjustments that U.S. policy-makers had favored, and the continuation of the U.S. deficit, in a kind of vicious circle, sharpened the political differences among the allies.

The 1957-59 period marked a significant turning point in postwar history; particularly dramatic in the case of Atlantic economic relations because the restoration of European convertibility, the beginning of the EEC, and the start of the U.S. gold drain all occurred within a relatively short period of time. But, somewhat less dramatically, the 1957-59 period was also a turning point in the politics of the Cold War. The passing of John Foster Dulles from the foreign policy scene in 1959 opened the way for new policy initiatives, and the trauma of Sputnik in 1957, the re-evaluation of American defense strategy during 1958, and the second Berlin Crisis all pointed to the changing nature of the global political environment. The critical aspect of the new environment was the possibility of a relaxation of the Cold War, including settlement of the problem of divided Germany.

The question of disengagement in Central Europe dominated foreign policy discussions in Europe and the United States in 1957 and 1958. Proposals were put forward by a variety of statesmen for settling the problem of divided Europe, and sentiment for a relaxation of tensions and for normalization in Europe was strong throughout Western Europe.[4] Nevertheless, there was no significant movement in the direction of relaxation or détente in this period. Whatever the responsibility of the Soviet Union for that lack of progress, it is significant that many Western politicians seem to have been haunted in this period by the fear that their allies would make a unilateral deal with the Russians. The fear that West Germany would seek a private understanding with the Soviet Union long predates this period, but it continued to worry the other Western powers. French foreign policy, particularly before De Gaulle's return to power, placed special emphasis on achieving détente. Although De Gaulle, in the late 1950s, took a hard line on East-West relations in order to consolidate the Franco-German relationship, his desire for an expanded French world-role created suspicions that he might attempt a dramatic rapprochement with the Russians. The British, in turn, were hoping at this point to salvage their international role—badly damaged by the Suez disaster—through the exercise of creative diplomacy. It was feared that their eagerness to become the pivot of East-West relations might lead them to make significant concessions to the Russians. Finally, even at this point, there was uneasiness in Western Europe about the possibility that the Soviet Union and the United States would make a deal over the heads of the Europeans. This kind of universal suspicion suggests that détente and a continuation of the Atlantic Alliance were dimly recognized as incompatible. The fear that one's allies might break ranks and make a deal with the enemy reflects an awareness that détente—a relaxation of Cold War tensions—would tend to destroy the raison d'être of the Alliance.[5]

None of the Western powers were willing to risk the Alliance by moving seriously toward détente with the Soviet Union, and in the United States there was still powerful resistance to the idea of a relaxation of the Cold War. In fact, the Eisenhower administration was under pressure to expand military spending considerably. The Gaither Report in late 1957, and a similar study commissioned by the Rockefeller Foundation, warned of the Soviet Union's ominous military strength and called for an increase in annual U.S. defense spending of $8-10 billion by 1961. Aside from military and strategic considerations, it appears that the call for increased arms spending was related to domestic economic considerations as well as fears of a premature relaxation of the Cold War. The domestic economy had weakened again after the capital goods boom in 1955, and Eisenhower eventually was forced to increase military spending in 1958-59 to cushion the effects of a recession. The rhetoric of these reports also suggests that increased military spending was a kind of inoculation against the virus of détente. Détente was perceived as dangerous because it could bring tensions to the surface, both in American society and the Atlantic Alliance, that had been repressed by the Cold War.[6]

Intertwined with the possibility or danger of détente in this period was increased conflict over Atlantic military strategy. The crux of the problem was that American insistence, during the period of "massive retaliation," that total war was the only possibility had served to undermine European faith in the American nuclear guarantee. The logic was as follows: If the only response to Russian aggression was all-out war, then the Americans would think twice before risking all-out war to defend a piece of Europe from Russian attack. The solution, from the European point of view, was simple; if the United States gave its European partners control over a part of the nuclear deterrent, the Europeans could rest easy that, even if the United States were reluctant to begin a nuclear war in response to aggression, the Europeans would have the capability to begin escalation themselves. This was objectionable to the United States because it would increase the chances of accidental war; more fundamentally, it would mean giving away the advantage of American military superiority. The response of the British and the French had been to develop their own nuclear weapons, on the theory that no matter how puny their nuclear arsenals they would still have the power to precipitate a general conflagration. This was also objectionable to the United States, because it meant proliferation and dilution of the American nuclear monopoly. The United States responded to this problem by orienting its strategy increasingly toward conventional warfare, in addition to the basic emphasis on nuclear war. The idea was that European fears about the reliability of the U.S. nuclear guarantee could be minimized if the NATO allies had the capacity to respond to limited aggression with a powerful conventional military response. This strategy, however, re-

quired the Europeans to provide increased military manpower to make
the conventional force convincing. To gain European acceptance of an
expanded conventional warfare effort, the United States moved toward the idea of creating a nuclear deterrent that would be controlled
collectively by all the NATO powers.[7]

The position of the Western European powers was difficult. Their
ability to move toward détente independently was limited by the unreliability of the American deterrent and the underdevelopment of their
own deterrent. The threat of the withdrawal of U.S. troops from
Europe lingered in the background, so the Europeans might find
themselves in a position of military weakness if they negotiated with
the Russians.[8] Similarly, if the Europeans moved too precipitously
toward the creation of their own deterrent, resisting the American
request for a coordinated effort to strengthen conventional forces, they
again risked the loss of American support if Soviet pressure were to
increase before their deterrent was ready. But the United States was
also tangled in this complex web. Pushing the threat of American
withdrawal could easily be counterproductive because it might convince the Europeans further of American unreliability as an ally.
Furthermore, Europe's fear of the Soviet Union could be minimized
by a highly conciliatory Soviet offensive, which would mean a severe
reduction in U.S. bargaining power. For this same reason, if the
United States moved toward détente with the Soviet Union, it would
be an invitation to the Europeans to pursue more independent
policies. Finally, even if several of the European powers moved slowly
toward the creation of their own deterrent, it would mean, over the
long term, a reduction in American power within the Alliance.

The other source of tension within the Atlantic Alliance was the
problem of relations between the industrialized and non-industrialized
world. This had been an area of conflict for some time, for the U.S.
commitment to "anti-imperialism" had run up against the desires of
Britain and France to maintain their special ties with colonies and
former colonies. While Suez had been a major blow to British and
French prestige, it did not mark a complete end to European ambitions for an independent foreign policy toward the Third World. The
French war in Algeria was another episode in the same history, with
the United States strongly critical of the French attempt to maintain a
colonial tie at the risk of widespread radicalization in Algeria and other
parts of the Arab world.[9] But by 1958-59, with the exception of

Algeria, the epoch of European colonial control was rapidly ending. The United States stood to gain from the elimination of direct European control over much of the Third World, because it was now more open to American economic penetration. However, American strategy shifted to an effort to enlist Europe's aid in keeping these areas open to foreign investment. The Cuban revolution and the strength of radical nationalism in the underdeveloped world made urgent the need for extensive aid programs and resources for possible military intervention.

For Europe, this American pressure for assistance in policing the Third World created two problems. First, public opinion within Western Europe placed severe constraints on the assumption of any new international obligations, particularly those that might lead to military involvement in the underdeveloped world. Second, European leaders were reluctant to accept responsibilities—in terms of aid obligations—for which they did not receive comparable benefits in increased influence and expanded opportunities for their country's businessmen. They were not about to grant aid to countries and then see those countries spend the aid money for U.S. goods. The long history of conflict with the United States for influence in certain parts of the underdeveloped world intensified mutual suspicions and made it difficult to develop a coordinated American-European policy toward the underdeveloped world.[10]

These problems of global political and military strategy overlapped with the more purely "economic" problems, such as the U.S. deficit, the trade consequences of the Common Market, and the stability of the international monetary order. The military and aid issues were closely intertwined with the problem of the U.S. deficit because, without European cooperation, the military and foreign aid burdens would make it more difficult for the United States to restore balance-of-payments equilibrium. It is because of this overlap that American policy toward Europe in this period has a unified quality that is summarized in the thematic phrase "Atlantic Partnership." While the rhetoric of Atlantic Partnership was a hallmark of the Kennedy administration, the policy dated back to the last few years of the Eisenhower administration. The essence of the policy was that Western Europe, having recovered its economic and political vitality, was now ready to join with the United States in the cooperative effort to solve the problems that faced the Alliance. But as a variety of critics of Partnership policy have noted, the unstated premise was that cooperation was not to mean an end to U.S. hegemony within the Alliance. It was to be a partnership without equality.[11]

ATLANTIC PARTNERSHIP AND
THE BALANCE OF PAYMENTS

Aid and Arms

The major initiative by the United States for coordinating and sharing the burden of foreign aid with the European allies focused on the Organization for Economic Cooperation and Development. The OECD was the direct descendant of the OEEC, the organization that had been created to divide Marshall Plan aid. The transformation of the OEEC into the OECD was a key part of the American effort to revive and strengthen the Atlantic Alliance. Through the 1950s the main activity of the OEEC had been the elimination of import restrictions within Europe and between Europe and the Dollar Area. The British proposal for a Europe-wide free trade area had been advanced within the OEEC, and the conflicts engendered by that proposal threatened the future of the organization. U.S. policy-makers had for some time considered the possibility of reorganizing and reviving the OEEC in order to make it an instrument for European-American international cooperation. In its old form its usefulness was limited because the United States and Canada were only associate members, and the organization's charter was relatively narrow. But with the emergence of the EEC, U.S. policy-makers saw an urgent need for an organization through which the United States could effectively influence the Common Market's direction. The United States proposed a transformation of the OEEC that would make the United States and Canada full members and that would revise the organization's charter. After a period of prolonged negotiations through 1959 and 1960, the new organization was officially launched in 1961.[12]

The Development Assistance Committee was the forum for coordinating aid policies in the new organization. The idea was to present a united front to the underdeveloped countries and to exert pressure on the European allies to increase their aid contributions and to pursue aid policies that contributed to international openness. While the group experienced some success in maintaining developed country solidarity and in increasing the European aid contribution,[13] there were still tensions over the kinds of economic relations the Europeans were developing with some of their former colonies. One critical question was the development of preferential trading agreements between the European Common Market and certain underdeveloped countries. In 1958, the United States had supported the EEC when other countries in GATT had protested against the proposed extension of Common Market preferences to the "associated overseas territories"—mostly former French colonies in Africa. By 1961, the U.S. line had shifted as anxiety grew over the development of a Eurafrican trading bloc. The U.S. anxiety had several dimensions. First, there was the fear that American access to those African markets would be limited by preferential trading arrangements. Second, the United States worried that other underdeveloped countries, especially those within the U.S. sphere of influence, would be unable to sell their tropical products in the European market because of the preferences granted to the associated territories.[14]

While the United States did apply pressure to limit the extent of these preferential arrangements, U.S. policy-makers were reluctant to push the issue to an open conflict. The problem was that the European countries had assumed the aid burden for these associated territories, a burden the United States was unwilling to carry itself. The goal of Atlantic Partnership, as European cooperation on American terms, was frustrated by European, and particularly French, resistance. The Europeans increased their aid contribution, but they did it in such a way as to consolidate their economic and political links to a part of the underdeveloped world. The United States was forced to tolerate another deviation from the fully multilateral trading structure it had advocated for so long.[15]

The pattern on defense issues was similar. The ambitious goal of partnership gave way to unsatisfactory compromises that left serious divisions within the Alliance. The American goal was to gain increased European spending for conventional forces, including funds to cover the foreign exchange costs of U.S. troops in Europe. To achieve this goal and to divert Europe from the effort to develop its own nuclear deterrent, the United States offered Europe the Multilateral Force, a nuclear deterrent that would be controlled collectively within NATO. But both parts of this plan ran into serious difficulties. The Europeans were extremely reluctant to increase their spending on conventional warfare, and they resisted the pressure put on them by the United States to pick up the tab for U.S. troops in Europe. The Multilateral Force died in its infancy because it failed to satisfy the European desire for military equality in the Alliance.[16]

The first major effort to gain European assistance in financing the American troops in Europe was the much publicized Anderson-Dillon mission to Germany in late 1960. The gold outflow from the United States had been going on for some time, and speculation against the dollar was intensifying. At the same time, the German mark was exceptionally strong, reflecting Germany's sizable balance-of-payments surplus. The purpose of the mission was to get German agreement to a cash payment for the foreign exchange costs of U.S. troops in Germany. Robert Anderson, the Secretary of the Treasury, was a hard bargainer because he believed that the U.S. balance-of-payments deficit was a structural, not a temporary, problem. This, a minority view in government circles, led him to demand an annual German payment of $650 million for the U.S. troops. The Germans responded with a package deal that included advance repayments of the German debt to the United States of $600 million and advance payment for all military equipment ordered by Germany through 1964. Anderson refused this offer and left Germany with threats of a U.S. troop withdrawal, but the State and Defense departments both indicated strong dissatisfaction with Anderson's threats to pull U.S. troops out of Germany.[17]

The outcome of the incident set the tone for American-German bargaining for quite some time. Though Anderson's authority was reaffirmed by Eisenhower, it was made clear that the demand for outright payment would not be raised again. Instead, the German counterproposal became the basis for the offset agreements that began in 1961. The result was that the German offsets did not involve any extra strain on the German federal budget. They were simply advanced repayments of debts or prepayments for military goods. To be sure, the Germans made other concessions: they increased their contribution to NATO, they launched a new foreign aid program, and in 1961 they revalued the mark upward by 5 percent—but they successfully resisted the American demand that they pay hard cash for the U.S. troops in Europe.

The increased German contribution to NATO was still far short of what the United States considered necessary to bring NATO's conventional capabilities up to an adequate level. The desire to induce increased European conventional efforts and the hope of staving off dissension in the Alliance over nuclear weapons stimulated the American proposals for some kind of multilateral nuclear force. The idea was first publicly suggested by Christian Herter, then Eisenhower's Secretary of State, in 1960. It was taken up again by the Kennedy administration, and it became a part of U.S. policy in the ill-fated Nassau Pact in

December 1962. The Multilateral Force involved the creation of a Polaris submarine fleet, armed with nuclear warheads, manned by a mixed force, and under NATO command. The United States, however, would retain veto power over the use of this NATO deterrent. The commitment to MLF came at a conference in Nassau between John F. Kennedy and Harold Macmillan, the British Prime Minister. Macmillan was angry over an American decision to cancel the production of the Skybolt missile system, which the British had been promised as a means to deliver their own nuclear weapons. To mollify Macmillan, Kennedy offered Polaris missiles to deliver British nuclear warheads. At least some of the British Polaris missiles were to become part of a multilateral NATO nuclear force, which the Americans understood to be a submarine fleet manned by a mixed NATO contingent. Kennedy offered the Polaris submarines to the French on the same terms, in part to make up for the American refusal a year earlier to assist France in the development of nuclear weapons.[18]

But De Gaulle rejected the American offer. The French would continue with the development of their own *force de frappe,* and they wanted no part of a nuclear partnership that meant continued European inferiority. The United States continued to push the MLF idea even without France, although the British as well began having second thoughts. The proposal's strongest appeal was to the Germans, who, in the midst of continuing Berlin crises, were most worried about military security. The offer of MLF had from the start been seen as a way of averting a Franco-German nuclear pact, so continued discussions were a means of strengthening U.S.-German ties. But although some progress was made in increasing consultation within NATO, technical obstacles and lack of domestic support within the United States effectively killed the MLF proposal. Lyndon Johnson finally tabled the MLF in 1965, signaling that a key element of Atlantic Partnership had run aground.[19]

Trade

In 1958 the United States had thrown its diplomatic support to the French and the EEC against the British proposal for a Europe-wide free trade area. To gain this support, the French and the EEC commission had stressed their eagerness to make the Common Market "outward-looking" in its trade policy. American foreign trade policy throughout the 1958-64 period was dominated by the effort to force the Common Market to live up to this commitment to an outward-looking trade policy. In the area of trade, the meaning of Atlantic Partnership was that Europe would live up to its responsibility to liberalize trade in industrial and agricultural goods. The catch was that Europe had to understand that parallel American progress toward further trade liberalization could proceed only slowly because of the continuing strength of protectionist interests in the United States.

When the American trade balance weakened in 1958, the first U.S. response was to intensify efforts to eliminate the remaining quantitative restrictions on dollar imports. But since these remnants of the period of dollar shortage had already been greatly reduced, removing the remaining restrictions in Europe provided relatively minor relief. The United States then moved to revive the GATT machinery and initiate a new round of tariff reductions. This round, proposed in 1958 and negotiated in 1961-62, was called the Dillon Round after Eisenhower's Assistant Secretary of State, Douglas Dillon. It was designed to reduce the European Common Market's external tariff, even before that tariff went into effect. It was widely feared that with a high external tariff—the average of the six countries' pre-EEC tariffs—the elimination of internal tariff barriers would lead to significant trade diversion. U.S. policy was oriented toward pushing the EEC to reduce its external tariff parallel with reductions in internal tariff barriers so that trade diversion would be minimized. The problem was that the Dillon Round was carried out under existing American trade legislation, so that the maximum possible reduction was 20 percent, and negotiations had to proceed on a laborious item-by-item basis.[20]

The limitations on the effectiveness of the Dillon Round negotiations led the Kennedy administration to push for new legislative authority for a new round of trade reductions. The result was the Trade Expansion Act of 1962 that increased U.S. tariff-cutting authority to 50 percent and allowed negotiations for across-the-board cuts. This proposed new round of trade liberalization was a continuation of the effort to make the EEC more outward-looking, but there were several additional subtleties. The Trade Expansion Act was a part of the Kennedy administration's design to push Britain into the EEC. The administration believed that British traditional interest in, and support for, liberal trade would greatly strengthen the outward-looking forces in the Common Market. The British support for liberalized trade in agricultural goods in particular would help open the EEC to large imports of non-tropical (that is, U.S.) agricultural goods. By this time it had become clear to American policy-makers that the comparative advantage of the United States in agricultural production could be an important support of the U.S. balance of payments if only foreign markets could be opened to U.S. agricultural exports. It was also hoped that liberalization of trade in industrial goods would strengthen the U.S. trade balance; Kennedy administration officials also argued that a reduction of EEC tariffs on industrial goods could slow the rate of U.S. direct investment in Europe. In short, another benefit of an outward-looking Common Market was that it would be less of a magnet for U.S. direct investment than an inward-looking market, and that would reduce the balance of payments drain caused by direct investment outflows.[21]

The Trade Expansion Act and the proposed Kennedy Round of tariff negotiations were centerpieces of the policy of Atlantic Partnership. The proposed round of trade liberalization was designed to create a high level of economic interdependence that would solidify the Atlantic Alliance. John F. Kennedy, in a speech before Congress calling for the passage of the new trade legislation, argued that "An integrated Western Europe, joined in trading partnership with the United States, will further shift the world balance of power to the side of freedom."[22] But as with the other dimensions of the Atlantic Partnership, the trade initiative resulted in disappointment.

The first blow came in January 1963 when De Gaulle announced, at the same press conference in which he rejected the MLF, that the French were vetoing British entry into the Common Market. A major setback to American policy, this meant that the Kennedy Round negotiations would be more difficult than anticipated. Furthermore, the actual negotiations were significantly delayed when the French won EEC agreement that the trade negotiations would not begin until the Six reached agreement on a common agricultural policy. This was a second blow, because it decreased the likelihood that the European market would be opened to American agricultural exports. Agreement on a common agricultural policy was, in turn, delayed by a major Common Market crisis over the development of supranational institutions. This crisis was not resolved until the middle of 1966, so that the Kennedy Round did not begin until 1967.[23]

When it finally took place, the Kennedy Round did result in major tariff reductions. However, the reductions were not as large as those anticipated before British entry into the Common Market was blocked, and little was done to liberalize agricultural trade. Furthermore, it is questionable whether the additional liberalization worked to U.S. advantage, since the trade balance moved into sharp deficit in the years after the Kennedy Round cuts went into effect. It is also uncertain whether the tariff cuts had the intended effect of slowing the rate of U.S. direct investment in Europe. That investment appears to have continued growing after the tariff cuts, and any slowing in the rate of growth could have been attributed as easily to government controls over foreign direct investment.[24] At any rate, it is certain that because of De Gaulle's objections the Kennedy Round "deteriorated from grand strategy for Atlantic interdependence to 'low-key commercial policy.'"[25]

Finance

Ironically, it was in the realm of international financial arrangements—most immediately linked to the balance of payments—that the strategy of Atlantic Partnership was most successful. But here as well, conflicts between the United States and European countries, particularly France, interfered with American plans and presaged more serious conflicts. The efforts in the financial area during the last years of the Eisenhower administration—the expansion of the IMF and the launching of the OECD—have already been described in other contexts. U.S. agreement in 1958 to expand the IMF quotas reflected an awareness that the Fund would have to be strengthened to deal with the problems generated by a restoration of convertibility in most of Europe. Whether or not U.S. policy-makers considered at that point that the United States might need to draw on the fund's resources in the event of a continued drain on U.S. gold, the decision represented a real shift from the earlier willingness to allow the fund to languish. Similarly, the decision to transform the OEEC into the OECD was informed by the desire to have a forum for discussions of balance-of-payments problems among the industrial countries. It was hoped that this discussion would help assure increased cooperation and avert serious crises.

With the start of the Kennedy administration, the effort to strengthen international financial cooperation became much more intense. The campaign was engineered by Robert Roosa, Undersecretary of the Treasury, and it proceeded on a number of different fronts. The first, reflecting Roosa's background at the New York Federal Reserve Bank, involved negotiating a series of swap arrangements between the major central banks. These arrangements were essentially standby credit lines, which could be drawn on by either side for the purposes of defending an existing exchange rate. If, for example, the Italian central bank was attempting to defend the exchange rate by buying lire (or selling dollars for lire), it could replenish its supply of dollars for this operation by drawing on its swap with the New York Federal Reserve Bank. The swap arrangements increased the capacity of the central banks to defend existing exchange rates against speculative pressure and hot-currency movements.[26]

A second front was the creation of the London gold pool in late 1961. The U.S. obligation to maintain the price of gold at $35 an ounce meant that the United States had to sell gold on the private market if demand began pushing the gold price above $35. Above and beyond the loss of U.S. gold to foreign central banks, lack of confidence in the dollar stimulated large-scale private speculative purchases of gold, forcing the United States to sell large quantities of gold to private buyers. To ease this situation, Roosa gained the agreement of Britain, Switzerland, and the Common Market Six to provide half of the gold necessary to stabilize the price. If gold purchases were necessary, in the event of a decline in the gold price, the same countries would acquire half of the gold bought to push the price up. The creation of the gold pool took some of the pressure off the United States' gold stock and made stabilization of the gold price easier. For the Europeans, the arrangement, in the context of Roosa's other initiatives, made sense as a way of increasing the stability of the international monetary system at a relatively low cost.[27]

A third front was another effort to expand the resources of the International Monetary Fund. This time, however, the route was not an expansion of quotas,[28] but an arrangement under which the fund could borrow additional resources from member countries. There was considerable conflict over the precise procedure for doing this, since the countries which would be lending the money wanted some voice in how it was to be used. The crux of the problem was an ironic shift in national attitudes toward international liquidity. Britain, because of her payments problem, had consistently in the 1940s, 1950s, and 1960s favored proposals that would expand the supply of international liquidity. Germany, since the triumph of Erhard's free-market economic policies in the early 1950s, had also remained consistent, but on the side of limiting the supply of liquidity to force governments to maintain economic discipline. The United States, however, had changed sides on the liquidity issue. After years of opposing any increase in international liquidity, the American balance-of-payments deficits forced the United States to look toward an expansion of the IMF resources if the U.S. position should become more serious. France, on the other hand, had favored increased liquidity until De Gaulle's economic measures in late 1958 had dramatically improved France's economic position.

Having successfully defeated inflation at home, the French adopted the German position of opposition to inflation everywhere and opposition to increases in international liquidity.

The emergence of a possible British-American common interest in increased and more easily available liquidity worried the French and the Germans. They feared that if they made an agreement to loan money to the fund, the money might be lent on easier terms than in the past. The fear was justified, because the United States and the British had a large share of the power in the fund. The Europeans were willing to put up the money, but they wanted to do it in such a way as to maximize their control over the fund's use of the money. The United States, precisely because of its enormous power in the fund, wanted an arrangement that left intact the fund's control of these supplemental resources. But because the United States was a potential borrower of these resources, its bargaining position was weak. The result of the negotiations was a compromise that strengthened the hand of the Europeans. The General Arrangements to Borrow (GAB), completed at the end of 1961, established a credit line to the fund of up to $6 billion, made up of quotas from ten countries (the gold-pool countries plus Japan, Sweden, and Canada). If any one of the ten was to draw from the fund on a scale that would force the fund to borrow from GAB, the Managing Director of the fund had to obtain the agreement of the GAB nations to the drawing and to the amount of each of their contributions. This amounted to an effective veto by the Group of Ten over a drawing by one of its members, and it created a new center of financial power on the periphery of the fund.[29]

Even though the arrangement involved some institutional concessions, the United States had succeeded in creating another structure to fortify the international monetary order. GAB diminished the possibilities that the fund's resources could be exhausted if two major currencies were simultaneously or sequentially under attack. The need for this was apparent when the fund was required, for the first time, to use some of its gold resources to purchase currencies for a British drawing of $1.5 billion in August 1961.[30] And while Britain's potential need for even larger aid to defend the pound was the immediate motivation for the GAB agreement, in the background lingered the possibility that the United States would need to draw massive amounts from the fund to defend against a major run on the dollar.

The other fronts of Roosa's diplomatic offensive were the negotiations of the offset agreement with the Germans, and the creation of the "Roosa bonds." The Roosa bonds were United States non-negotiable

government bonds, denominated in foreign currencies, that were sold
to foreign central banks. They were guaranteed against loss through
devaluation of the dollar and were immediately redeemable at the
option of the holder. The idea of this instrument was that it transformed "excess" dollar holdings by foreign central banks into a longer-
term debt. Or, in other words, they were designed to slow the converting of foreign official dollar holdings into gold by giving cooperative
foreign governments a sound alternative to gold. The problem was that
those governments most eager to convert dollars into gold—France
and Spain—were unwilling to buy the Roosa bonds. Nevertheless,
they probably made it somewhat easier for other central banks to
justify larger dollar holdings.[31]

Roosa's efforts ran out of steam by the middle of 1962. He had
done much to strengthen the international monetary system and to
bolster the dollar. His period of activity coincided with a revival of
cooperation and consultation among central bankers that was crucial in
increasing the international monetary system's ability to deal with destabilizing capital flows. But Roosa's measures and other government
policies had failed to halt the U.S. deficit, and voices in the U.S.
government began arguing for more fundamental changes. While
Roosa's diplomacy fits into the overall context of Atlantic Partnership,
Roosa was oriented to bilateral negotiations and bilateral arrangements
between the United States and its individual allies, exemplified by the
swap arrangements and the Roosa bonds. The new voices favored a
policy that was more multilateral: they proposed something on the
order of an Atlantic Payments Union, with pooled reserves or the
creation of an international central bank along the lines proposed by
Robert Triffin. In sum, these new voices, centered in the State Department and the Council of Economic Advisors, favored the creation
of a new international monetary order that involved a somewhat diminished international role for the dollar and the need for the United
States to surrender some monetary sovereignty to an international
body.[32]

The would-be reformers were politically weak, and their plans
never got off the ground. During the brief period in which the dream
of Atlantic Partnership flourished, Roosa and Secretary of the Treasury
C. Douglas Dillon effectively blocked any initiative in the direction of
multilateral reform. For example, at the annual meeting of the IMF in
September 1962, Reginald Maudling, Britain's Chancellor of the Exchequer, made an ingenious proposal for a system by which excess

holdings of certain currencies could be turned over to the IMF for a guaranteed claim on a "mutual currency" account. This device would both increase available liquidity and protect U.S. gold reserves. Nevertheless, the proposal was resoundingly rejected by Dillon and Roosa because of its multilateral overtones and probably because of its similarities to the plans of the American reformers. The vehemence of Dillon and Roosa flowed from their fears that any plan that diminished the dollar's role as an official reserve would endanger its role as a key currency in international trade and finance. Their aim was to improve the balance of payments and strengthen international cooperation without making any concessions that would lessen the dollar's official role or that would restrict U.S. monetary sovereignty.[33]

Although Roosa and Dillon succeeded in blocking multilateral reform moves, they failed in solving the problem of the deficit.[34] In 1962, Dillon made an effort to persuade the Europeans to develop their own capital markets so that they could reduce their borrowing in New York and the consequent strain on the U.S. payments balance. This was apparently an effort to avoid direct controls on the outflow of capital from the United States, but Dillon's exhortation accomplished little and the capital outflow continued to grow. In July 1963, Kennedy proposed an Interest Equalization Tax that would discourage foreign bond offerings in the United States. The IET was part of a package of measures that included new economy moves in foreign aid and defense. Although the IET was not passed by Congress until September 1964, the period during which it was considered marked a turning point in U.S. balance-of-payments policy.[35] The resort to capital controls indicated that the strategy of improving the payments balance by tinkering with the Atlantic Alliance had failed. In fact, by the time the IET legislation became law, the idea of Atlantic Partnership had already received such critical setbacks as De Gaulle's veto of British entry into the EEC, the delay of the Kennedy Round, and the decline of European interest in the Multilateral Force. Starting in 1964, capital controls replaced Atlantic Partnership as the central theme of U.S. balance-of-payments policy.

PHASE 2—VIETNAM AND HOLDING ACTIONS: 1964-1968

In the period from 1964 to 1968, the earlier optimism that the deficit could easily be eliminated gave way to an embattled holding action to prevent a serious worsening of the deficit. The continuous escalation of the Vietnam War in these years placed increasing strains on the U.S. payments balance, and a steady escalation of the capital controls that had begun with the IET in 1964 was required just to prevent a disastrous leap in the size of the deficit. The effort to hold the deficit in check was part of a struggle fought on several fronts to protect the international value of the dollar and to defend the dollar's special role within the international monetary system. On all fronts, the effort was to gain time on the theory that U.S. victory in Vietnam was just around the corner, and once victory had come it would be possible to strengthen the balance of payments and relieve the pressure on the dollar.[36]

The holding-action mentality extended in this period to the Atlantic Alliance as well. Instead of proposing ambitious schemes for Atlantic Partnership, U.S. policy-makers fought a rear-guard action to prevent a further deterioration in the Alliance, while they focused most of their attention on Southeast Asia. Rather than an attempt to revitalize NATO, the U.S. effort was simply to keep NATO together in the wake of the French withdrawal. The rhetoric of burden-sharing in aid and arms was minimized, and emphasis was placed instead on reassurances about the U.S. contribution to European security designed to keep Germany from drifting too close to Gaullist France.[37] De Gaulle's explicit anti-Americanism and the gradual emergence of détente diplomacy indicated the seriousness of the strains in the Alliance in this period. De Gaulle had begun the drift toward improved relations with the Soviet Union, and his example inspired West German efforts at détente in 1967-68.[38] U.S.-Soviet relations were also improving in the period after the Cuban missile crisis, although the Vietnam War interfered with a general Soviet-American understanding. To be sure, approaches to the Soviet Union were still characterized by extreme caution, and American urgings for allied cooperation in détente diplomacy were sometimes heeded. But the Cold War framework, and with it the basic justification for the Atlantic Alliance, was breaking down.

VIETNAM AND CAPITAL CONTROLS

The impact of the Vietnam War on the balance of payments was both direct, through increased overseas military costs, and indirect, through the impact of increased defense expenditures on the overall economy. While the major impact, both direct and indirect, came in 1966-68, the effect of the war on the dollar concerned policy-makers as early as

1963. Arthur Schlesinger, Jr., quotes a facetious memorandum that purports to describe a typical Kennedy administration cabinet meeting on Vietnam in the fall of 1963. Dillon's contribution to the discussion, presumably typical of his viewpoint, was a cautioning that public discussion of certain Vietnam-related expenditures should be minimized lest it further weaken confidence in the dollar.[39]

Serious anxiety that the Vietnam War would further weaken the dollar probably began in 1964, when a decision was made to escalate American involvement, after a period in which the American presence in Vietnam had gradually decreased.[40] Since U.S. escalation in Vietnam was almost always based on exaggeratedly optimistic expectations of the effectiveness of the escalation, any damage to the dollar from an increase in U.S. involvement was perceived to be a temporary problem of a year or two's duration. Thus, balance-of-payments policy from 1964 on was characterized by the hope that, if disaster could be averted this year and the next year, successful conclusion of the war would relieve the pressure on the dollar. Consistent with this faith, the controls over capital movements that paralleled the escalation in U.S. involvement were generally justified as temporary measures made necessary by the war effort.

The first capital controls— the imposition of the Interest Equalization Tax—went into effect in September 1964, shortly after the Tonkin Gulf incident. The next controls—voluntary restraints on banking and corporate transfers of funds abroad—were imposed in February 1965, when the air war against North Vietnam began in earnest. The program was tightened at the end of 1965, when there were close to 200,000 troops in Vietnam. Another tightening came at the end of 1966, after a troop level of 469,000 had been authorized. The continued escalation and worsening of the war's balance-of-payments effect forced the administration to make the "voluntary" program mandatory and much tougher at the beginning of 1968.[41]

On the domestic side, the Vietnam War strained the federal budget and led to over-rapid expansion in the domestic economy. Especially in comparison to the economic restraint of the 1960-63 period, the 1965-68 period was strongly inflationary. And the inflationary pressure had the effect of worsening the trade balance by pushing up demand for imports and slowing export growth. The administration was reluctant to cut back other parts of the federal budget, insisting that the economy could afford both guns and butter. The administration was also opposed to a tax increase to limit the inflationary impact of government deficits for fear that would consolidate opposition to the war. In 1966, there was strong pressure for anti-inflationary actions, and Johnson finally responded with a call for an income tax surcharge in January 1967. However, the tax was not passed until July 1968, and that was too little, too late, as the inflationary pressure caused by the war severely weakened the dollar.[42]

OTHER BALANCE-OF-PAYMENTS POLICIES

Another thrust of U.S. international monetary policy in this period was a holding action involving bilateral agreements under which other governments agreed not to turn in their dollars for gold. In much the same way as Britain had been forced to offer incentives for countries to continue holding their reserves in sterling, so the United States had to provide a quid pro quo for other countries' continued willingness to hold on to their dollars.[43] At an earlier point in each nation's history, central banks needed no special inducements to hold either of these currencies, but as confidence dissipated countries were able to exact concessions from the reserve currency countries. The contents of most of these bilateral arrangements are shrouded in secrecy, but in a few cases the nature of the quid pro quo is clear. For example, in the 1967 negotiations over offset payments for the cost of U.S. troops in Germany, the Germans agreed to stop turning in dollars for gold. The German concession was clearly a response to mounting pressures in the United States for reductions in U.S. troop levels in Germany. The German government perceived any reduction in these troop levels to be a threat to its security, and hence was willing to make concessions that would avert troop withdrawals.

At the time of the imposition of the Interest Equalization Tax, both Canada and Japan, nations that were heavily dependent on the New York capital market, pleaded for exemption from restrictions on their borrowing in the United States. Exemption was granted to Japan, apparently in exchange for Japan's agreement to continue holding its reserves largely in dollars. Canada accepted an even more limiting condition in exchange for its exemption: the Canadians agreed to prevent their currency reserves from rising above a certain specified limit. This meant that the Canadians would have to take actions, in certain conditions, deliberately to worsen their balance of payments to assure continued access to U.S. capital markets.[44] It is probable that the United States used a number of similar inducements to discourage other countries from turning dollars in for gold. However, the United States also indicated that it was attempting to control its deficit and assure the continued strength of the dollar. The bilateral deals had to be supplemented by a concrete balance-of-payments program to convince other countries that the cost of holding dollars would not be prohibitive. The balance-of-payments program included further restrictions on duty-free imports, export expansion programs, and so forth, but the capital controls remained the heart of the administration's effort to prove its sincere effort to defend the value of the dollar.

THE DEFENSE OF THE POUND

While the bilateral agreements could slow official conversion of dollars for gold, the problem of private speculation against the dollar remained. When confidence in the dollar was weak, private holders would trade dollars for gold. The gold pool agreement of 1961 relieved the United States of the obligation of providing all of the gold necessary to keep the gold price from rising above $35 an ounce, but the danger remained that if private gold purchases became too great the other countries would drop out of the pool. Furthermore, it was feared that, if private purchases of gold led to a sharp drop in the size of the U.S. gold stock, this would generate a massive run on the dollar by both private and official holders. American efforts to limit the size of the deficit and to halt official purchases of U.S. gold served to bolster confidence in the dollar in the private markets. But there was another element to the U.S. defense against a speculative assault on the dollar—the pound sterling. During this period the pound served as both a lightning rod for speculative pressure and a bulwark in defense of the dollar. As long as the pound was relatively weak, speculative pressure was likely to concentrate on the pound, since a devaluation of the pound with its potential for speculative profits was much more likely than a devaluation of the dollar. But, at the same time, it was recognized that once the pound was devalued the speculative assault would then turn against the dollar with greater intensity. Hence, the defense of the pound at its existing exchange rate was a central part of U.S. international monetary policy between 1964 and 1967.

The defense of the pound at the $2.80 parity dated back to the sterling crises of the 1950s, but the attack on the pound that began with the accession to power of the Labour government in 1964 was by far the most serious and sustained attack since the 1949 devaluation. As in 1945, the Labour government came to power after a prolonged period—this time thirteen years—out of power. The Labour government's lack of experience in dealing with international monetary problems was once again a factor in its handling of the balance-of-payments crisis the Conservative government had left it. There was also the inevitable fear by international bankers and currency speculators that a Labour government would prove irresponsible. The new government faced a loss of confidence even before it assumed office.⌉

The situation that the Labour government had inherited from the Conservatives was extremely grave: the balance-of-payments deficit was projected at 800 million pounds for the year, a record level. Beginning particularly in 1957, the Conservatives had pursued a stop-go economic policy. When the pound was under attack, extremely restrictive domestic economic policies were pursued, and then, when the situation improved, measures encouraging economic expansion were implemented. Deflationary measures were put into effect in 1957 and 1961, and attempts to expand the economy came in 1959 and 1963. During 1964, the Chancellor of the Exchequer, Reginald Maudling, was reluctant to take actions to halt the expansion of the economy. His motives appear to have been a combination of electoral considerations—another deflation would have assured Conservative defeat in the elections—and a sincere commitment to economic growth. But the result was that by October, the balance-of-payments situation was desperate.[45]

The heart of the problem, however, was not Maudling's slowness in applying the brakes to the economy, but the underlying weakness of the pound and the long-term consequences of the stop-go policy. The weakness of the pound had four major components. The first was the continued existence of large sterling balances held by foreign governments. Although the sterling balances had changed hands since the end of World War II, they continued to be a source of weakness. Private speculation against the pound was always intensified by the fear that official sterling holders would move to convert their pounds for dollars. To prevent this, the British had to make a number of concessions to the sterling holders to avert massive conversions. These concessions included military protection and assurance of continued access to the British capital market—the second and third components of the pound's weakness. Britain, through the early 1950s and early 1960s, maintained a sizable and expensive overseas military presence.

Despite extensive economy campaigns, the foreign exchange cost of this foreign military presence had doubled from 1956 to 1964, to 250 million pounds.[46] These overseas military commitments were a concrete quid pro quo for the continued willingness of the Sterling Area nations to hold sterling balances. Similarly, access to British capital markets was a way of keeping those countries in the Sterling Area. The magnitude of the capital outflows to the Sterling Area tended to be obscured by the inflow of U.S. direct investment into Britain, but even with capital inflows continuing capital export placed a major strain on the British balance of payments.

The final component of Britain's problem was the chronic weakness of the trade balance. The stop-go policy—the alternation of managed reessions and managed expansions—was primarily directed at improving the trade balance, since a slowing of domestic business activity would slow imports and encourage businessmen to seek markets abroad. However, it is probable that the stop-go policy exacerbated the underlying problems of the British economy by discouraging new business investment. For businessmen, the inevitability of another recession created doubt that new investments would prove profitable, since the market would contract again. The rate of new investment in Britain remained below that on the Continent, and British industrial productivity rose more slowly than the EEC's or Japan's. Moreover, it seems likely that Britain's continuation of Commonwealth preference arrangements after World War II gave British industrialists safe foreign markets which undermined their competitiveness. In fact, Britain's applications for membership in the Common Market were based on the theory that the fresh wind of competition from the Continent would ultimately lead to a modernization of British industry and a rate of economic growth similar to those of the Continental countries.[47]

Britain's accumulated economic difficulties, as well as the immediate balance-of-payments crisis, greeted the new Labour government in October 1964. It was clearly a moment for bold action to relieve the external pressure on the pound and begin a program of domestic economic modernization, free of the constraints of stop-go policies. This would mean devaluation, as much to relieve pressure on the pound as for any hope of increasing exports and discouraging imports. Devaluation would provide the opportunity as well for liquidating the pound's reserve role through some kind of funding arrangement. Ending the pound's reserve role would also make possible savings on foreign military expenditures and severe control of the export of capital. This done, there would be both resources and increased freedom to carry out a domestic reform program.

However, this path was not taken by the Labour government, whose tiny electoral majority made any kind of radical departure politically dangerous. Furthermore, Harold Wilson's politics had changed significantly from the time in 1951 that he, in alliance with Bevan, had resigned from the government in protest against rearmament plans. At one time a severe critic of Britain's dependence on the United States, Wilson had come to accept the centrality to British foreign policy of the Special Relationship with the United States. Wilson realized that any retreat from Britain's world role would be considered a hostile act by the American government and that the devaluation of the pound was strongly opposed by American policy-makers because of its potential impact on the dollar. This American opposition to devaluation coincided with Wilson's own tendency to see devaluation as a humiliation to be avoided at all costs. [48]

Within its first few days, the new government decided against devaluation and proceeded to formulate an alternative economic policy. The first major measure was the imposition of a 15 percent import surcharge in late October. While this led to considerable protest from Britain's trading partners, particularly in the EFTA, there was relative calm in the foreign exchange market. The calm did not last for long. In mid-November, the government's budget speech stimulated speculation against the pound as foreigners began to worry that the government's commitment to welfare was greater than its commitment to the pound. The fear deepened as the government was slow to respond to the crisis with the usual increase in the bank rate. As pressure on the pound mounted, the government was forced to turn to the international bankers for assistance. The U.S. Federal Reserve Bank quickly organized a credit line of $3 billion from a group of major central banks. The Fed's willingness and eagerness to help was based on the perception that the dollar's fate was linked to the pound's, so that every possible measure should be taken to defend the pound's parity. [49]

The sterling crisis of November 1964 set the pattern for the next three years. By April 1965, the British had used $1.1 billion of the central bank credit line to defend the pound. Britain then drew $1.4 billion from the IMF, requiring the first activation of the GAB agreement, in order to repay the short-term central bank credits. The government began mildly deflationary policies and some controls on capital exports, but another sterling crisis broke out in the summer of 1965. The government was now increasingly dependent on the international bankers, and they pressed for further deflationary actions and controls over wages. Gradually, any pretense the government had had of pursuing growth without resort to stop-go policies disappeared. There was a gradual improvement through the rest of 1965, and the government took advantage of the opportunity to increase its majority in a general election in spring 1966. But a new sterling crisis broke out in the summer of 1966, and the government was forced to take its most drastic deflationary actions. Another $1.3 billion of short-term central bank credits were drawn on to protect the pound during this prolonged crisis. There was another recovery as the deflationary measures increased confidence, and the improvement in the payments balance made it possible for the government to repay the short-term credits.[50]

The final crisis began in May 1967. It was quickly aggravated by the economic impact of the closing of the Suez Canal during the Arab-Israeli War. The government was extremely reluctant to take new deflationary actions, and the crisis intensified as the trade balance worsened dramatically. The continued defense of the $2.80 parity appeared increasingly quixotic. Nevertheless, another $1.4 billion of central bank credits were used to defend the rate. And even after the Labour government had decided that devaluation was unavoidable, the United Stated urged another major international support effort. But this time the British refused and the pound was devalued to $2.40 on November 18. This was, of course, not the end of the pound's problems, as the British moved agonizingly slowly after the devaluation to end the pound's international role. It was, however, the end of the U.S. attempt to prop up the pound as the front line of defense for the dollar. While the effort had been extremely useful in protecting the dollar for three years, it had proved very costly for Britain. Valuable time had been lost in which the modernization of the British economy could have been attempted, and Britain now found herself deeper in debt with the very same structural problems.[51]

THE LIQUIDITY DEBATE

The last front of the U.S. balance-of-payments holding action was political defense of the dollar's international role. This defense was waged in the course of negotiations on liquidity and international monetary reform. The continuing U.S. deficit and the danger of a run on the

U.S. gold stock had led to a variety of proposals for an alternative to the dollar as the basis of the international monetary system. Critics of the dollar's international role generally argued either for a return to gold at a significantly higher price or for some kind of internationally created asset that would be the basis of national reserves. As the dollar continued to weaken, these proposals for alternatives to the dollar became increasingly respectable. It was recognized that a continuing expansion of the supply of international liquidity was necessary to support steady growth in the level of international trade, but through most of the postwar period the expansion of liquidity had been provided by an increase in foreign dollar-holdings. Since further expansion of foreign dollar-holdings would probably increase the threat of a run on the U.S. gold stock, it was clear that the world economy would eventually need another source of international liquidity. The sooner the U.S. controlled its deficit and halted the growth of foreign dollar-holdings, the sooner would the need for a new source of international liquidity be manifest.[52]

The issue of an alternative source of liquidity was complicated by two additional factors. First, the imposition of restrictions on capital exports from the United States worried countries that had become accustomed to borrowing large sums of capital in New York. The closing of New York as an international capital market would make it difficult for them to finance balance-of-payments deficits with private borrowing abroad. The United States had worked hard to create an international monetary order in which private capital flows played an equilibrating role, but the responsibility of the United States within that order was to keep its private capital markets open for foreign official and private borrowers. If the United States was no longer willing to accept that responsibility, other countries were likely to question the continuing special international role of the dollar. Second, the United States had its own special interest in expanding international liquidity. American policy-makers worried that the IMF's resources would prove insufficient if the pound and the dollar came under simultaneous attack. While the General Arrangements to Borrow did provide the fund with additional funds to cover such a contingency, GAB rules gave the Western Europeans a veto on the use of these resources. To protect the pound and the dollar the United States wanted international resources that would be freely available without placing limits on American freedom of action internationally.

The U.S. response to the complexities of the liquidity issue was to push for an expansion of IMF quotas while resisting proposals for the creation of new reserve assets. But this position became more difficult to maintain as the Europeans became increasingly impatient with the U.S. deficit. The French and the Germans objected to the Americans' proposed quota increase, and although the increase did go through there was much hard bargaining involved. To increase the pressure, the French, in September 1964, made public their support for the idea of a Composite Reserve Unit (CRU). This CRU would be made up of the major currencies and would be issued by the International Monetary Fund. Countries could then hold their currency reserves in some combination of gold and CRUs. By the French proposal, CRUs would completely replace holdings of dollars or sterling, so that the dollar would no longer have a reserve currency role.[53]

The United States resisted this pressure for international monetary reform. While opposing the call for multilateral action, Dillon and Roosa continued to advocate measures that would increase bilateral cooperation. Finally, as pressure for reform mounted, Dillon and Roosa left the administration. Henry Fowler, the new Secretary of the Treasury, in June 1965, after only three months in office, called for a world monetary conference to discuss reform of the monetary system—a new Bretton Woods conference. Such a conference did not take place, but there was a definite shift in U.S. policy. The United States began, for the first time, pushing actively for negotiations to create a new reserve asset. These negotiations got under way in late 1965 and finally reached fruition in September 1967 when the IMF accepted the proposal for the creation of Special Drawing Rights (SDRs).[54]

The motives behind the U.S. policy shift are complex. Fowler and others saw that creation of a new international asset could fulfill the same function as expansion of the IMF: it would give the United States an additional cushion against a major run on the dollar. It would also give the United States more room for the pursuit of domestic economic expansion. The launching of new negotiations was also seen as a tactical device designed to gain the monetary initiative for the United States. In a period in which existing monetary arrangements and the U.S. deficit were the subjects of mounting international criticism, the United States could best defend itself by appearing to take the lead in organizing international monetary reform. The launching of complex international negotiations on a new reserve asset could be a way of diverting attention from other key international monetary issues.[55]

Significantly, the U.S. policy shift came at the time of the most intense crisis in the history of the Common Market. It is probable that U.S. policy-makers decided to take the initiative at a moment when their chief international opponent—France—appeared most isolated. With France politically isolated, the risk that the negotiations would result in a reform that would challenge the dollar's international role would be minimized. De Gaulle's campaign against the dollar climaxed in early 1965, when he announced his belief that the world should return to a strict gold standard. But whatever De Gaulle's intention in making that statement, the Common Market crisis that climaxed in June 1965 made it impossible for him to rally support within the EEC for reform of the international monetary order. Instead, it was easy for the United States to argue that De Gaulle was out of line on both the organization of the Common Market and the international role of the dollar.[56]

In fact, the United States began its new diplomatic efforts only after the publication of the Ossola Report, a technical study (1965) prepared by the deputies of the Group of Ten, indicated that France was isolated in its desire to displace the dollar completely as a reserve currency. As long as negotiations took place with the premise of creating a supplement to existing international reserves, there was little for the United States to lose and much to gain. Actual negotiations moved slowly during 1966, focusing on the creation of a composite reserve unit as a supplement to the dollar and gold. There was considerable debate over whether the new asset would be available to the Group of Ten alone or to all members of the IMF. The United States opportunistically argued for universal distribution in an effort to gain the support of the liquidity-starved poor nations as a counterweight to the financially conservative Europeans. But though this maneuver was successful, the American position was considerably weakened when, in early 1967, the French altered their tactics.[57]

The French conceded, for the first time, that some kind of liquidity planning was desirable while the United States remained in deficit, but they called for a system of drawing rights in the IMF rather than a new reserve unit. The French quickly solidified a common position with Germany, and this, in turn, became the bargaining position of the EEC. The new position included demands that 85 percent of the IMF's weighted votes would be needed to approve important policies, including the creation of new liquidity. This gave the EEC, with its 16.5 percent of the total vote, effective veto power. The position also called for stricter repayment provisions for the special drawing rights, making the instrument less expansionary, less liberal, than the United States would have liked. The United States attempted to resist the EEC demands by convincing Germany to drop its support for the French position. But with minor compromises, the Franco-German version was accepted. The United States had gained agreement on a new reserve device but had also ceded a good deal of power to the EEC. The actual agreement left the creation of the SDRs to the initiative of the Group of Ten, and the EEC had effective veto power. Nevertheless, the United States had succeeded in defusing the liquidity issue through the creation of an international reserve asset that did not threaten the international role of the dollar. The new arrangements left the United States free to continue running deficits, and the SDRs, when issued, could provide additional resources for the defense of the dollar against speculative attack.

PHASE 3—CHRONIC CRISIS: 1968-1975

As anticipated, the devaluation of the pound in November 1967 set off a wave of speculation against the dollar in the form of massive gold purchases in the European gold markets. The gold pool countries were forced to sell $1 billion worth of gold in November, and another billion in December, to keep the price from rising above $35 an ounce. The United States, bound to provide 59 percent of the gold, suffered an enormous drain on its gold stock and attempted to negotiate a number of changes in the gold pool arrangement to relieve the situation. But other countries rejected the idea of broadening participation in the pool, of creating a three-tier market that would separate the official price from the free market price, and of a gold accounting system that would allow countries to continue to count, as part of their total reserves, gold that they had already sold. President Johnson attempted to slow the speculative attack with his new program of mandatory capital controls announced in January 1968, but the situation was quickly worsened by the explosion of the Tet offensive in South Vietnam. The possibility of a new U.S. escalation of its war effort stimulated a new wave of speculative gold purchases.[58]

The severity of the international monetary crisis played a crucial role in the refusal of General Westmoreland's request for another 200,000 troops and in the decision to reverse the course of escalation in Vietnam. But even those in policy-making circles who welcomed the reversal of the Vietnam policy were horrified by the realization that U.S. foreign-policy options were being dramatically restricted by the weakness of the dollar. To reverse this trend, the United States embarked on an aggressive campaign to regain the international monetary initiative. This meant relieving the pressure on the dollar by forcing the Europeans to take actions to curtail their balance-of-payments surpluses. The first step was the formulation of plans for a tariff surcharge of 5-10 percent on imports and a tax rebate plan that would encourage exports. The intent of these measures was to force the Europeans to make economic concessions by threatening a trade war. The United States wanted the Europeans to agree to an acceleration of the Common Market's tariff concessions in the Kennedy Round and to expand their economies at a more rapid rate. It was assumed that a higher rate of economic activity in Europe would take pressure off the dollar. The Common Market did make the tariff concessions, and some European countries did make gestures toward domestic expansion. The United States did not have to carry through on the threat at this time.[59]

It is probable that the threat of U.S. tariff action also served to force European acquiescence to a second U.S. move, the unilateral ending of the gold pool. In March 1968, the United States simply announced that it would no longer support the price of gold at $35 an ounce in the free market. From that point on, there would be a two-tier gold market, with official transactions at $35 an ounce and the free market allowed to reach its own level. This amounted to renunciation of a U.S. obligation under the Bretton Woods Agreement. It stopped short, however, of a unilateral U.S. refusal to redeem all dollars held by foreign central banks for gold. No doubt relieved that the United States did not take the more radical step, the European governments accepted the idea of two gold markets insulated from each other.[60] But the new arrangements meant that the only way to speculate against the dollar was to sell dollars for other currencies. Foreign central banks that were attempting to maintain their currencies' exchange rates would have to absorb as many dollars as speculators were willing to sell. In contrast to the gold pool arrangements, the two-tier market meant that there was little pressure on the United States when speculation against the dollar mounted. When confidence in the dollar weakened, the United States could just sit on the sidelines and watch as foreign central banks were forced to absorb huge quantities of dollars. The elimination of direct pressure on the United States of private gold purchases laid the basis for the policy of "benign neglect."

While the term "benign neglect" was not applied to U.S. balance-of-payments policy until somewhat later, the more aggressive policy of early 1968 marked the beginning of a new phase in U.S. foreign economic policy. The United States did continue in this period to take steps to limit the size of its deficit, but the context had changed. The idea that balance-of-payments equilibrium was just around the corner—the light at the end of the tunnel—faded away. Instead, the United States would use its still formidable economic power to resist foreign pressures for balance-of-payments adjustment, especially when adjustment meant abandoning U.S. global aims or accepting significantly higher levels of domestic unemployment. The economic power would also be used to pressure countries with balance-of-payments surpluses to bear the burden of adjustment themselves. Furthermore, since the U.S. trade balance had begun to deteriorate, U.S. economic power would be used to force other countries to make concessions, such as tariff reductions or exchange rate increases, that would improve the U.S. trade position. The key to this economic power was what Henry Aubrey called the "financial deterrent," the threat to halt completely the official convertibility of the dollar into gold. This step would give other countries the unpleasant choice of either accepting a total dollar standard, in which there were no constraints on U.S. freedom of action, or of provoking some kind of international financial conflagration. By threatening other countries with the choice, the United States could significantly expand its options in the present.[61]

Although this new policy began to emerge in 1968, it had its roots in analyses and arguments put forward in the 1964-67 period. One significant strand was the analytic contribution of Kindleberger, Salant, and Despres. These three economists advanced the idea that it was inappropriate to see the U.S. payment position as one of deficit. The fact that foreigners, central banks, and private holders were willing to accumulate dollars indicated that they found those dollars to be of use for a variety of international purposes. The fact that foreigners wanted to expand their dollar holdings did not indicate a U.S. deficit, but rather a significant difference in the kind of assets that Europeans and Americans preferred to hold. While American investors preferred direct investments in Europe, there was a significant European preference for more liquid holdings, hence their desire to hold dollars. In short, what appeared to be a U.S. deficit was the normal consequence of the flow of capital between two financial centers with different liquidity preferences.[62]

The proponents of this international financial intermediation hypothesis tended to favor far less restrictive balance-of-payments policies than those the government was pursuing. In particular, they opposed capital controls, since they tended to sever the beneficial links between the U.S. and foreign capital markets. But while the proponents of this view could argue that the dominant European understanding of the U.S. position was mistaken, they had no clear plan for forcing the Europeans to accept this new analysis and to stop acting as though the United States was running a deficit. A second strand of analysis provided an important supplement to their position. This was the argument that unilateral action by the United States to demonetize gold would restore the U.S. bargaining position in the international monetary system. The United States could force the Europeans to accept the U.S. deficit by unilaterally ending the link between the dollar and gold. When this position was put forward in 1965, it was generally considered extreme and possibly dangerous for the Atlantic Alliance.[63] But as time went on, the position became more respectable. In late 1967, Eugene Birnbaum, then senior economist at Standard Oil of New Jersey and later vice president of Chase Manhattan, published an influential essay called *Changing the United States Commitment to Gold.* In it, he called for U.S. renunciation of the obligation to supply gold for dollars. Under certain conditions, other countries could demand that the United States redeem dollars by paying them their own currency, but that would be the limit of the U.S. obligation.

These ideas were built upon during 1968-69 and reached their highest expression in an article by Lawrence Krause, published in 1970, entitled "A Passive Balance of Payments Strategy for the United States." Krause's view was that the United States no longer had the power to manage the international monetary system directly. But the United States could continue to achieve its goals, despite its relative weakness, by adopting a passive balance-of-payments strategy. This meant that the United States would run its domestic economy at an optimal level and make little effort to control the size of the deficit. Foreign countries would then have to adjust their interest rates and exchange rates so as to avert unwanted dollar inflows. Krause was relatively contemptuous of the counterstrategies that other countries could use to resist this kind of policy, especially since they had to worry about some kind of international economic collapse if they responded to U.S. passivity too aggressively.

The Nixon administration followed the broad outlines of the Krause strategy, although the controls over U.S. foreign investment were retained. The new administration did move quickly to slow down the domestic economy in 1969 and 1970, and that helped ease pressure on the dollar. However, it is probable that domestic considerations were paramount in the management of the 1969-70 recession, because when domestic political considerations dictated turning to a more expansionary economic policy the Nixon administration did not hesitate to move in that direction, despite the worsening of the balance-of-payments deficit. The crisis came in the spring of 1971, when massive speculation against the dollar took the form of huge dollar flows into Germany, the country with the strongest currency in Europe. The official U.S. position was that this was Germany's problem and the United States was not going to take action to slow the U.S. deficit. The U.S. intent was to force the Germans and other countries to revalue their currency upward so as to improve the U.S. foreign trade position. The Germans resisted as long as they could, but they were reluctant to continue buying dollars to defend the existing parity. They finally allowed the value of the mark to float upward, so that they no longer had to absorb dollars. With the mark, other currencies were also revalued upward, although the Japanese continued to resist U.S. pressure for an upward shift in the price of the yen.[64]

The United States dropped the second shoe in August 1971, when Nixon announced his new economic policy. Since the policy of benign neglect had already led to some currency realignments, it was decided to finish the job by forcing other countries to accept new and fixed U.S.-dictated exchange rates. The United States announced the closing of the official gold window, as Birnbaum had suggested, so that the world was now placed on a dollar standard. Having used the financial deterrent, the United States also imposed the 10 percent import surcharge that had first been considered in March 1968. The lifting of the import surcharge was to be a quid pro quo for negotiating satisfactory new exchange rates. The intention of the United States was that its major trade competitors would revalue their currencies upward while the dollar remained fixed to gold at $35 an ounce. Finally, to sweeten a bitter pill, Nixon imposed a system of domestic wage and price controls to prove American seriousness in eliminating its domestic inflation.

The situation that Europe and Japan faced was clearcut. Either they could move toward full-scale economic conflict with the United States, beginning with a tariff war, or they could attempt to negotiate the best possible settlement, given a bad situation. They chose the latter course, and the period between August and December was one of intense diplomatic maneuvering. The Europeans and the Japanese had three priorities: to limit the amount their own currencies would be revalued, to force the United States to devalue relative to gold, and to get the United States to agree to reopen the gold window at some later time. They made some progress on the first two demands as the United States finally agreed to change the gold price to $38 an ounce. The United States had preferred to have the exchange-rate adjustment come by everyone else revaluing while the dollar stayed put. This preference arose from a desire to avoid the humiliation and the precedent of a change in the dollar's price relative to gold. But while the United States made this concession to get as large a total exchange-rate shift as possible, U.S. officials refused to make any concessions on the issue of gold convertibility. The new exchange rates were settled at an international conference at the Smithsonian in Washington in December 1971. President Nixon proclaimed the event as "the most significant monetary achievement in the history of the world."[65]

Despite Nixon's hyperbole, the new exchange rates failed to stabilize the international monetary system. Within less than half a year, a speculative attack on the pound forced the British authorities to let the pound float downward, and in early 1973 a new run on the dollar began. The loss of confidence in the dollar was stimulated by the upsurge in the U.S. rate of inflation after Nixon's removal of Phase III wage and price controls and the continuing weakness of the U.S. trade balance. Billions of speculative dollars again poured into West Germany; in one seven-day period, "the Bundesbank had to buy nearly $6 billion to resist another devaluation of the mark."[66] The United States responded to the crisis by negotiating another realignment of currencies that included a new devaluation of the dollar by 10 percent. Most European currencies remained unchanged, and the Japanese agreed to allow the yen to float even higher relative to the dollar. While this second dollar devaluation involved some further humiliation for the United States, it was consistent with its passive strategy. Rather than directly controlling the deficit, the United States forced other countries to accept a realignment of exchange rates designed to produce a dramatic improvement in U.S. competitiveness in foreign trade. Yet this second devaluation failed to halt the speculation against the dollar and the Germans were again forced to absorb huge quantities of unwanted dollars. Finally, the Germans gained the agreement of the other EEC countries to attempt a joint float against the dollar. The EEC countries would maintain fixed rates among their own currencies while floating relative to the dollar. With this decision, the age of fixed exchange rates came to an end.

While the Europeans initiated the move to floating exchange rates in a period when U.S. policy still favored a regime of fixed rates, the reality was that floating rates were more consistent with the passive strategy. With freely floating rates, other countries had no choice but to see their currencies appreciate in value relative to the dollar when the U.S. deficit was expanding. In other words, the stage of diplomatic pressure to force exchange rate changes was eliminated, since the exchange rate changes occurred virtually automatically. It is hardly surprising then that U.S. position shifted, so that by 1975 it was official Treasury Department policy to defend the regime of floating exchange rates against European pressures for a return to more fixed exchange rates.[67] One of the important steps that floating rates facilitated was the elimination of U.S. capital controls in January 1974. In late 1973, the dollar's exchange rate began moving upward because currency traders assumed that the Arab oil embargo would do more damage to the Western European and Japanese economies than to the American. U.S. policy-makers did not want the dollar's value to rise too far and wipe out the competitive gains from its earlier depreciation. So they took advantage of the occasion and eliminated the capital controls, the last real vestige of an active balance-of-payments policy designed to limit the size of the U.S. deficit.

EVALUATING THE PASSIVE STRATEGY

Any evaluation of U.S. balance-of-payments policy in recent years must acknowledge the enormous success of U.S. policy-makers in expanding American freedom of action. The unilateral termination of dollar convertibility into gold deprived foreign governments of their major threat against the United States. With the threat eliminated, the United States has been able to eliminate the controls on the outflow of capital from the United States. The petro-dollar crisis made that step easier, but it probably would have come in any event, because without convertibility there was no reason for the United States to continue controls that might impede the foreign expansion of U.S. multinationals. The coming of floating rates has also meant that the United States cannot be intimidated by massive selling of foreign dollar balances. If other countries want to allow the dollar to depreciate relative to their currencies, the United States will be glad to reap the advantages of improved trade. In short, foreign governments gain nothing from initiating or tolerating a general run on the dollar. This is particularly true of foreign governments that do not want to see a further diminution of their substantial dollar holdings. Foreign governments are not completely powerless to exact financial concessions from the United States, but most of the weapons they still retain have a high probability of backfiring. For example, extensive controls can be imposed to prevent the inflow of dollars, but these controls might interfere with the normal international economic transactions of the country that imposes them.

Floating rates have not, however, been an unalloyed blessing for the United States. Floating exchange rates have led in international money markets to some periods of extreme uncertainty that threatened to disrupt normal economic transactions. Even though such periods have been relatively rare, floating rates have made it more difficult for international businessmen to make firm calculations on the allocation of resources internationally. In fact, a rash of huge losses by international banks on their exchange-rate operations coincided with the transition to floating rates, and there have been repeated complaints by some businessmen that floating rates are a real threat to profits, since the costs of insurance against substantial exchange-rate changes are quite steep.[68]

Some of the uncertainty has been diminished through a revival of intervention by central banks, including the Federal Reserve, to make the foreign-exchange markets more orderly. While such intervention can limit the size of exchange-rate fluctuations, it raises other problems. The border line between interventions to make the market orderly and interventions to influence a nation's exchange rate (dirty floating) is very hazy. As soon as intervention in the market becomes a daily occurrence, the danger is great that nations will intervene to set their exchange rates at desired levels, and many of the advantages of a regime of floating rates will thus be lost. In fact, a competitively motivated depreciation of a nation's currency is relatively easier to carry out in a system of dirty floating than in a regime of fixed rates. In short, freely floating rates have proven too chaotic, but a system of regulated floating reopens all the political difficulties involved in fixed rates.

There is still another problem that has emerged to indicate that floating rates are not the panacea they were advertised to be by some American academics. Evidence has mounted that downward movements of the exchange rate of the dollar, such as the 1971 and 1973 devaluations, have contributed to domestic inflationary pressures. When devaluation occurs, workers and producers attempt to neutralize the reduction in their real incomes by striving to push wages and prices up further. If devaluation is accompanied by strong deflationary actions, these attempts might be thwarted; but in the absence of deflation, as in 1973, both workers and producers raise their prices and accelerate inflation. In fact, the resulting rise in prices might easily obliterate the initial trade gains from the devaluation. To the extent that devaluations produce this kind of inflation, floating exchange rates become very dangerous. Rather than being an equilibrating device that strengthens a country's trade balance, a decline in the exchange rate might simply speed inflation, leading to a further drop in the exchange rate, and a new spiral of inflation. The supposed virtuous cycle becomes a vicious cycle.[69]

The problems created by the devaluation-inflation link challenge a basic aspect of the American passive balance-of-payments strategy. Basic to the strategy has been the idea that if the United States can force other nations to accept a depreciation in the value of the dollar, the result will be a dramatic improvement in the American international trade position that will make it easier for the United States to finance its international governmental and corporate activities. The other basic part of the strategy has been the attempt to expand U.S. freedom of action by eliminating the capacity of other nations to place international monetary pressure on the United States. However, the two parts of the strategy are linked because U.S. policy-makers have been aware that other nations will not accept indefinitely an international monetary system that gives the United States the freedom to behave totally irresponsibly. Gradual improvement in the U.S. trade balance, brought about by dollar depreciation, would prove to other countries that the United States should be allowed to continue its international economic dominance. However, if dollar depreciation causes domestic inflation rather than a marked improvement in the U.S. trade balance, then the passive strategy becomes a pointless exercise in global bullying.

The key issue then is the effect of dollar depreciation on the American international trade position. The important point to recognize here is that, even if depreciation leads to domestic inflation, the shift in price levels does not occur in uniform ways. It is probable that some producers will gain a competitive advantage from devaluation, even while others find themselves adversely affected by the consequent inflation. It seems likely that exchange rates do have a particularly important influence on international trade in a variety of heavy capital goods, where international competition for contracts is intense. But whether exchange-rate reductions will improve a nation's overall trade balance, rather than simply benefiting certain producers, depends on the overall structure of the nation's trade. While the evidence is still not in, it seems unlikely that the competitive gain for the United States from the 1973 devaluation, for those goods where price is important in determining foreign demand, was enough to outweigh the consequences of the later inflation.[70]

These problems with floating rates—uncertainty in exchange markets, the problem of dirty floats, the worsening of inflation, and the uncertain advantages of currency depreciation—make it easy to understand the intensification of debate within the United States about the desirability of floating rates, as opposed to a return to fixed rates. However, the proponents of fixed rates must contend with the problem that fixed rates would limit U.S. freedom of action and force acceptance of greater balance-of-payments discipline. The contradiction remains: How can the U.S. simultaneously pursue its global aims and live within the rules of an international monetary order?

EIGHT. *The International Monetary Order in Crisis*

The struggle of the United States to increase its freedom of action in international monetary affairs destroyed the old Bretton Woods system. Step by step, the United States either broke the rules of the old order or forced other countries to break them. The rule-breaking was deemed necessary at each step to save the international monetary system from an even greater crisis. The first major alteration of the rules was the creation of the gold pool in 1961, which relieved the U.S. of part of the responsibility of maintaining the gold price at $35 an ounce. The next step was the unilateral renunciation by the United States in 1968 of the obligation to provide gold to private purchasers at the $35-an-ounce price. This was followed three years later by the decision to close the gold window to official purchasers as well. The United States also renounced its informal obligations as a reserve currency country by blocking access to its capital markets, and the imposition of the 10 percent import surcharge in August 1971 was a blatant violation of rules governing international trade. Finally, the United States was largely responsible for the final significant rule violation, the end of the regime of fixed exchange rates. The continuation of the U.S. deficit left foreign countries that did not want to accumulate additional dollars with only two options: instituting potentially dangerous controls over capital inflows or floating their currencies. Since the second alternative seemed less risky, it was the one for which Western Europe and Japan eventually opted.

It can be argued that each of these rule changes is part of a gradual evolution to a new monetary order, but there can be no doubt that the evolutionary process is still far from complete. The international monetary system, as it presently exists, lacks the institutional structure to deal smoothly either with special shocks such as the oil price rises or with the day-to-day problems of inflation and balance-of-payments adjustment. Even though the international monetary system survived the strain of financing the huge trade deficits of the oil-consuming nations during 1974, there were some periods when that

203

survival seemed problematic. And it remains to be seen how the system will be able to cope with some of the shocks that certainly lie ahead. But the most telling critique of the present international monetary system is that the system has heightened the problem of global inflation. An analysis of the problem of inflation also provides a glimpse of the kinds of reforms that are necessary to create an international monetary order that minimizes, rather than maximizes, the strain between national economies and the world economy.

THE PROBLEM OF INFLATION

It hardly needs repeating that mounting inflationary pressure has been the characteristic problem of developed capitalist nations in the past fifteen years. While there are a multitude of explanations for this inflationary pressure, it is increasingly recognized that the inflationary dynamic is deeply rooted in the structure of contemporary capitalism. [1] It seems that the very success of advanced capitalism in using Keynesian techniques to moderate the severity of the business cycle has created the current problem with inflation. Since World War II, the developed economies have not experienced the "purification" of a major depression that lowers wages, prices, and interest rates. Instead, all of those have risen, if not steadily, relentlessly. In fact, it appears that in contemporary capitalism almost any strain generates new price rises and parallel wage gains. Even during periods of economic recession, significant price rises occur as capitalists attempt to make up for lagging profits by increasing their profit per unit sold. Such violations of the law of supply and demand, and parallel violations on the side of wages, are made possible by the market power exercised by giant corporations and the more powerful of the trade unions. This market power is a major factor in making contemporary capitalism so prone to inflationary pressure.

This means also that the capacity of governments to take effective action to control inflation is limited. The orthodox cure for inflation is a deliberate effort to slow the pace of economic activity through fiscal or monetary action. However, since market power makes it possible for firms and unions to increase prices and wages even in periods of recession, the economic slowdown might have to be quite severe before such wage and price rises are halted. The problem is that the lower the level of economic activity and the higher the rate of unemployment, the greater the social and economic risks. Not only is there a threat of social unrest or rebellion resulting from high rates of unemployment, but there is the clear danger of a general economic collapse if economic activity drops too far. A severe reduction in the level of economic activity threatens to produce widespread corporate, personal, and governmental bankruptcies that could easily spiral out of control. Finally, even if deflation is relatively successful in eliminating inflation, it might well mean that inflationary pressures, once economic expansion begins again, will be stronger than before. This can happen because low levels of investment during the period of deflation can lead to strains on capacity once expansion begins anew.[2]

The major alternative to deflation as an anti-inflationary strategy has been the development of an incomes policy, a government-imposed system of wage and price controls. The idea of such controls is to maintain a constant relationship between profits and wages through administrative measures rather than through market forces and inflation. While controls of this sort appear to have some initial success in halting inflation, they tend to break down over time. The continued existence of the controls places the state in the center of the struggle over the distribution of the social product. In this position it is difficult for the state to preserve its pretense of neutrality in the class struggle while simultaneously defending the existing distribution of income between wages and profits. To protect their electoral base, politicians usually opt for an end to controls in order to extricate themselves from a dangerous position. However, the pressure for elimination of controls is often exerted by capitalists as well as by labor. Capitalists attempt to raise profits by subverting the controls through the downgrading of product quality and the creation of artificial shortages. These efforts mean that the logic of long-term price controls points to increased government regulation of product quality, investment decisions, and profit levels. However, this is a logic that capitalist firms strenuously resist, because it threatens their decision-making autonomy. So instead of pursuing a logic of expanded controls, the state usually simply abandons the experiment with wage and price controls.

The inadequacy of the standard policy tools for controlling inflation in advanced capitalism would be a serious problem even if each of these economies existed in isolation. However, the openness of the world economy to flows of goods and capital across national boundaries makes the inadequacy of the anti-inflation tools even more dramatic.

Illustrating the complexities that flow from the openness of the world economy, to take one example, are the potential, ironic consequences of domestic monetary policies. The normal use of monetary policy to prevent an overheating of the domestic economy involves pushing interest rates up. However, higher interest rates can attract capital from abroad, which will act as a stimulus to the domestic economy. A country that has been able to avoid inflation with a tight money policy can find itself overwhelmed by an inflow of capital attracted by high interest rates and a low rate of inflation. The inflow of capital can quickly destroy the government's work in holding inflation in check. Similarly, government efforts to slow the rate of economic activity by making credit scarce and expensive can be subverted by the ability of major corporations, particularly multinationals, to finance new expansion with capital borrowed at lower interest rates abroad. The national government's ability to control the domestic economy—already limited by the relative ineffectiveness of anti-inflationary tools— is further impaired by the openness of the international economy.[3]

Inflationary pressures in one national economy can also spill over into other economies through spreading shortages of commodities. Agricultural shortfalls, production bottlenecks, sharply increased speculative purchases, and even sudden growth in consumer demand can lead one country to increase its imports of certain products rapidly, resulting in parallel shortages in other countries. Inflation is exported by bidding up the price of certain commodities, and the increased price of those goods sets off price rises for related products. Again, a country that has kept to a relatively low level of inflation might find its price structure thrown into disarray by booming foreign demand.[4]

The problem of inflation has been further complicated in recent years by the relatively anarchic organization of international liquidity. At times, an excess of international liquidity has heightened the inflationary pressure on national economies. Excessive international liquidity more or less assures that there will be large capital inflows into low-inflation countries, and it also facilitates worldwide price increases in the same way that an excess of domestic liquidity contributes to inflation. The anarchic organization of international liquidity can be traced to American failure to perform adequately the tasks of an international financial center. The quantity of dollars pumped abroad through the U.S. deficit often bore little relation to the quantity needed for gradual increments in official and private reserves. Furthermore, U.S. policies encouraged the rise of the Eurodollar market that provides another important source of international liquidity. However, the expansion or contraction in the Eurodollar market's contribution to global liquidity is not subject to governmental regulation. In fact, there is some evidence that the supply of Eurodollars expands at precisely the time when the U.S. authorities are attempting to slow the growth of the domestic money supply.[5]

There are, then, a variety of ways in which inflationary pressures can be transmitted from one country to another in the present system. If these various processes equalized the rate of inflation in all countries, the problem of balance-of-payments adjustment would be greatly reduced. However, that equalization does not occur. National rates of inflation vary according to specific national conditions, and the vulnerability of economies to imported inflations also differs dramatically. The consequence is that nations will have widely different rates of inflation depending on their own level of business activity, their vulnerability to imported inflation, the ability of their authorities to moderate wage demands, the rate of productivity advance, and other factors. Sharp differences in inflation levels most often lead to balance-of-payments problems for high-inflation countries. Not only do high rates of inflation tend to weaken the balance of trade, but inflationary pressure also results in capital outflows as investors switch to assets in more stable currencies.

Overcoming this kind of inflation-induced balance-of-payments deficit is the heart of the adjustment problem in contemporary capitalism. And it is the ineffectiveness and unreliability of the major anti-deflationary tools that makes this kind of adjustment so difficult. The process is further complicated by the reluctance of low-inflation countries with balance-of-payments surpluses to share the burden of adjustment. If low-inflation countries allowed their rates of inflation to rise by a portion of the difference between the low and high rates, the task of high-inflation countries would be more manageable. However, there is no institutional mechanism for forcing the low-inflation countries in this direction, and they are extremely reluctant to increase their rates of inflation through deliberate action. Low-inflation countries tend to see their success in holding inflation in check as an indicator of social health, and taking action to stimulate more inflation is seen as the equivalent of planning an epidemic of a dangerous disease. The fear is that a higher rate of inflation would destroy the existing delicate balance between labor and capital and begin a period of intense conflict over the distribution of the social product that could push the rate of inflation completely out of control.[6]

EXCHANGE RATE ADJUSTMENTS

The orthodox economic solution to balance-of-payments deficits caused by high rates of inflation is a downward shift in the deficit country's exchange rate. As we have argued previously, the problem is that this mechanism often fails to work in the way that economic theory indicates it should. Devaluations are designed to restore international equilibrium through a market device. Lower prices abroad for a country's exports are supposed to increase the volume of exports, while higher prices for imported goods will diminish total import volume. Increased exports and decreased imports mean a reduction in overall consumption. However, if a country's labor movement is anxious to preserve the existing level of real income, it will fight for wage increases to compensate for the losses due to devaluation.[7] If successful, this could set off a new inflationary spiral that would easily eliminate the potential trade gain from devaluation. Even when devaluations are combined with efforts to control inflation through monetary or fiscal restraint, the strength of unions in key sectors can still prevent the reduction in real incomes that devaluations are intended to produce.

Another problem with devaluations is their uncertain effects on the trade balance. A variety of products are not particularly responsive to price changes. Imports of crucial raw materials, many agricultural goods, petroleum, and other commodities might well continue at the same volume despite higher prices, since demand is not sensitive to price changes of 5 or 15 or 25 percent. Similarly, exports of a similar range of products might not increase in volume despite lower unit prices, resulting in a drop in total export receipts for those goods. Another range of products are traded internationally under conditions of oligopolistic pricing, so that these goods are also relatively insensitive to price changes. Producers of certain goods, for example, might not even bother to reduce the foreign-currency cost of export goods that have been priced in another currency, increasing their profits per item regardless of volume. Depending on the specific composition of a country's exports and imports, it is possible that the impact of a devaluation on a country's trade balance might be the reverse of what was intended. The increased cost of necessary imports and decreased receipts on certain exports might outweigh the savings from discouraged imports and the gains from increased receipts for price-sensitive exports. But it is difficult to assess in advance whether the impact of a devaluation on the trade balance will be negative, neutral, or positive. The outcome depends significantly on the willingness or eagerness of a country's exporters to cut their foreign-currency prices and to pursue aggressively the new opportunities for expanded exports. It also depends on the nation's success in inducing the working class to accept a reduction in real earnings.

Since exchange rate changes do not automatically restore balance-of-payments equilibrium and sometimes even have adverse effects, floating exchange rates are not the universal panacea that they have been alleged to be.[8] An international monetary order in which exchange rates are free to find their "correct" level in the free market could work only if real-wage levels could be readily lowered. For real incomes to be successfully reduced without inflation in contemporary society seems to require, at the very least, a concerted and conscious policy by business and government. The advocates of floating exchange rates, however, generally assume that the market will accomplish this reduction by itself. In fact, it seems possible that, instead of facilitating adjustment, freely floating exchange rates would contribute to inflationary pressure because they would eliminate a traditional incentive for anti-inflationary actions—the defense of the existing exchange rate and the country's stock of currency reserves.

But whether exchange rates float freely or are more fixed, the problem remains that exchange rate changes, the major means of balance-of-payments adjustment, can serve to intensify inflationary pressures. The same is true of the other major techniques of balance-of-payments adjustment. Deflation, as already noted, can increase inflationary pressures over the short term or the long term. Attempts to adjust the balance of payments by raising domestic interest rates to attract capital flows can accelerate inflation when borrowers pass along the costs of higher interest rates to customers.[9] Even efforts to restrict imports, such as the import surcharges used temporarily by Britain and the United States, can have the effect of driving up certain critical prices. The consequence of all of these adjustment techniques is a classical vicious circle: rising domestic prices require balance-of-payments adjustment, but balance-of-payments adjustment leads to rising domestic prices. The severity of this cycle can be attenuated, since the rate of domestic inflation is affected by a wide variety of different factors. Yet the point remains that the adjustment mechanisms within the present international monetary system can work to intensify the tendency toward inflation, which is already the most critical economic problem of advanced capitalism.

THE NEED FOR REFORM

The problem of inflation provides a dramatic illustration of the inadequacy of the present international monetary system, dramatic because accelerating inflation poses a fundamental threat to political and social order. To the extent to which present international monetary arrangements actually accelerate inflation or simply make it more difficult to control, it is clear that those arrangements are in need of repair. Still, there are those who take a sanguine view of today's international monetary system and argue that reform is not urgently needed because there is a gradual evolution toward a stronger, more stable order based on a high level of international cooperation. However, this optimistic view rests on the assumption that domestic solutions will work to curb inflationary pressures and that, with the problem of inflation reduced, the present system will work adequately. Such a view is unrealistic if, in fact, strong inflationary pressures are endemic to capitalism at its current stage of development. To be sure, the intensity of inflation will rise and fall over time, but I would argue that it is utopian to expect a sudden return to an era of stable prices or price rises limited to 2-3 percent a year. Once high levels of inflation are seen as virtually inevitable, it follows that international monetary reform is necessary to create a monetary order better fitted to the task of neutralizing these inflationary pressures.

The problem of inflation and the related issues of exchange rate adjustment and international liquidity do not exhaust the reasons for international monetary reform being urgently needed. The crisis created by the increase in petroleum prices in 1973-74 revealed that the institutional apparatus for international crisis management is underdeveloped. For one thing, there is no adequate supervision of the Eurodollar banking system that had to bear much of the burden of recycling the petrodollars. For another, the IMF's resources are too limited for the kind of bailing-out operations that might have proved necessary. Of course, the world economy did survive the crisis, and a number of ad hoc measures succeeded in staving off disaster. But a sanguine view is justified only if one believes that the oil price crisis was simply a once-only phenomenon. If one sees other major international economic crises as likely,[10] it follows that the international monetary system needs an institutional structure powerful enough to cushion the impact of such crises. Such an institutional structure would minimize the need for last-ditch diplomacy to devise ad hoc means of crisis management. The strengthened institutional structure would decrease the danger that is always present in ad hoc arrangements—that one or two key nations might demand too high a price for cooperation in the ad hoc solution, thus creating a diplomatic deadlock that would make effective intervention impossible.

THE SHAPE OF REFORM

The type of international monetary reform necessary to neutralize inflationary pressures and to facilitate global crisis management would involve both strengthening of supranational institutions and a higher level of economic coordination among the developed nations. Supranational institutions would be necessary to regulate smoothly the supply of international liquidity and to regulate international capital markets, such as the Eurodollar market. A strengthened supranational agency would also provide a first line of defense in crisis management, because it would control enough resources to perform bail-out operations without complex negotiations. Improved economic coordination among nations would ease the adjustment problem by dividing the burden among surplus and deficit nations. Coordination would also mean a much higher level of exchange of information about economic conditions and intended policies, so that deficit nations would be able to formulate a mix of policies for balance-of-payments adjustment based on the best possible information about the economic environment. Coordination would have to go far beyond the relatively low level of consultation that has already been achieved, and it would have to involve agreement on the acceptability of different types of economic intervention.[11] The supranational institutions would then be able to enforce those agreements.

While it is relatively easy to specify the types of reforms necessary for the successful management of an open world economy, it is extremely difficult to imagine the means by which those reforms would be implemented. Historically, the successful efforts at international monetary reform have been those organized by a single hegemonic power, but there exists today no single nation or group of confederated nations that has that kind of economic and political dominance. In the absence of a hegemonic power, there seem to be only two possible political foundations for effective international monetary reform. The first is the concerted exercise of political leverage by the multinational corporations. The second is the development of a joint partnership among the United States, Japan, and the major nations of Western Europe that would include a common program for international monetary reform. I will argue, however, that neither of these alternatives is likely to provide the necessary political base for reform.

THE GLOBAL CORPORATIONS AND INTERNATIONAL MONETARY REFORM

Those who celebrate the rise of the multinational corporation have often argued that the nation-state is no longer a viable economic unit. The nation-state, they assert, acts as a fetter on economic progress in the same way that principalities and duchies slowed the rise of capitalism before the creation of national markets. Multinationals must waste endless resources contending with dozens of different governments, each with a complex web of specific regulations that limit the ability of the multinational to organize its global activity in the most rational and efficient way.[12] While abolishing the nation-state seems unrealistic, the creation of a series of international institutions that would allow multinationals to operate as though the capitalist world economy were one nation has been advocated. This would involve an international system of corporate charters, patent arrangements, and antitrust and tax regulations. These arrangements would require mechanisms for adjudication and for enforcement on an interational level. Along with the supranational structure required for these purposs, it would make sense to create an agency that would regulate international capital markets and an international central bank that would regulate the world's supply of liquidity. This would involve the creation of a formidable network of supranational economic agencies that would gradually relieve national governments of almost all authority over international economic matters.[13]

This is simply a modern version of the nineteenth-century utopian vision of a self-regulating international market. The only difference is that the contemporary view recognizes that the world market cannot adequately regulate itself, so that a supranational authority is required. Yet this authority would be fundamentally similar to the self-regulating

market because it would be above politics; it would allow economic
activity to proceed without interruption, except for the minimum
necessary to assure order. Implicit here is the myth that there is basically one natural way of organizing the world economy, which would
ultimately bring equal benefits to all classes and all nations. The whole
thrust of the present study has been to argue that the specific way in
which the world economy is organized has important consequences for
the distribution of resources among nations and within nations, and
this means that the specific organization of that world economy can
never be "above politics." It *is* politics.

Just as the nineteenth-century effort to establish a self-regulating
international market was based on Great Britain's international political and military hegemony, so the contemporary vision of supranational regulation of the world economy has flourished in the context of
U.S. international hegemony. American political, economic, and military power has been critical in making the world safe for multinational
enterprises. But as the international position of the United States has
begun to slip, it is increasingly argued that the same safety for multinational enterprises can be assured by a supranational authority divorced
from the political and military power exercised by nations. Yet such an
argument must be based on either extreme naiveté or self-interested
cynicism. The men who run the multinationals are well aware that the
exercise of political, economic, and military power is necessary to give
them the freedom to continue their global operations.[14] Unless a supranational agency were invested with such powers, which seems quite
unlikely, the agency would have to co-exist with the exercise of those
powers by national governments. But under such conditions, it would
be extremely improbable that the supranational agency would be able
to disregard differences in national power in making its decisions. If
several major nations were carrying the bulk of the military burden of
keeping the world safe for multinational enterprises, could a supranational agency avoid favoring the corporations based in those nations?
And if it did, why should those nations continue to bear the burden
without gaining advantages?

The issue is starker if one looks at the idea of supranational regulation from the point of view of a particular multinational corporation. In
the present order, that corporation gets a certain amount of support
from the government of its base country. That support, whether it
takes the form of preferential access to government contracts, diplomatic clout, or tax benefits, is useful in competing with foreign-based

firms, especially those whose governments are able to provide less adequate support. If, however, a transition were made to supranational regulation, all of these forms of support would have to be eliminated to lessen the impact of national politics on the world economy. Each company would face the supranational agency on an equal footing. It seems obvious that American-based multinationals, in particular, would stand to lose a great deal by no longer having exclusive access to U.S. diplomatic power.

In reality, the idea of supranational regulation of the world economy is simply an ideological smoke screen that the multinationals use in their campaign to lessen governmental regulation of their activities. It is certainly true that the multinationals want to minimize regulation by governments at home and abroad, but it does not follow from that that they have no interest in national governments. They want diplomatic and economic support from their home nation, but they want it with no strings attached. So they use an anti-nation-state ideology when they want to avoid regulation, but usually become quite patriotic when they need something from the government. No matter how hypocritical, the patriotism indicates their fundamental dependence on the power of their particular home government. That dependence makes it extremely unlikely that the multinationals will throw their weight behind efforts to replace national governmental regulation with supranational regulations.

This does not mean that any form of internationalization of economic regulation is impossible. International conventions and even effective international regulations can be developed in areas such as patents where the common interest among nations is strong and national practices are relatively similar. It is also possible that some limited form of supranational central banking could evolve, as long as it concentrated on creation of reserves and the management of international capital markets, leaving governments free to determine their own policies. The point is that the more ambitious vision of international economic management or of a highly interventionist international central bank will not be realized. And any progress toward effective international institutions would likely be interrupted or reversed when one nation feels that its international position is being undermined or unfairly limited by the international arrangements. In sum, the rise of multinational corporations does not increase the likelihood that international economic coordination will be handed over to a supranational agency, because conflict of interests among nation-states continues unabated. The only viable foundation for the further elaboration and development of supranational institutions would be some form of relatively stable political cooperation among the major capitalist powers. If such cooperation for the purpose of smoothly managing the world economy developed, one could expect a flowering of supranational regulations. The important question is whether the conditions exist for the development of the kind of political cooperation necessary for the joint management of the world economy.

REFORM THROUGH JOINT MANAGEMENT

Reform through joint management would mean that several of the strongest capitalist nations would have to agree to manage the world economy collectively and carry out the reforms described earlier. They would jointly play the role performed by a hegemonic power in earlier periods, but they would have to do so with a higher level of responsibility and with new skills appropriate to the more complex problems of the contemporary world economy. While it is impossible to predict whether this kind of joint management will evolve, it is possible to analyze the major obstacles from the point of view of the United States, Western Europe, and Japan.

The United States

In the two previous chapters, I have argued that the breakdown of the postwar monetary order was rooted in the inability of the United States both to pursue its global aims and to live within the rules of international monetary behavior it had earlier devised. Joint management, however, would necessarily mean the development of a new set of rules that the United States would be expected to obey. It seems very likely that the conflict between the pursuit of U.S. global aims and the "rules of the game" would re-emerge, especially because the partners in joint management have an interest in rules that place serious constraints on U.S. economic freedom. In short, it seems extremely likely that joint management would force the United States at least in certain periods, to accept some combination of global and domestic retrenchment. Global retrenchment means a reduction in the cost of public and private U.S. international activities, while domestic retrenchment means a willingness to accept more stringent anti-inflationary actions, including higher levels of unemployment. Since both forms of forced retrenchment can be hazardous, it would seem that U.S. policy-makers have good reason to avoid the constraints that joint management would most probably involve.

The danger of global retrenchment in a period of intensifying international competition is that it could further worsen the international economic position of the United States, forcing continually more serious retreats, in a kind of snowballing effect. A cutback in U.S. overseas political and military presence could cause U.S.-based firms to lose economic opportunities to foreign-based firms. The loss of major construction contracts and control or access to lucrative raw materials could hurt the profits of U.S.-based firms and lead to higher prices of U.S. raw material imports. Similarly, limitations on the ability of U.S. firms to continue their overseas growth by exporting capital from the United States could result in a relative strengthening of foreign-based multinationals. Again, this would be most costly in competition for raw materials, construction projects, and sales of heavy equipment, but it might also damage the ability of U.S. firms abroad to compete profitably in other manufactured goods.

In addition to strengthening the relative position of Western European and Japanese capitalists, American retrenchment might also mean a strengthened position for the socialist bloc and for the revolutionary and nationalist forces in the underdeveloped world. If U.S. retrenchment is not matched by a complementary extension of political and military efforts by Western Europe and Japan, there would be increased opportunities for countries to opt out of the capitalist world economy. Underdeveloped countries that did not move that far would still have greatly increased bargaining power in relation to the developed capitalist countries. And as long as Japan and Western Europe did not fill the political vacuum left by retreating U.S. power, China and the U.S.S.R. would increase their own bargaining power in relation to both the developed and underdeveloped world.

These risks involved in retrenchment compound the difficulties facing a state apparatus that would have to design a strategy for imperial retreat that combines maximum balance-of-payments savings with minimum damage to the U.S. international position. If the state were free to pursue the most rational strategy, the job would be merely difficult, but the state must formulate its policies in the context of pressures by a variety of powerful interest groups, many of which are strongly represented in the state apparatus itself. For example, the decision to reduce the American political, military, and foreign-aid presence in a country where a handful of U.S. multinationals have investments would be strongly contested by those firms and by a lobby of people with strong political, cultural, and economic ties to that particular country. It is difficult for the government to resist this kind of pressure simply on the grounds that it is attempting to pursue the most efficient and economic global policy. Just as the extension of U.S. power internationally was orchestrated through a series of crises, so it would seem that its retreat might be accomplished only through a series of crises that make the need for retrenchment painfully obvious. In short, it would require a powerful counterpressure for the state to be willing or able to sacrifice the interests of those firms that would stand to lose from a retreat from a particular area.[15]

If global retrenchment seems too costly, American policy-makers could respond to foreign pressure by relying on more intense domestic retrenchment. However, domestic retrenchment has serious costs of its own, because unemployment and lower rates of economic growth create a multitude of new problems. Even without joint management, the United States already suffers from levels of unemployment that are substantially higher than those in other developed capitalist countries. And unemployment rates among the urban black population are usually about twice the rate for the whole nation. While it is true that the social and political response by blacks and others to the high levels of unemployment in the 1974-75 recession was remarkably mild, domestic retrenchment could well require that, in certain periods of balance-of-payments difficulties, the United States would have to tolerate unemployment rates substantially above the 8-9 percent range. Furthermore, any U.S. administration would be foolish to anticipate that the quiescent response to the high levels of unemployment in 1974-75 will become a permanent feature of the political landscape. It is far more likely that future administrations will be under very strong domestic pressure to bring unemployment back down to the 4-5 percent range. In that context, pressure from abroad for domestic retrenchment would be politically explosive.

The other problem is that domestic retrenchment, with its slower rates of economic growth, could easily heighten the inflationary pressure that results from labor's struggle to defend and expand its share of the total product. In sum, externally imposed economic discipline would increase the likelihood that the United States would follow the British pattern of economic stop-go. Brief periods of inadequate and

inflationary economic growth would alternate with periods of high unemployment, and the economy's underlying problems would only worsen. The greatest danger for U.S. policy-makers in such a pattern is the
possibility that, as in Britain, the consequences of stop-go would be
intensification of class conflict and radicalization of the labor movement. Because of this risk and because of the dangers involved in
international retrenchment, it is of considerable advantage to the
United States to avoid the constraints on its action implicit in joint
management. The United States is likely to acquiesce in a system of
joint management that would probably entail substantial sacrifices only
if Western Europe and Japan could apply convincing pressure.

Western Europe and Japan

The relation of Western Europe and Japan to joint management is
complex. While their governments and strongest firms have much to
gain from coordinated management of the world economy and the
consequent American retrenchment, there is likely to be strong
domestic resistance to the expanded international role required by
joint management. The use of economic resources for expanded political-military roles and the adoption of the style of global powers will
generate domestic conflicts. Yet this expanded political-military role is
necessary, first to convince the United States to accept joint management, and then to make a jointly managed system work. To complicate
matters further, the struggle by Japan and Western Europe for an
expanded international role occurs in the context of military and
economic dependence on the United States. This dependence can be
manipulated by the United States to discourage pressures by the
Europeans and Japanese for concessions on economic management.

The most immediate gain for Western Europe and Japan from
joint management would be greater ease in domestic economic management. Limits on American ability to export its deficits and its inflation would help reduce the inflationary pressure elsewhere. Agreement with the United States on new rules for adjustment would help
depoliticize the adjustment process and would make the control of
inflation easier. Similarly, cooperation would reduce the risk of major
currency crises, competitive devaluations, or international debt crises.
The process of economic integration in Europe could then proceed
without the disruption of periodic currency crises,[16] and Europe and
Japan could be surer that their dollar holdings would eventually be
redeemed for real resources. Western European and Japanese

capitalists would also gain from the extension of their home countries' political influence and the retreat of U.S. power. They would be in a better position to win construction contracts and raw-materials concessions abroad, and they would be able to extend even further the geographical range of their investments. Limitations on capital exports from the United States would decrease the threat of takeovers and competitive investments by U.S. multinationals. And joint management would probably mean that the international capital market would become less biased toward U.S. firms, so that Japanese and Western European firms would be better able to borrow to finance their own expansion.

Despite these advantages, the obstacles to this kind of extension of power are formidable. For Western Europe the issue is tightly intertwined with the prospects for economic and political integration. For Japan, the issue is closely knit with the legacy of World War II and the popular reactions against a militaristic and aggressive foreign policy. In both cases, the strength of left-wing political forces at home operates as a double limitation on an ambitious foreign policy. The Left tends to oppose the expansion of international political-military commitments out of anti-imperialist and anti-militarist motivations. At the same time, demands by the Left and by the labor movement for higher wages and increased social spending make it difficult to free resources for international purposes. Strong domestic pressures can make it difficult for a nation to operate in the international sphere—fulfilling such obligations as providing credit to other countries or honoring military commitments—with the consistency expected of a major power.

For Western Europe the pursuit of a coherent international policy depends either on the further development of a supranational authority or on the emergence of a cohesive alliance among its most powerful nations, West Germany and France. The first development is problematic for the near future for many of the same reasons that make the emergency of international economic management unlikely—most fundamentally, the reluctance of states to cede sovereignty over crucial economic policy decisions. The latter development is more likely, but there is the continuing possibility that an alliance can be shattered by international conflicts of interest or by domestic pressures that block agreement on critical issues. But without a reasonably stable alliance at the center, the European nations would be left to formulate independent foreign policies. Only Germany, acting independently, could make a claim to joint partnership, but it would be difficult for her to make that claim credible. Given the present political alignments within Germany, the exercise of independent political power on a global basis would place a real strain on available resources.

Japan would also find it difficult to make a claim to global joint partnership if Western Europe as a region did not participate in the effort. But even under the most ideal circumstances, it is uncertain whether domestic resistance to a greatly expanded international role for Japan would be overcome. The rapid pace of Japan's post-World War II industrial growth has left a huge backlog of social demands that might interfere with an expanded world role. More significantly, the strength of the opposition to militarism in Japan could preclude the rapid expansion of political-military influence that would have to be a condition for gaining and sustaining a jointly managed world economy. A country whose military forces are constitutionally defined as "Self-Defense Forces" has trouble establishing its credibility as a reliable world power.[17]

Western Europe and Japan can also be dissuaded by the United States from pressing too hard for an effective global partnership. As long as joint management is seen by the United States as an undesirable alternative, the United States can attempt to play on internal division in and between Western Europe and Japan to block an effective challenge. In Western Europe, this can be accomplished by a divide-and-conquer policy that attempts to prevent the emergence of a unified EEC. The United States can also use the threats of withdrawing military protection and of heightened economic conflict to counter European and Japanese pressures. An overly aggressive use of these threats could backfire, because it might result in strengthening the impulse in Western Europe and Japan toward a more independent policy. However, the point remains that internal divisions, lack of adequate economic resources, and American counterpressures will make it difficult for Western Europe and Japan to press successfully for joint management of the world economy despite the advantages to them of such a regime.

THE UNREFORMED FUTURE

I have tried to show that neither of the frequently cited paths to international monetary reform is likely to produce results in the foreseeable future. Yet I have also argued that the need for reform is critical if the system is to function. If international monetary reform is both necessary and unlikely, it follows that the international monetary system will suffer severe and chronic crises in the years ahead. Such a prediction, however, does not imply that there will be an international financial crisis on the scale of the Great Depression of the 1930s. While that possibility is no longer unimaginable, the resources available for crisis management are formidable enough for an economic collapse to be avoided under most circumstances.[18]

The common interest among the major capitalist nations in avoiding an international economic collapse is strong enough so that ad hoc measures can be found for dealing with almost all crisis situations. This makes it possible for the international monetary system to survive for some time despite its fundamental weaknesses. It is even possible to imagine that ad hoc cooperation among the major capitalist nations could quickly undo the damage if an international financial collapse unfolded before governments could act to halt it. If, for example, a series of major bankruptcies led to an international financial panic similar to the one in 1931 that forced Germany to adopt exchange controls, it might be still possible for governments to intervene to provide financing for international trade. Such intervention, combined with measures to save the banking system, could prevent the collapse from leading to a rapid decline in business activity internationally.

This type of crisis management can be extraordinarily effective if the major nations are willing to put aside their differences long enough to rescue the international economy. If, however, one or more nations attempt to extract concessions from the others as a condition for cooperation in efforts at crisis management, serious problems can arise. When the nation holding out for concessions is indispensable to an effective rescue, and when other nations are unwilling to grant the concessions, effective crisis management can be blocked. This could mean that the negotiations dragged on past the deadline for effective action, or simply that efforts at crisis management were abandoned.[19] In either event, the consequence could be that a potentially manageable crisis escalates out of control, leading to a collapse of international trade and global deflation. Obviously, such an outcome would be damaging to all nations, including those that blocked effective action initially, so it is unlikely that a group of national policy-makers would take such an intransigent stance lightly. I would argue that they would take such a risk only when they perceived a fundamental threat to their nation's political stability. If, for example, a regime was being challenged by powerful domestic opposition movements of the Left or of the Right, its policy-makers might feel that the regime's survival depended on gaining certain concessions internationally, such as the freedom to reduce unemployment despite adverse balance-of-payments effects. In such a case, national policy-makers might consider that the burden of causing an international economic collapse would fall on those nations that were too shortsighted to grant the concessions necessary for national stability.

At present, few governments of major capitalist powers face serious threats from dangerously disloyal opposition movements. The threat posed in Italy and France by the Communist party's insistence on its right to play a role in the government is hardly enough to justify disruptive international actions by Italian or French policy-makers. The danger in these cases is minimal, because these parties have pledged themselves to parliamentary methods and there is little likelihood that they will act to dismantle the structures of Italian or French capitalism. However, far more threatening movements might arise in these nations and in others if present economic conditions continue. High levels of unemployment and inflation can strengthen radical political movements of the Left and of the Right that are unwilling to respect established institutional structures in their eagerness to respond to economic and social problems. Such movements could force national policy-makers to change the way they negotiate internationally, with the consequence of destroying the minimal level of international cooperation required for effective global crisis management.[20]

It is here that the major effects of the present international monetary system might be felt. The unreformed international monetary system heightens advanced capitalism's tendency toward stagflation—the coexistence of high unemployment and high inflation. It does this in part because of the vicious circle described before; almost all measures of balance-of-payments adjustment can serve to intensify inflationary pressures. The present system also works to transmit inflationary pressures from one nation to another, even to nations that have already reduced their levels of economic activity. But the more intense the inflationary pressures, the worse the trade-off between inflation and unemployment. So policy-makers must worry in periods of relatively low inflation that a reduction in unemployment might dangerously accelerate inflation, and they must be willing to impose even more severe unemployment in periods of high inflation.

As the problem of stagflation worsens, governments will be forced to resort to politically unpopular policies, such as prolonged high unemployment and reductions in government services. These measures can generate mass support for opposition movements that challenge the political and economic status quo. Such threats to national political order can work to undermine international economic order, and by doing so they can heighten the possibility of even more disruptive international economic developments. Further international disruptions would be likely to create more economic havoc internally, which would also strengthen the hand of the domestic opposition movements, and so on. It is through this kind of complex pattern that the present international economic order is likely gradually to self-destruct: domestic political responses to the problem of stagflation —a problem that has been exacerbated by the international monetary system—will effectively destroy the conditions for the international economic cooperation that is essential for the system's continued survival.

ALTERNATIVES

In the meantime, however, a number of political alternatives are open to nations that perceive the mounting costs of continued participation in the existing international monetary system. All these alternatives involve a sharp break with liberal economic principles, because they use extensive government intervention to insulate the domestic economy from the pressures of the world economy. In the near future, these alternatives are most likely to be advocated by those opposition movements that arise to protest the consequences of stagflation. But if international monetary reform continues to prove illusory and the domestic costs of the present system mount, all nations will have to face these alternatives. Even if only one major nation chose to opt out of the present system, it would have a major impact on the others.

While the range of actual policy devices that can be used to insulate economies from international market pressures is almost unlimited, the alternatives that use such devices systematically can be reduced to a number of "ideal types."[21] It is not possible here to fill in the political dynamics and class forces involved in each of the ideal types, but I will attempt to outline schematically the major dimensions of these political alternatives.

The first alternative is actually much less feasible now than it was in the 1930s and 1940s. This is the idea of national capitalism, by which I mean a system that leaves ownership of the means of production in private hands while almost all international economic transactions are organized by the state. Foreign trade would be controlled by the state and the outflow of capital would be severely restricted. However, if the government of a developed capitalist nation attempted to impose this solution, presumably as a response to severe domestic disruptions caused by the world market, it would immediately come into conflict with all the multinational corporations operating within its borders. These corporations would be unable to function within a national capitalist system, and we could expect to see ferocious opposition on their part. If the government refused to back down, it is likely that the economy would be severely disrupted by the multinationals. For the government to stand its ground, it would probably have to take direct control of large sectors of the domestic economy and mobilize popular support. It seems most likely that victory in the conflict with the multinationals would lead quickly to full socialization of the domestic economy, because the government and its supporters would have lost patience with the prerogatives of private capital. If, on the other hand, the multinationals were victorious, the society would likely return to liberal capitalist principles.

If the national capitalist form of insulation is no longer viable, that still leaves two other ideal types from the 1930s and 1940s: fascism and socialism. While it is naive to anticipate a form of fascism identical with its earlier incarnations, the basic outlines of Nazi economic policy in the pre-World War II period remain a viable, but temporary, solution to the problems facing developed capitalist nations today. In the fascist form of insulation, the nation does not close itself off from international transactions, but it uses the state to organize those transactions to maximize the national wealth with little regard for the "rules of the game" of liberal capitalism. The state works closely with the nation's most powerful firms to boost exports, expand access to cheap foreign raw materials, and increase the return of profits from overseas operations. This might be combined with strict controls on other capital flows and restrictions on foreign multinationals operating within the nation's boundaries. Those measures are backed by an aggressive foreign policy that makes full use of military and political threats to intimidate weaker nations. A large share of the nation's resources is devoted to military purposes, and a garrison society that represses dissent is constructed on the grounds of severe external threats.

The logic of this solution is that the problem of stagflation would be resolved by military spending and direct government intervention to control wage levels. The control of wages would require a direct assault on the trade union movement, which could be justified by the external crisis. At the same time, the aggressive foreign economic policy could help relieve internal pressures by providing resources to appease certain sectors of the population. While this neofascist form of insulation would require a sharp break with current policies and an increased danger of war, it still remains a possibility, because it provides immediate solutions to a number of interlocking problems. In other words, the danger of fascism cannot be lightly dismissed, because it provides measures to resolve temporarily the contradictions created by liberal capitalism.

Another response to these contradictions is the final form of insulation, the socialist solution. Socialism eliminates the problems created by national capitalism because it combines strict governmental control over all international transactions with socialization of the domestic economy. It does not require the aggressive foreign economic policies of fascism, because the radical reorganization of the domestic economy can bring the national economy closer to self-sufficiency. Socialism can exist in more authoritarian or in more democratic forms, but all forms would employ centralized control over international transactions with the criteria for decision-making based on a comprehensive economic plan designed to optimize certain goals. Authoritarian and democratic socialism would differ in the ways in which the goals and techniques of the economic plan would be formulated. In authoritarian forms, the political elites have broad opportunities to direct the planning process in their own favor. In a democratic form of socialism, popular participation in the decision-making process could work to assure a close fit between the plan and the actual needs of the population.

The ideal of socialism has been that humanity would one day be able collectively and consciously to control economic processes, rather than remain subject to the whims of uncontrollable natural and market forces. The struggle by the United States to restore an open world economy in the period after World War II has created a world system in which those market forces increasingly conflict with the welfare of the world's population. If our goal today is the improvement of human welfare, this requires subordinating market forces to conscious human will, but there are profound dangers if that will is exercised predominantly by new or existing elites. Only democratic socialism holds the promise of fulfilling the historic goal of conscious *and* collective control of the economy.

NOTES

Chapter One. Introduction

1. The open/closed distinction is implicit in Polanyi, *The Great Transformation* (1944). The major techniques for closing an economy are import restrictions (only a certain quantity or money value of a commodity can be imported during a given period), capital controls (limitations on the quantity, conditions, and destination of capital flows), exchange controls (earnings of foreign currencies must be surrendered to the central government, which will determine their use), bilateral trading (under government supervision an attempt is made to balance a country's foreign trade on a country-by-country basis), and state trading (a central authority controls import or export transactions in certain commodities). Tariffs are usually not used for closing an economy; they are designed to influence the market rather than to suspend its operation. However, extremely high tariffs can be used to close an economy off from international market influences.

2. The distinction between international monetary system and international monetary order is suggested by Mundell, "The Future of the International Financial System", (1973).

3. The gold standard became almost universal in the last quarter of the nineteenth century, as many countries abandoned silver-based currencies or bimetallism and adopted fixed gold parities. Lindert, *Key Currencies and Gold 1900-1913* (1969), p. 33.

4. Hirsch, *Money International* (1969), p. 16.

5. Hirsch, *Money*, especially pp. 15-23; Bloomfield, *Monetary Policy Under the International Gold Standard 1800-1914* (1959).

6. Emmanuel, *Unequal Exchange* (1972), pp. xii-xx, argues that Friedrich List's defense of protection for infant industries did not challenge the basic assumptions of the free trade orthodoxy.

7. See, for example, Amin, *Accumulation on a World Scale* (1974).

8. The clearest statement of this position was Keynes, "National Self Sufficiency" (1933). Evidence that this view had its adherents in the United States is in Hawley, *The New Deal and the Problem of Monopoly* (1966), pp. 169-186.

9. Keynes, "Self Sufficiency," p. 758.

10. "Some type of socialism" could mean anything from an extremely hierarchical and authoritarian form of state socialism to an egalitarian democratic form of socialism that placed power in the hands of the people.

11. Jacob Viner, quoted in Warren Hickman, "Genesis of the European Recovery Program" (1949), p. 137.

12. This insight has been at the core of the revisionist critique of traditional Cold War historiography. See, for example, Williams, *The Tragedy of American Diplomacy* (1962) and Kolko, *The Politics of War* (1968).

13. Hayter, *Aid as Imperialism* (1972), and Payer, *The Debt Trap* (1974).

Chapter Two. The Decline of the Nineteenth-Century Gold Standard

1. This is the theme of Brown, *The International Gold Standard Reinterpreted* (1940).

2. The classical works by Polanyi, *The Great Transformation* (1944) and Feis, *Europe: The World's Banker* (1965) describe Britain's financial role. Also, Hobsbawn, *Industry and Empire* (1968) and Robinson and Gallagher, "The Imperialism of Free Trade" (1953), analyze the British trading role. The analysis in Strange, *Sterling and British Policy* (1971), ch. 1, is also extremely useful here.

3. This contrast is made in Feis, *Banker,* pp. 83-186.

4. The British willingness to sacrifice domestic economic stability is analyzed in Bloomfield, *Monetary Policy . . . 1880-1914* (1959), p. 25, and Hirsch, *Money International* (1969), pp. 16-17. Of course, the bankers did not have to bear the cost of domestic deflation themselves. There is reason to believe that the political power of the British internationalist bankers was so great that they could impose policies that damaged the interests of domestic industrialists. See Block, "Expanding Capitalism: The British and American Cases" (1970), pp. 140-141.

5. Polanyi, *Transformation,* p. 19. The retreat from freer trade is described in Kenwood and Lougheed, *The Growth of the International Economy 1820-1960* (1971), pp. 80-85.

6. Lindert, *Key Currencies and Gold 1900-1913* (1969), p. 76, notes that by 1913 the German mark had become a more popular reserve currency asset on the European continent than sterling. This suggests that the intense trading rivalry between Germany and Britain in the period leading up to World War I was paralleled by a financial rivalry in which Germany was threatening London's central financial role in the world system.

7. Lindert, *Currencies,* pp. 74-75, 79.

8. Brown, *Gold Standard,* I, pp. 127-247.

9. The chaos in the early post-World War I years is described in Kindleberger, *The World in Depression 1929-1939* (1973), pp. 31-54.

10. Brown, *Gold Standard,* I, pp. 342-357.

11. While the increase in holdings of foreign currencies from $1.1 billion in 1913 to $3 billion in 1928 is less dramatic than had earlier been believed, there is a significant shift in the geographical distribution of those currency reserves. Before the war, 60 percent of the currency reserves were held by Japan and India alone, but after the war a large share of the holdings were in European hands. Lindert, *Currencies,* pp. 13-15, and Triffin, *The Evolution of the International Monetary System* (1964), pp. 21-23.

12. The stabilization process is reviewed in Meyer, *Banker's Diplomacy* (1970), and in Clarke, *Central Bank Cooperation 1924-1931* (1967), ch. 4.

13. Wolfe, *The French Franc Between the Wars* (1951), describes the French return to parity. Also Kindleberger, *Depression,* pp. 48-52.

14. The British return to parity is exhaustively analyzed in Moggridge, *British Monetary Policy 1924-1931* (1972), especially chs. 3 and 4.

15. Clarke, *Cooperation,* p. 72; Moggridge, *British,* pp. 51-52.

16. Clarke, *Cooperation,* pp. 75-85.

17. Keynes, *Economic Consequences of Sterling Parity* (1925).

18. Foreign investment as a percentage of British national income fell from 9.3 percent in 1910-1913 to 2.3 percent in 1920-1924 and 1.6 percent in 1925-1929: Brown, *After Imperialism* (1963), pp. 108-109. The deterioration in Britain's export position and the liquidation of some foreign investments during World War I meant that Britain could no longer afford on balance of payments terms to continue a high level of foreign investment. Moddridge, *British,* pp. 28-36.

19. The classical statement of the contrasting international economic positions of the U.S. and Britain is Lary, *The United States in the World Economy* (1943), pp. 1-12. The argument about the political consequences of that difference draws heavily on Wilson, *American Business and Foreign Policy 1920-1933* (1973), and Kindleberger, *Depression.* Brown, *Gold Standard,* is also relevant.

20. Wilkins, *The Emergence of the Multinational Enterprise* (1970), is valuable for understanding the internationalist thrust of U.S. firms in this period. My analysis also relies on Williams, *The Tragedy of American Diplomacy* (1962), pp. 104-159, and Parrini, *Heir to Empire* (1969), a detailed examination of the divisions within the international banking community.

21. Wilson, *American Business,* especially pp. 69-100, 123-256.

22. Wilson, *American Business,* uses the term "independent internationalism," pp. x-xi.

23. Weinstein, *The Decline of Socialism in America 1912-1925* (1969), ch. 3, describes the Left's agitation against the war and the repression unleashed by the Wilson administration.

24. Wilson, *American Business*, pp. 22-23.

25. Wilson, *American Business*, ch. 5. It also seems likely that the issue of the bonus for the veterans of World War I was closely intertwined with the issue of the war debts. The succeeding administrations could not very well continue resisting the bonus demands of the veterans (that culminated in the Bonus March of 1933 that was attacked by Generals MacArthur and Eisenhower) if they gave in to foreign demands for renunciation of the war debts.

26. Wilson, *American Business*, p. 126.

27. Wilson, *American Business*, p. 127, discusses the failure of the United States to gain parallel concessions. She analyzes the Dawes and Young loans on pp. 144-147. For more on the Dawes loan, Clarke, *Cooperation*, ch. 4. Kindleberger, *Depression*, discusses the Young loan on pp. 78-82 and U.S. foreign lending in general on pp. 56 and 71.

28. Arndt, *The Economic Lessons of the 1930's* (1963), pp. 28-29.

29. Salter, *Foreign Investment* (1951), pp. 15-17, describes the speculative nature of foreign bond sales in the United States. Wilson, *American Business*, devotes chapter 4 to Hoover's unsuccessful effort to establish a program of foreign loan supervision.

30. Wilson, *American Business*, ch. 3, describes the struggles over tariffs. The relationship between imports and debts can be understood as follows: If several countries, A, B, and C, want to pay interest on loans or to repay the principal borrowed from country D, they must either run a trade surplus with country D or continue borrowing ever greater amounts from country D. The United States, when in the role of country D, refused to let other countries run a trade surplus with it; instead, the United States ran a large trade surplus. This meant that the only alternative open to countries A, B, and C was to continue borrowing heavily from the United States to finance interest payments or debt repayments. When the United States stopped lending abroad, countries A, B, and C attempted to deflate so as to run an overall trade surplus. The idea was that they might be able to earn dollars from each other which they could use to pay the United States. However, since they were all in the same position, this strategy was bound to fail. Its only consequence was the intensification of deflationary pressure.

31. The most-favored-nation principle governed most European trade at this time. It meant that tariff concessions granted to one country would be granted to all countries with which one had most-favored-nation agreements. The European reluctance to make tariff concessions is noted in League of Nations, *Commercial Policy in the Interwar Period* (1942), p. 123.

32. Mikesell, *United States Economic Policy and International Relations* (1952), pp. 22-23. The refusal of the United States to allow an inflation in response to gold inflows of flight capital is paralleled in the post-World War II period by the West German refusal to inflate when foreign speculative capital flowed across the border in large quantities. While such a refusal is sound from a domestic standpoint, it is still a violation of the norms of the international monetary order.

33. This debate is reviewed in Kindleberger, *Depression*, chs. 5 and 6.

34. Clarke, *Cooperation*, p. 183. The Austrian crisis is described in Clarke, *Cooperation*, pp. 185-189, and Kindleberger, *Depression*, pp. 148-152.

35. Clarke, *Cooperation*, pp. 189-195.

36. These negotiations are discussed at length in Bennett, *Germany and the Diplomacy of the Financial Crisis, 1931* (1962).

37. Bennett, *Diplomacy*, pp. 153-285; Clarke, *Cooperation*, pp. 193-201. The German choice of exchange controls resulted from the impossibility of further deflation or devaluation. It was assumed that letting the mark float downward would result in intense inflation, and the Germans could not contemplate a repetition of the hyperinflation of the early 1920s. Further deflation was out of the question because of the intensity of the gathering social crisis and because deflation was unlikely to halt the flight of capital. The exchange controls are described in Ellis, *Exchange Controls in Central Europe* (1941), pp. 158-289.

38. The sterling crisis is described at length in Skidelsky, *Politicians and the Slump* (1967). Also Clarke, *Cooperation*, pp. 201-218, and Kindleberger, *Depression*, pp. 157-162.

39. Clarke, Cooperation, pp. 218-219; Kindleberger, *Depression,* pp. 167-172.

40. Carr, *International Relations Between the Two World Wars 1919-1939* (1966), pp. 147-149; Kindleberger, *Depression,* ch. 9; Gardner, *Economic Aspects of New Deal Diplomacy* (1971), pp. 26-30.

41. Roosevelt's nationalist economic policies were rooted in some of the same interest groups that had opposed internationalism in the 1920s, but the pressure for nationalist solutions was much stronger because of the depth of the economic crisis. It should also be recognized that there were intense conflicts among the economic nationalists.

42. The quote is from Gardner, *Economic Aspects,* p. 29. See also pp. 30-33.

43. Arndt, *Lessons,* pp. 37-40; at pp. 75-76, Arndt argues that the dollar devaluation placed deflationary pressures on other countries, but Kindleberger, *Depression,* pp. 228-231, notes that the U.S. devaluation was a clumsy but necessary step in a universal devaluation of currencies relative to gold. If everyone devalues—raising the price of gold—the gold profits will be available for spending, which could encourage a revival of international demand.

44. Harrod, *The Life of Keynes* (1971), especially pp. 509-520; Arndt, *Lessons,* pp. 73-77, 96-110.

45. Arndt, *Lessons,* pp. 50-70. In previous cyclical downturns, a revival of business-fixed investment led the process of recovery. In the United States in the 1930s, this revival failed to occur. A number of theories have been offered to explain this failure; the major explanations are lack of business confidence and stagnation. The first argument is that the business community was hostile to the New Deal's pro-labor policies and engaged in a kind of general strike of capital by restraining investment. The stagnation argument is that given existing or anticipated levels of demand, there simply were not enough profitable investment opportunities.

46. Arndt, *Lessons,* ch. 4.

47. Arndt, *Lessons,* chs. 6 and 7; Neumann, *Behemoth* (1966), pp. 327-337. German trade policy came to be dominated by the drive to obtain and maintain access to raw materials necessary for the war effort. But the devices used to maximize imports and the devices used to maximize exports are very similar.

48. Average monthly imports of 75 countries, in millions of dollars: 1929—$2,858; 1930—$2,326.7; 1931—$1,667.7; 1932—$1,122. Kindleberger, *Depression,* p. 127.

49. League of Nations, *Commercial,* p. 59; Arndt, *Lessons,* pp. 83-88.

50. League of Nations, *Commercial,* pp. 80-90, 143-149; Arndt, *Lessons,* pp. 83-88.

51. Each country maintained an exchange stabilization account that was used to intervene in the foreign exchange market to limit the fluctuations of its currency's value. The Tripartite Agreement made this intervention easier. Between May 1935 and July 1938, the British pound fluctuated between $4.89 and $5.04, a rather limited range. Hinshaw, *Toward European Convertibility* (1958), p. 4.

52. Mikesell, *Economic Policy,* pp. 55-57; Kindleberger, *Depression,* pp. 257-261. The Tripartite Agreement represented only the slightest shift away from Roosevelt's economic nationalism, since it did little to restrict U.S. freedom of action.

53. The view that World War II was a consequence of the breakdown of the world economy is shared by Marxists and American internationalists such as Cordell Hull: "unhampered trade dovetailed with peace, high tariffs, trade barriers, and unfair economic competition, with war. Though realizing that many other factors were involved, I reasoned that, if we could get a freer flow of trade—freer in the sense of fewer discriminations and obstructions—so that one country would not be deadly jealous of another and the living standards of all countries might rise, thereby eliminating the economic dissatisfaction that breeds wars we might have a reasonable chance of lasting peace." Quoted in Gardner, *Sterling-Dollar Diplomacy* (1969), p. 9.

54. The key changes in capitalism were the increasing difficulty of adjusting wages downward and the widespread and effective opposition to high levels of unemployment.

55. This was Keynes' position in the 1930s: Keynes, "National Self Sufficiency" (1933).

56. Harrod, *Keynes,* pp. 601-607, 617-620. The idea is that each country would have a limit on how large a cumulative deficit it could run, as well as a limit on how much

foreign paper it would be forced to hold. Countries running a surplus would be induced to return to balance because they were simply accumulating IOUs.

57. The main example was the early White Plan for a Stabilization Fund. Horsefield, *The International Monetary Fund 1945-1965* (1969), vol. III, pp. 37-96.

58. One analyst who argued for a second chance for the United States wrote, "The fault, dear Brutus, was not that our bankers made loans; it was that they stopped making them." Schoepperle, "Future of International Investment: Private vs. Public Foreign Lending" (1943), p. 338. Some of the major statements of the internationalist position are Feis, *The Sinews of Peace* (1944); Condliffe, *Agenda for a Post-War World* (1942); National Planning Association, *America's New Opportunities in World Trade* (1944).

Chapter Three. Bretton Woods and the British Loan

1. This interpretation of the political divisions within the Roosevelt administration relies on Hawley, *The New Deal and the Problem of Monopoly* (1966), for the prewar period, and on a number of published memoirs and diaries for the World War II period. These include Hull, *The Memoirs* (1948); Blum, ed., *From the Morgenthau Diaries* (1959-67); Berle and Jacobs, eds., *Navigating the Rapids 1918-1971, From the Papers of A.A. Berle* (1973); Blum, ed., *The Price of Vision: The Diary of Henry A. Wallace 1942-1946* (1973).

2. Divine, *Second Chance* (1967), describes the triumph of U.S. internationalism during World War II.

3. A fairly standard estimate was that with relatively full employment the American economy could produce 50 percent more in 1946 than in 1940. Bureau of Foreign and Domestic Commerce, *Markets After the War* (1943).

4. Analysts who predicted an inflationary boom for several years before the danger of depression materialized include Backman and Gainsbrugh, *Deflation or Inflation* (1946); Clark, "Financing High-Level Employment" (1945); Condliffe, *Agenda for a Post-War World* (1942).

5. See Hawley, *New Deal*, pp. 170-177, for a description of the national economic planners. For examples of the thinking of national economic planners, see Reuther, "The Challenge of Peace" (1945); National Planning Association, *Guides for Post-War Planning* (1941)—Note that the National Planning Association underwent a political transformation during the course of the war; it began as an outpost of national planning and ended as an advocate of multilateralism; National Resources Planning Board, *Report for 1943*, Part 1.

6. Henry A. Wallace was the most prominent political figure associated with na- ·tional economic planning. He played an extraordinarily important role in dramatizing the issue of postwar full employment. Yet Wallace's concern with foreign markets for American grain often led him into a free trade rhetoric that conflicted with the views of some of his colleagues on the left of the New Deal. See Wallace, *Sixty Million Jobs* (1945), and Blum, *Vision*.

7. Hawley's discussion of the NRA makes clear the business community's preference for some kind of "business commonwealth" in which businessmen organize themselves into some kind of cartel structure with little interference from government or labor. Hawley, *New Deal*, pp. 36-43. The classic critique of national economic planning was Hayek, *The Road to Serfdom*, first published in 1944 and extremely popular in American business circles.

8. The links of the national economic planners to the CIO come across clearly in Blum, *Vision*, especially pp. 33-35. For a statement of American business ideology, see Sutton et al., *The American Business Creed* (1956), especially 184-207.

9. The Committee on Economic Development was a business group founded with the purpose of assuring full employment after the war. Yet it is striking that the Committee's 1945 report, *Toward More Production, More Jobs and More Freedom*, betrays a surprisingly high level of uncertainty about how full employment would be maintained. The fact that the CED, the business group with the strongest commitment to high employment, was reduced to calling for further study at that late date is significant,

It is important to realize that there was a tremendous range of views in the business community about the best way to achieve high levels of employment after the war. The National Planning Association's *National Budgets for Full Employment* (1945), is interesting in this respect. It offers three alternative models of how full employment could be maintained. Eakins, "Business Planners and America's Postwar Expansion" (1969), discusses some of the divisions among business planners. Other sources for contemporary discussions of the problem are Pabst Brewing Company, *The Winning Plans in the Pabst Postwar Employment Awards* (1944), and Homan and Machlup, eds., *Financing American Prosperity* (1945).

10. The stagnationists were those economists who argued that the lack of investment opportunities in the United States meant that the economy would slip back into depression without extensive government spending. See Hansen, *Full Recovery or Stagnation?* (1938), especially chs. 16-19.

11. Most discussions of the export surplus centered around a figure of $3-5 billion a year, but it was generally argued that an even larger surplus, if possible, would be advantageous for domestic employment. It must be remembered that the tools of economists for predicting the impact on employment of a given level of exports were quite crude. It is quite possible that this lack of certainty led policy makers to err on the side of an even larger export surplus in their eagerness to avoid a new depression. National Planning Association, *America's New Opportunities in World Trade* (1944), and Lary, "Domestic Effects of Foreign Investment" (1946).

12. "There has been during the war an enormous expansion in manufacturing capacities in the United States, and this expansion has been concentrated very largely in heavy industry. Unless foreign markets for the products of American heavy industry can be found during the period which lies immediately ahead, many war-expanded industries will be obliged severely to curtail their operations and accordingly to reduce their employment of labor." Leo Cowley in Department of State, *Foreign Relations of the United States*, 1946, vol. I, p. 1397.

13. Two representative discussions of the difficulties involved in a sustained export surplus are Feis, *The Sinews of Peace* (1944), pp. 115-125, ·168, and Buchanan, *International Investment and Domestic Welfare* (1945), pp. 125-180.

14. The centrality of multilateralism to United States foreign policy is stressed by Williams, *The Tragedy of American Diplomacy* (1962), and Gardner, *Economic Aspects of New Deal Diplomacy* (1971). Note that the terms "multilateral," "liberal," and "open" are used synonymously.

15. Harry Dexter White of the Treasury Department, whose views I take to be representative of the national economic planners, believed that a high level of domestic activity "would do far more for our foreign trade than a complete wiping out of our tariff rates, or 100 trade treaties." Gardner, *Sterling-Dollar Diplomacy* (1969), p. 15. White also wrote somewhat later that the belief that the United States needed expanded foreign markets to assure prosperity was a "Marxist fallacy." Quoted in *New York Times*, November 14, 1953, and cited in White, *Harry Dexter White—Loyal American* (1956), p. 218.

16. A statement from the National Resources Planning Board, a stronghold of the national economic planners, captures their idealistic internationalism:

> We stand on the threshold of an economy of abundance. This generation has it within its power not only to produce in plenty but to distribute that plenty. Only a bold implementation of the will-to-do is required to open the door to that economy. Give the American people a vision of the freedoms that we might enjoy under a real program of American and *world-wide* development of resources, and all of the opposition of blind men and selfish interests could not prevent its adoption. (Emphasis added)

National Resources Planning Board, *Report for 1943*, Part I, p. 4.

17. Gardner cites Ansel Luxford as saying that the fund's major historical function was to pave the way for American internationalism. Gardner, "The Political Setting" (1972), pp. 32-33.

18. This controversial issue has generated much debate, but rarely has the point about the potential productive impact of government social service spending been made.

See Hirschhorn, "Toward a Political Economy of the Service Society" (1974). It should also be remembered that Keynes anticipated the "euthanasia of the rentier" as capital became increasingly productive. See Keynes, *The General Theory of Employment, Interest, and Money* (1964), pp. 375-377.

19. While the secondary sources rarely acknowledge that there was more at stake in the conflict between State and Treasury than a jurisdictional dispute, there is evidence that fundamental policy issues were at stake. Hints at the conflict can be found in passim, in Blum, *Morgenthau*, III; Rees, *Harry Dexter White* (1973); Gardner, *Sterling-Dollar;* Eckes, *A Search for Solvency* (1975). A particularly clear statement was that of A.F.W. Plumptre, who was in the Canadian delegation to Bretton Woods. He recalled that "Certain persons in the Treasury, Harry White outstanding, and Frank Coe, an ex-associate of mine at the University of Toronto, again were very much left-wing 'New Deal' in their thinking." Plumptre, "Canadian Views" (1973).

20. For Morgenthau's views, see Blum, *Morgenthau.* His views and relationship to Roosevelt are described briefly in Rees, *White,* pp. 49-52.

21. Blum, Morgenthau, III, p. 149.

22. Biographical information on White is drawn from White, *Loyal American,* and Rees, *White.* White's personality is mentioned by Gardner, *Sterling-Dollar,* p. 111, and Harrod, *The Life of Keynes* (1971), pp. 613-615.

23. The charges against White centered on the passing of certain critical documents to the Russians and some complicated financial transactions with the Chinese. Morgenthau provides a defense of White on the Russian charge in his diaries, see Blum, *Morgenthau,* III, pp. 177-194. The White case continued as a political issue long after White's death. Eisenhower's Attorney General, Herbert Brownell, was repeating the charges against White in 1953, and, even later, Congressional committees were still poring through the White and Morgenthau papers for definitive evidence of subversion. The failure of these prolonged investigations to turn up definitive evidence would suggest that the charges were basically unsubstantiated. But the issue was politically useful for the Republicans because Truman's appointment of White to work at the fund, even after charges had been made against White, made Truman and the Democrats vulnerable to the charge of being "soft on Communism."

The Rees biography of White takes the charges against White very seriously, but Rees fails to explain why credence should be given to the charges of Chambers and Bentley. It is hoped that the opening of the government's files on the White case may finally prove that White was the victim of an early "Watergate" conspiracy.

24. For the wartime line of the American Communist party, see Starobin, *American Communism in Crisis 1943-1957* (1972), pp. 51-70.

25. Quoted in Gardner, *Sterling-Dollar,* p. 9.

26. Acheson's testimony before the Special Subcommittee on Postwar Economic Policy and Planning of the House of Representatives, cited in Williams, *Tragedy,* pp. 235-236.

27. Quoted in Hutchison, *Rival Partners* (1946), p. 53. For more on Clayton, see Gardner, *Architects of Illusion,* (1970), ch. 5, and Dobney, ed., *Selected Papers of Will Clayton* (1971).

28. Adolf Berle's diaries give a hint of the confusion and intrigue within the wartime State Department: Berle and Jacobs, *Navigating,* especially pp. 442-468. Also Notter, *Postwar Foreign Policy Preparation 1939-1945* (1949), documents the continuing reorganization of the State Department during the war years.

29. The logic was that only with Germany's export capacity could Western Europe as a whole run a large enough export surplus with the underdeveloped world to finance a sizable share of its import surplus with the United States. Gardner, *Economic Aspects,* pp. 275-282; Gardner, *Sterling-Dollar;* pp. 16-22; Kuklick, "American Foreign Economic Policy and Germany, 1939-1946" (1968), pp. 51-57; Kolko, *The Politics of War* (1968), especially pp. 320-333.

30. Gardner, *Sterling-Dollar,* pp. 18-20, pp. 40-47.

31. Kuklick, "Germany," pp. 116-121; Gardner, *Economic Aspects,* p. 268; Rees, *White,* pp. 240-265, 300-307.

32. Mansfield, "The Origins of the International Monetary Fund" (1960), pp.

219-221; Rees, *White*, pp. 52-54; Eckes, *Solvency*, pp. 41-42.

33. Gardner, *Sterling-Dollar*, p. 77. This section draws on Gardner, *Sterling-Dollar*, pp. 71-77, and Horsefield, *The International Monetary Fund 1945-1965* (1969), I, pp. 10-14. It should also be noted that part of White's shrewdness involved adapting his rhetoric to his audience. When attempting to sell the Bretton Woods Agreement, he, on occasion, slipped into the rhetoric of an open world economy. See, for example, White, "The Monetary Fund: Some Criticisms Examined" (1945).

34. Most of this April 1942 draft is published in Horsefield, *Fund*, III, pp. 37-82.

35. Gardner, *Sterling-Dollar*, pp. 74-75. For a more detailed description of the early Bank draft, see Oliver, *Early Plans for a World Bank* (1971).

36. Oliver, *Plans*, pp. 30-35.

37. Horsefield, *Fund*, III, p. 44. A country's vote in the fund would be roughly proportionate to the size of its quota. The United States would have something like 25 percent of the vote, although its share of the quota was larger. See p. 75.

38. Wolfe, *The French Franc Between the Wars* (1951), pp. 147-170.

39. Horsefield, *Fund*, III, p. 44.

40. Horsefield, *Fund*, III, pp. 67, 49-50.

41. Horsefield, *Fund*, III, pp. 67, 64, 70, 73.

42. For the 1943 draft, Horsefield, *Fund*, III, pp. 83-96; Gardner, *Sterling-Dollar*, p. 77.

43. Although White's provision that four-fifths of the votes were necessary to oppose any domestic economic action was probably designed to protect against opposition to any U.S. domestic policies because the United States would have more than one-fifth of the total votes.

44. In negotiations in August 1941, Keynes shocked American officials with a statement that Britain would be forced to adopt bilateral solutions in the postwar period. Gardner, *Sterling-Dollar*, pp. 41-42.

45. Keynes' draft from February 1942 is printed in Horsefield, *Fund*, III, pp. 3-18. The critique of bilateralism is on pp. 9-10.

46. Before the war, Britain financed a major portion of her imports with earnings from foreign investments, shipping services, and other invisible services—insurance, merchant banking, etc. For the 1936-38 period, Britain averaged imports of $3.5 billion, exports of $1.95 billion, and invisible earnings of $1.35 billion. But during the course of the war, Britain was forced to liquidate some $4.5 billion of foreign investments and had incurred some $412 billion of new sterling debts. It was generally recognized that Britain would have to increase exports by 75-100 percent over the prewar level, while keeping imports down, in order to make up for the loss of invisible earnings. Gardner, *Sterling-Dollar*, pp. 178, 200, 306-307.

47. Keynes' views are outlined in Harrod, *Keynes*, especially pp. 559-666.

48. The quotas in the 1943 version of the Keynes plan were as follows (in $ millions):

Great Britain	4,978
United States	4,040
France	1,931
Germany	3,129
USSR	411

Schumacher, *Export Policy and Full Employment* (1943), p. 13.

49. The text of the Joint Statement of Experts is in Horsefield, *Fund*, III, pp. 128-135.

50. Gardner, *Sterling-Dollar*, pp. 110-121.

51. Horsefield, *Fund*, III, p. 132. Gardner, *Sterling-Dollar*, pp. 113-114, implies that the compromise gave more or less equal weight to provisions stressing free access and provisions stressing conditional access to fund resources. It seems that this view is too charitable to the later American position, when the United States wanted to make access highly conditional. The intent of the provisions in the Joint Statement and in the Articles of Agreement of the fund was that access to fund resources would be basically unconditional. The later American position depended on making provisions that were designed for extraordinary circumstances appropriate for all circumstances. See Birn-

baum, *Gold and the International Monetary System: An Orderly Reform* (1968), pp. 14-17.

52. Blum, *Morgenthau*, III, pp. 259-265.

53. Quoted in Hudson, *Superimperialism* (1972), p. 70.

54. Birnbaum, *Reform*, pp. 14-17.

55. Most of the relevant articles are published in Williams, *Post-War Monetary Plans* (1947).

56. For the international bankers' critique of the fund, see Aldrich, *Some Aspects of American Foreign Economic Policy* (1944), and American Bankers Association, *Practical International Financial Organization* (1945). The ABA document was the product of several different bankers' committees, including the Bankers Association for Foreign Trade—Study Committee on Post-War Problems and the Committee on Federal Fiscal Policy of the Association of Reserve City Bankers.

57. This analysis is implicit in the testimony of Randolph Burgess, head of the American Bankers Association, before the Senate Committee considering the Bretton Woods Agreement. U.S. Congress, Senate Committee on Banking and Currency, *Bretton Woods Agreement Act*, pp. 468-490.

58. "It was no secret that Clayton was displeased at the wide latitude for currency restrictions left by the monetary compromise of Bretton Woods." Gardner, *Sterling-Dollar*, p. 196. Morgenthau charges that Winthrop Aldrich and Thomas Lamont, both prominent bankers, attempted to sabotage the fund as early as the Bretton Woods conference. Blum, *Morgenthau*, III, p. 258.

59. Blum, *Morgenthau*, III, pp. 427-432; Eckes, *Solvency*, pp. 174-179, 190-197.

60. It is also significant that administration defenders of the fund before Congress were less than candid in their insistence that the fund would be useful in the transition period and that no further large scale U.S. aid to Europe was contemplated. Gardner, *Sterling-Dollar*, pp. 139-140.

61. Burgess, quoted in Senate, *Bretton Woods*, p. 474; see also pp. 491-499.

62. Gardner, *Architects*, pp. 232-269.

63. Department of State, *Foreign Relations of the United States*, 1945, VI, especially pp. 54-119.

64. Gardner, *Sterling-Dollar*, pp. 40-47, 174.

65. Penrose, *Economic Planning for the Peace* (1953), p. 192; Gardner, *Sterling-Dollar*, pp. 18-20.

66. "1. If the U.K. is forced to maintain rigid exchange controls, other countries in the sterling area and in Western Europe will also be obliged to maintain them. Such action will give a pronounced impetus to state control of foreign trade in a large area of the world. A substantial dollar credit to the U.K., therefore, will help to preserve free enterprise, especially in foreign trade." From a memo by the Executive Committee on Economic Foreign Policy of the State Department, September 7, 1945, *FRUS*, 1945, VI, pp. 120-121.

67. By the end of the war, the sterling balances had reached $14-15 billion, while Britain's gold and dollar reserves were in the neighborhood of $2-2.5 billion. Gardner, *Sterling-Dollar*, pp. 324-327. For a description of the dollar pool, see Bell, *The Sterling Area in the Postwar World* (1956), pp. 51-54.

68. Penrose, *Planning*, pp. 87-103; Gardner, *Sterling-Dollar*, pp. 101-109.

69. Kolko makes this point about the need to keep Britain neither too weak nor too strong: Kolko, *Politics*, pp. 283-287. Also Morgenthau notes a role reversal between State and Treasury on the issue of Britain's balances: Blum, *Morgenthau*, III, pp. 123-124, 132-133, 314.

70. Penrose, *Planning*, pp. 106-107; Gardner, *Sterling-Dollar*, pp. 150-153.

71. Gardner describes the opponents and supporters of multilateralism in Britain, *Sterling-Dollar*, pp. 24-35. A good statement of the Left critique of multilateralism is Schumacher, *Export Policy*.

72. This argument was made skillfully by L.S. Amery, a long time defender of the Empire. Amery used full employment arguments to bolster his position. Amery, *The Washington Loan Agreements* (1946).

73. During the war, the City of London was largely closed down because of the extensive economic controls. However, the political influence of these interests was still formidable and was directed largely toward multilateralism. See *The Banker*, 1945-1947.

74. Much of the positive discussion in Britain of the Bretton Woods Agreements centered on the fact that Britain would retain her freedom of action, at least during the transition period. Gardner, *Sterling-Dollar*, pp. 127-129.

75. Rees, *White*, pp. 278-279.

76. Gardner, *Sterling-Dollar*, pp. 181-187. The August cutoff of Lend-Lease had been prefigured by a brief cutoff in May that appears to have been primarily aimed at the Soviet Union. Truman argues that the May cutoff was a mistake, while Kolko sees it as a deliberate ploy. Truman, *Memoirs* (1955-56), vol. I, pp. 227-229, 234; Kolko, *Politics*, pp. 397-398.

77. This is implicit in the memoirs of the Labour Chancellor of the Exchequer, Hugh Dalton: *High Tide and After* (1962), pp. 68-69.

78. *FRUS*, 1945, VI, pp. 79-87, 97-101, 156-157, 188-189; Dalton, *High Tide*, pp. 68-89.

79. Dalton, *High Tide*, p. 85. Because of the important role of the British financial community in causing the run on sterling in 1931, Keynes was not warning simply of an externally caused crisis.

80. Dalton, *High Tide*, p. 85.

81. Keynes' use of such a threat is documented in *FRUS*, 1945, VI, pp. 97-101. His strategy is indicated in Moggridge, "From War to Peace—How Much Overseas Assistance" (1972).

82. Vinson, a conservative Democrat, had little sympathy with many of the views that Morgenthau had tolerated or supported. There was relatively little distance between Vinson's views and Clayton's. Gardner, *Sterling-Dollar*, pp. 193-194.

83. Current account convertibility meant that the British would assure that sterling earned through trade transactions anywhere in the world could be converted to dollars, or other currencies, at a fixed exchange rate. Current account convertibility assumed continuing controls over sterling balances held abroad. Unless otherwise specified, convertibility will refer to current account convertibility.

84. *FRUS*, 1945, VI, pp. 79-87, Dalton, *High Tide*, pp. 68-69; Gardner, *Sterling-Dollar*, p. 204.

85. Gardner, *Sterling-Dollar*, pp. 204-205.

86. The political sensitivity of the sterling balances is suggested by Hirsch, *The Pound Sterling: A Polemic* (1965), pp. 42-43; Polk, *Sterling: Its Meaning in World Finance* (1956), p. 67; Gardner, *Sterling-Dollar*, pp. 169-170.

87. Gardner, *Sterling-Dollar*, pp. 205-206; Dalton, *High Tide*, p. 82-83; Moggridge, "From War to Peace—The Sterling Balances" (1972).

88. Gardner, *Sterling-Dollar*, p. 146.

89. Gardner, *Sterling-Dollar*, pp. 145-152, analyzes the commercial policy negotiations.

Chapter Four. The Marshall Plan and Rearmament

1. The British had made the loan a condition for approval of the Bretton Woods Agreement, so the two agreements were sent to Parliament at the same time. However, December 31, 1945, was the deadline for Britain to accede to the Bretton Woods Agreement. A delay in the vote on the Loan would have severely jeopardized the Bretton Woods institutions. Gardner, *Sterling-Dollar Diplomacy* (1969), pp. 224-236.

2. Gardner, *Sterling-Dollar*, pp. 236-253; Freeland, *The Truman Doctrine and the Origins of McCarthyism* (1972), pp. 61-69.

3. Gardner, *Architects of Illusion* (1970), pp. 128-132; Freeland, *Doctrine*, pp. 67-68.

4. See Radosh, *Prophets on the Right* (1975), pp. 147-195.

5. The Export-Import Bank was a government institution that had been created to finance exports during the depression. It was designed to supplement private financing of exports. In 1945, Congress passed legislation extending its lending authority to $3.5

billion. Much of this capital was used to finance a continuation of aid that had earlier been financed through Lend-Lease. Mikesell, *United States Economic Policy and International Relations* (1952), pp. 207-215. On the decision not to ask for a further increase in lending authority in 1946, see Department of State, *Foreign Relations of the United States,* 1946, I, pp. 1413, 1435.

6. Freeland, *Doctrine,* pp. 55-56. The IBRD was scheduled to begin operations in early 1947.

7. White was already under FBI surveillance in connection with the allegations made against him by Elizabeth Bentley: Rees, *Harry Dexter White,* pp. 380-381. In a sense, however, the investigation into his past was irrelevant in determining White's qualification for the managing directorship of the fund. His public position on the left wing of the New Deal was sufficient to disqualify him in the eyes of Vinson, Byrnes, and Truman.

8. Harrod, *The Life of Keynes* (1971), pp. 709-724; Gardner, *Sterling-Dollar,* pp. 257-268; Horsefield, *The International Monetary Fund 1945-1965* (1969), I, pp. 129-135.

9. Gardner, *Sterling-Dollar,* pp. 269-286.

10. It is an oversimplification to discuss Western Europe as a homogenous unit since there were great variations in the war's impact.

11. Freeland, *Doctrine,* pp. 71-72. In France, the Netherlands, and Italy, total production in 1945 was about half the level attained in the prewar period. Kuznets, *Postwar Economic Growth* (1964), pp. 91-95.

12. In 1947, 61 percent of Western Europe's trade was organized bilaterally, and the extent of state trading is indicated by the fact that in France, between 1948 and 1952, 33 percent of all imports went to government-controlled agencies: Frank, *The European Common Market* (1961), pp. 42, 61. The network of bilateral agreements is described in Patterson and Polk, "The Emerging Pattern of Bilateralism" (1947).

13. Brown, *The United States and the Restoration of World Trade* (1950), p. 2, describes the situation after the war as follows: "Aside from the United States and Canada, and in lesser degree Belgium and a few other countries, almost all the leading participants in international trade were, to say the least, doubtful and reserved about the feasibility or even the desirability of abandoning centralized controls over foreign trade and payments . . . Some countries, like the United Kingdom, saw definite and perhaps permanent advantages in retaining freedom to bargain bilaterally with other countries and to consolidate regional and other special economic arrangements."

14. This is one of the basic themes of Kolko, *The Politics of War* (1968), and Kolko and Kolko, *The Limits of Power* (1972).

15. The political nature of the inflation in France and Italy is indicated in Baum, *The French Economy and the State* (1958), pp. 43-51, and Holbik, *Italy in International Cooperation* (1959), pp. 28-29.

16. Open inflation existed particularly in Italy and France. The Italian cost of living index in 1948 was 55 times the 1938 level: Foa, *Monetary Reconstruction in Italy* (1949), p. 65. In France, the index of retail prices (1938—100) went from 300 at the Liberation to 2000 by 1948: Piatier, "Business Cycles in Post-War France" (1957), p. 108. In countries such as Britain, inflation was suppressed by an elaborate system of price and wage controls, which also included controls over most international transactions: Harris, *The European Recovery Program* (1948), pp. 42-43. Belgium was one of the only Western European countries that had solved the problem of inflation before the Marshall Plan. A currency reform carried out in 1944, while the country was occupied by the Allies, effectively deflated the economy.

17. The danger from the Left diminished considerably when conservative governments came to power in Italy and France in 1947. However, even before then, the Left's lack of a coherent strategic response to Europe's economic crisis weakened it considerably. In retrospect, it seems that a strategy for the gradual socialization of the economy that took advantage of the controls over international transactions might have succeeded in creating a real alternative to liberal capitalism or Eastern European socialism.

18. Some of these intra-European transactions increased Britain's dollar deficit; for example, food for the Germans usually was bought from the United States.

19. Gardner, *Sterling-Dollar,* p. 294. A rough sense of the shift in Europe's accounts with the rest of the world can be derived from the following (figures in billions of dollars):

	1938	1947
Europe's imports	4.2	7.8
Europe's exports	3.1	5.5
Trade balance	−1.1	−2.3
Income from investments	1.1	.6
Income from transportation	.4	.3
Income from other invisibles	—	− .5
Balance on goods and services	.4	−1.9

Note that this includes all of Europe, not just Western Europe, and its trade with all of the rest of the world, except the United States. United Nations, Department of Economic Affairs, *Economic Survey of Europe in 1948* (1949), p. 112.

20. U.S. trade in goods with the countries of Western Europe that were recipients of Marshall Plan aid developed as follows (figures in millions of dollars)

Year	U.S. Exports to Marshall Plan Countries	U.S. Imports from Marshall Plan Countries
1946	4,252	767
1947	5,728	843
1948	4,733	1,212
1949	4,272	1,026

United States, *Report to the President on Foreign Economic Policies* (1950), pp. 105-106.

21. This kind of bilateral arrangement was most tempting and most probable in the case of Britain and the Sterling Area. However, it might have been possible to negotiate an agreement under which all the Western European countries would pool access to their colonies and former colonies in an extended bilateral system.

22. Bilateralism would be an effective obstacle to U.S. investment abroad because there would be no way to assure that profits from investments in such areas could be repatriated.

23. A bilateral trade agreement between countries A and B might be based on the assumption that a certain quantity of a key commodity would be available for export to Country A. However, if Country B were also heavily involved in multilateral trade, all of its exportable supplies of that commodity might well be purchased on the free market. The decision as to which purchasers should be given priority raises policy difficulties that might best be resolved by orienting policy in either a bilateral or a multilateral direction.

24. "The danger facing the International Trade Organization is not Russia's failure to participate in it, but rather her increasing tendency to extend her state-trading and joint-enterprise system over countries with more or less mixed economies. Her influence over the trade of Europe is not negligible." Letiche, *Reciprocal Trade Agreements in the World Economy* (1948), pp. 55-56. "What if the Soviet Government should negotiate economic collaboration agreements with the countries of Western Europe or of this hemisphere of the kind that it has with Hungary and Rumania?" Feis, "The Conflict over Trade Ideologies" (1947), p. 227.

25. U.S. Exports of Goods and Services by Quarters 1946-49 (in millions of $):

	Goods and Services			
	Exports	Imports	Export Surplus	U.S. Gov't. Grants & Loans
1946				
I	3338	1677	1661	1154
II	3897	1651	2246	1415
III	3784	1764	2020	1542
IV	3722	1871	1851	866
Total	14741	6963	7778	4977

25. U.S. Exports Continued

Goods and Services

	Exports	Imports	Export Surplus	U.S. Gov't. Grants & Loans
1947				
I	4800	1988	2812	1316
II	5628	2103	3525	2011
III	4830	1986	2844	1731
IV	4898	2212	2686	784
Total	19796	8289	11507	5842
1948				
I	4484	2492	1992	1343
II	4322	2488	1834	959
III	4029	2735	1294	1132
IV	4257	2641	1616	1634
Total	17092	10356	6736	5068
1949				
I	4323	2550	1773	1676
II	4442	2418	2024	1661
III	3685	2346	1339	1469
IV	3506	2401	1105	1141
Total	15956	9715	6241	5947

Survey of Current Business, June 1950. See also Blyth, *American Business Cycles 1945-50* (1969), pp. 133-136.

26. *FRUS,* 1947, III, pp. 210-211.

27. *FRUS,* 1947, III, pp. 202-219. "Danger to American plans lay in permitting Europe to recover by itself, and in so doing develop bilateral trade agreements, exchange controls, and regional blocs as protection. Then when the backed up demand of the domestic market was filled, the United States would turn to sell abroad only to find all markets closed to American goods." Hickman, "Genesis of the European Recovery Program" (1949), p. 138.

28. William Clayton wrote that "The Marshall Plan was like one of those inventions that several people came up with at the same time." Dobney, ed., *Selected Papers of Will Clayton* (1971), p. 206.

29. Freeland, *Doctrine,* p. 89. The account of the Truman Doctrine here relies heavily on Freeland, *Doctrine,* pp. 70-114.

30. Acheson also noted in this speech, "When the process of reconversion at home is completed, we are going to find ourselves far more dependent upon exports than before the war to maintain levels of business activity to which our economy has become accustomed." Quoted in American Assembly, *United States–Western Europe Relationships* (1951), p. 35.

31. Foa, *Reconstruction,* pp. 104-120; Price, *The Marshall Plan and Its Meaning* (1955), pp. 274-277.

32. This was the maximum authorized under U.S. trade legislation but, given the high levels of U.S. tariffs, a halving of the tariff often left a still formidable obstacle to foreign products.

33. Gardner, *Sterling-Dollar,* pp. 348-361.

34. In the final week of the convertibility experiment, Britain lost dollars at an annual rate of $11 billion. Hinshaw, *Toward European Convertibility* (1958), p. 11; Gardner, *Sterling-Dollar,* pp. 306-325.

35. Britain's balance of payments deficit in 1947 was 545 million pounds: Gardner, *Sterling-Dollar,* p. 207. Distrust of the Labour government's domestic economic policies and the strain on the British payments balance of the rising prices of dollar goods also played a role in the failure of convertibility.

36. Agreements were reached between Britain and India, Pakistan, Iraq, and Ceylon on the rate at which the sterling balances could be drawn down, but these agreements were not stringent enough to ease the burden of the balances. Bell, *The Sterling Area in the Postwar World* (1956), pp. 23-24.

37. There were always significant strains in the U.S.-British relationship, but Britain's support for U.S. anti-Soviet policies was of decisive importance. See Manderson-Jones, *The Special Relationship* (1972).

38. Treating Western Europe as a region represented a significant shift in U.S. foreign policy away from strict multilateralism. During the war, State Department policy makers had discussed plans for a Western European region, but these proposals were rejected in favor of the multilateral, universal approach of the United Nations and International Trade Organization. Schmitt, *The Path to European Union* (1962), pp. 13-15.

39. Freeland, *Doctrine*, pp. 246-287; Price, *Marshall Plan*, pp. 49-69.

40. "There was every prospect that without further large-scale American aid an economic crisis would develop in Europe that would accentuate every form of economic nationalism, produce social upheavals, and strengthen extreme political movements in many countries. Such a crisis could hardly fail to bring with it ever stricter controls over trade and foreign exchange. The direction of European economic policy would, in such an event, have become more and more incompatible with the achievement of the long-range objectives of American foreign economic policy." Brown, *Restoration*, p. 306. Clayton wrote to Acheson in May 1947 that what Europe could afford to import at that point "represents an absolute minimum standard of living. If it should be lowered, there will be revolution." *FRUS*, 1947, III, p. 230.

41. Between 1947 and 1950, U.S. aid financed one-quarter of Western Europe's total imports and two-thirds of merchandise imports from the dollar area. OEEC, *Ninth Report* (1958), p. 33.

42. The European Recovery Program was the official name of the Marshall Plan. Western Europe's trade with Eastern Europe peaked in 1948-49 and then declined. This was partly a result of U.S. pressures on Western Europe to avoid trade with the East in certain commodities considered to be strategic. Adler-Karlsson, *Western Economic Warfare 1947-1967* (1968), pp. 158-178.

43. Manderson-Jones, *Relationship*, pp. 51-57.

44. Brown and Opie, *American Foreign Assistance* (1953), pp. 177-179, 235-246.

45. The intervention in the European labor movement is described in Radosh, *American Labor and United States Foreign Policy* (1969), pp. 310-347. The extent of U.S. influence in Western European politics is hinted at in Price, *Marshall Plan*, especially pp. 264-286.

46. Scammell, *International Monetary Policy* (1961), pp. 279-285.

47. Price, *Marshall Plan*, pp. 313-320. The Secretary of the Treasury testified before the Senate in January 1948 as follows: "We have a direct interest in assuring that the aid we provide to Europe makes a maximum contribution to the reduction of inflationary pressures and the restoration of stability. To this end we propose that each participating country deposit in a special account the local currency equivalent . . . of the goods supplied through grants in aid." Cited in *Report of Activities* of the National Advisory Council on International and Monetary Financial Problems, August 4, 1948.

48. "The ECA, by its stand, had given needed support to a realistic group within the French government who themselves wished to carry out the formidable measures essential to bringing the [inflationary] crisis under control. In effect, the ECA helped to take the 'heat' off those leaders at a time of great political difficulty." Price, *Marshall Plan*, p. 105. See also Luthy, *France Against Herself* (1955), pp. 143-157. The Italian deflation is described in Foa, *Reconstruction*, pp. 104-113; Holbik, *Italy*, pp. 26-27. All of these accounts stress the critical role of bankers in the deflationary policies. The German deflation was carried out by means of the 1948 currency reform, described in Wallich, *Mainsprings of the German Revival* (1955), pp. 68-73. Wallich notes that a currency reform of such severity could not have been put through by a parliamentary government.

49. Radosh, *American Labor,* pp. 310-347. The Marshall Plan did mean increased pressure on the working class of Western Europe; benefits for the working class were to be deferred until recovery had proceeded further. Arkes, *Bureaucracy, The Marshall Plan, and the National Interest* (1972), pp. 318-319.

50. The centrality of industrial investment is stressed by Price, *Marshall Plan,* p. 98: "Welfare needs—in residential housing, schools, and hospitals—though pressing, were widely deferred in favor of more strictly productive investments . . ." Cohen, *Modern Capitalist Planning: The French Model* (1969), pp. 104-108, notes that in France investment for housing was generally sacrificed for industrial investments.

51. Brown and Opie, *Assistance,* pp. 239-242.

52. Brown and Opie, *Assistance,* pp. 236-238.

53. This dilemma is noted in Foa, *Reconstruction,* p. 126: "For if deflationary policies are permanently clamped down upon the various national economies, recovery becomes a practical impossibility even when the actual underlying conditions are favorable to it."

54. But Cohen's account indicates that this tension continued in France: *Planning,* pp. 91-103.

55. The difficulties that the Western Europeans encountered in their efforts to agree on a distribution of U.S. aid money suggests that the far more demanding coordination required for coordination of investment decisions was beyond their reach. At a time when most governments were struggling desperately to avoid social turmoil or political chaos, it was difficult to pursue international planning. Van Der Beugel, *From Marshall Aid to Atlantic Partnership* (1966), pp. 139-170.

56. OEEC, *Second Report* (1950), especially pp. 247-251, provides a pessimistic analysis of Europe's dollar needs after the Marshall Plan.

57. Vatter, *The U.S. Economy in the 1950's* (1963), pp. 66-68; Blyth, *Business Cycles,* pp. 120-124, 134-136.

58. See *Business Week,* 1949-1950, especially March 4, 1950, pp. 19-20. In this article, *Business Week* points out that productivity increases mean that the economy has to expand very fast to reduce unemployment. Normal levels of prosperity will likely mean politically unacceptable levels of unemployment.

59. Truman's Council of Economic Advisers proposed an economic expansion bill in July 1949 that included a $15 billion reserve fund for public works and a proposal for government investment in new capacity for basic industrial commodities: *Fortune,* May 1950, pp. 71-74. While there were indications of an economic upturn in early 1950, we have no way of knowing whether that upturn would have continued or petered out. The start of the Korean War in June 1950 assured that the economy would move toward full employment.

60. *Business Week,* August 27, 1949, p. 79; Balogh, *The Dollar Crisis* (1949), p. 117.

61. Bell, *Sterling,* pp. 55-61.

62. The weakness of the pound in 1949 could not be attributed entirely to sterling balances; the internal economy had its problems as well. The Labour government had resisted American pressure to deflate the economy, and the continuation of full employment policies must have created problems for foreign trade in a period when most European countries were deflating their economies drastically. The relaxation of some internal controls also made possible an unintended jump in British imports during 1949 and some diversion of exports to satisfy domestic demand. Finally, the absence of controls over the export of capital to the Sterling Area made possible significant flights of capital in the period from 1946 on. These flows were particularly strong in times of crisis as investors attempted to hedge against a devaluation. Balogh, *Dollar,* pp. 114-117; Bell, *Sterling,* pp. 373-375.

63. *Business Week,* July 9, 1949, p. 101; Bell, *Sterling,* p. 60; *Business Week,* July 16, 1949, p. 101; Van Der Beugel, *Marshall Aid,* pp. 162-165.

64. Van Der Beugel, *Marshall Aid,* pp. 157-165.

65. *Business Week,* July 16, 1949, p. 98; August 20, 1949, p. 100; August 27, 1949, pp. 19-20; January 28, 1950, p. 15; February 4, 1950, p. 15; March 4, 1950, p. 119.

66. The theory behind the devaluations is indicated in the following: "There was

serious danger that unless such action [devaluations] were taken, the marked disparities in cost-price structures existing between the soft-currency-area countries and the dollar-area countries on the one hand, and among the soft-currency-area countries themselves on the other, would tend to become set, the strains of altered creditor-debtor relationships increasingly burdensome, and the distortions of international trade and the disequilibria in European balances of payments increasingly intractable." *Report of Activities* of the National Advisory Council on International Monetary and Financial Problems, January 20, 1950. That this was predominantly a Treasury policy is indicated in *Business Week*, July 2, 1949, p. 67; July 9, 1949, pp. 99-100; July 16, 1949, p. 97. But it probably would not have succeeded in its aims without support from the Marshall Plan Administration: see *FRUS*, 1949, IV, pp. 377-383, 391-394, 397-399.

    67. See *Report* of the NACIMFP, July 5, 1949.

    68. Horsefield, *Fund*, I, p. 235.

    69. Manderson-Jones, *Relationship*, pp. 58-59; *Business Week*, July 16, 1949, p. 97.

    70. *Business Week*, August 6, 1949, p. 83.

    71. *Business Week*, October 8, 1949, p. 103.

    72. Tew, *International Monetary Co-operation 1945-1965* (1965), pp. 169-170.

    73. *Business Week*, September 17, 1949, pp. 19-20.

    74. Quoted in Van Der Beugel, *Marshall Aid*, p. 183.

    75. This theory was developed in an ECA document cited by Price, *Marshall Plan*, pp. 120-121.

    76. Scammell, *Policy*, p. 277.

    77. The EPU is described by Robert Triffin, its architect, in *Europe and the Money Muddle* (1957), pp. 161-179, 199-208.

    78. Manderson-Jones, *Relationship*, pp. 46-51.

    79. Manderson-Jones, *Relationship*, pp. 46-47.

    80. *Business Week*, July 23, 1949, p. 79.

    81. Manderson-Jones, *Relationship*, pp. 61-63; Kennan, *Memoirs 1925-1950* (1967), p. 458.

    82. Dobney, *Clayton*, pp. 258-262. It should also be noted that the idea of the Atlantic Union of Democracies was a way of making the U.S. commitment to the NATO alliance more palatable to the U.S. public, and, as such, the idea of some kind of Atlantic Community has had considerable influence.

    83. Arkes, *Bureaucracy*, pp. 195-196. *Business Week*, September 17, 1949, pp. 19-20; September 24, 1949, p. 116.

    84. The decision to embark on the H-bomb project was complicated by the fear that the United States would be blamed for escalating the arms race.

    85. Acheson, *Present at the Creation* (1969), pp. 451-457; Hammond, "NSC-68: Prologue to Rearmament" (1962), pp. 287-297.

    86. Schilling. "The Politics of National Defense: Fiscal 1950" (1962), especially pp. 103-114, 141-164; Acheson, *Creation*, pp. 486-488.

    87. Hammond, "NSC-68," pp. 304-307; Acheson, *Creation*, pp. 488-492; Huntington, *The Common Defense* (1961), pp. 47-64.

    88. Huntington, *Defense*, pp. 49-50; Hammond, "NSC-68," pp. 318-321. Hammond also discusses the debates within the State Department over the nature of the Soviet threat, in which Kennan argued that the military threat was by no means as apocalyptic as "NSC-68" suggested. See pp. 312-313.

    89. This logic is explained in Bell, *Negotiation from Strength* (1963), pp. 3-30.

    90. NSC-68 was finally declassified during 1975. It includes passages that indicate that domestic economic considerations played a role in shaping the rearmament decision. This is consistent with Acheson's continuing sensitivity to the problems of the domestic economy. However, it seems logical that by the time of NSC-68, Acheson and his aides would have deliberately avoided closely linking rearmament to domestic employment needs, so as to avoid giving credence to the Marxist charge that capitalism requires war or armament spending for prosperity.

    91. Dean Acheson wrote in a memo to Truman in early 1950: "The time is rapidly approaching when the Government and the people of the United States must make critical and far-reaching decisions of policy affecting our economic relationships with the

rest of the world. . . . It is expected that unless vigorous steps are taken, the reduction and eventual termination of extraordinary foreign assistance in accordance with present plans will create economic problems at home and abroad of increasing severity. If this is allowed to happen, United States exports, including the key commodities on which our most efficient agricultural and manufacturing industries are heavily dependent, will be sharply reduced with serious repercussions on our domestic economy . . . as ERP is reduced, and after its termination in 1952, how can Europe and other areas of the world obtain the dollars necessary to pay for a high level of United States exports, which is essential both to their own basic needs and to the well-being of the United States economy? . . ." Cited in Kolko and Kolko, *Limits*, pp. 471-472. Shortly thereafter, a presidential commission reported: "The impact of United States rearmament will be to enlarge greatly the available markets for European exports and the ability to earn dollars both in the U.S. and in third areas. Adequate markets are in prospect for some time and this removes at least temporarily what was, prior to the decision to accelerate rearmament, the major threat to achieving European self-support." United States, *Foreign Economic Policies*, p. 35.

92. While this intention was not stated explicitly, the United States did attempt to integrate military procurement among NATO members. This would have the effect of making Western Europe dependent on the United States for certain kinds of military goods. A good statement of the political dimension of NATO, from the U.S. point of view, is Fox and Fox, *NATO and the Range of American Choice* (1967), pp. 34-46.

93. At the time that news of NSC-68 began leaking to the press, *Business Week* wrote as follows: "Don't be surprised if the Administration resorts to phony war crises to get its way in Congress on foreign policy legislation. A real enough crisis exists. But it isn't a war crisis now. And apparently the crisis has sunk in in only a few high places. Witness the House vote, last week, to ban aid to Britain unless Ireland is unified. Scare talk may first be drummed up over Indo-China." April 8, 1950, p. 112.

94. Huntington, *Defense*, p. 55.

95. On the Defense Production Act, see Director of Office of Defense Mobilization, *Report to the President* (1953).

96. There were fears that the military expansion of the economy would create new problems of excess capacity: National Industrial Conference Board, *Post Defense Outlook* (1952), especially pp. 19-26. The Eisenhower administration found out very quickly that cutbacks in the level of defense spending led to serious recession.

Chapter Five. Toward European Convertibility

1. The supply of international liquidity is the sum of international assets held in national reserves and readily available credits in international currencies.

2. Horsefield, *The International Monetary Fund 1945-1965* (1969), I, p. 189. This discussion draws on chs. 8 and 9 of Horsefield, *Fund*, I.

3. Horsefield, *Fund*, II, p. 462.

4. Horsefield, *Fund*, II, pp. 191-194; *The Banker*, May 1954, p. 279.

5. Horsefield, *Fund*, I, pp. 287-288; the first report was United Nations, Department of Economic Affairs, *National and International Measures for Full Employment* (1949).

6. Horsefield, *Fund*, I, pp. 287-288; the first report was United Nations, Department of Economic Affairs, *Measures for International Economic Stability* (1951).

7. Horsefield, *Fund*, I, pp. 334-335; Bernstein, "The Evolution of the IMF" (1972), pp. 61-62.

8. The advantages of making access to the fund's resources conditional was graphically illustrated in 1956 when the United States made British withdrawal from Suez a condition for British drawings on the fund. See Macmillan, *Riding the Storm 1956-1959* (1971), pp. 164-167. For the fund's relation to underdeveloped countries, see Hayter, *Aid as Imperialism* (1972), and Payer, *The Debt Trap* (1974).

9. Lewis, *The United States and Foreign Investment Problems* (1948), pp. 146-150.

10. These investment incentives are discussed in Mikesell, ed., *United States Private and Government Investment Abroad* (1962), especially ch. viii.

11. Brown and Opie, *American Foreign Assistance* (1953), pp. 455-465, 483. Transfers of goods and services under U.S. military grant programs changed as follows (in millions of dollars):

Year	Aid	Year	Aid	Year	Aid
1949	211	1953	4176	1957	2418
1950	520	1954	3362	1958	2286
1951	1439	1955	2588	1959	1974
1952	2582	1956	2567		

Survey of Current Business, October 1972. This represents only a part of U.S. military assistance, because other military aid was not tied to the export of goods and services.

12. Off-shore procurement developed as follows (in millions of dollars):

Year	Amount	Year	Amount
1953	326	1956	515
1954	595	1957	371
1955	640	1958	212

International Economic Policy Association, *The United States Balance of Payments* (1966), p. 102. The usefulness of these dollar flows in strengthening the European economies is noted in Elliot et al., *The Political Economy of American Foreign Policy* (1955), p. 313.

13. *Survey of Current Business,* October 1972. Note that these figures include the off-shore procurement dollars but not the transfers of goods and services.

14. See Department of State, *Foreign Relations of the United States,* 1949, IV, pp. 469-472, 489-490.

15. For fears of German neutralism, see *Business Week,* March 10, 1951, pp. 125-129. In 1955 a prestigious foreign policy study said, "The political problem is rather that the frustration of German exports would tend to lead important business and other groups in West Germany to support a neutralist or even an anti-Western foreign policy in the illusory hope of buying with political concessions greater market opportunities in Soviet Europe": Elliot, *Political Economy,* p. 125.

16. "This Germany is almost in her entirety created and maintained by the occupation and by the East-West conflict. . . . There is no doubt that the present picture has little resemblance to the actual social and political forces." Marcuse, "Antidemocratic Popular Movements" (1951), p. 112.

17. On the Social Democrats, see Edinger, *Kurt Schumacher* (1965), pp. 190-258; Hanrieder, *The Stable Crisis* (1970), pp. 134-136; the orientation of the business community is discussed in Feld, *Reunification and West German-Soviet Relations* (1963), pp. 49-50.

18. The seriousness with which U.S. policy-makers looked at the German and European situation in 1949 is indicated in *FRUS,* 1949, VI, especially pp. 426-429, 434-435, 469-472, 485-486, 489-490. Rearmament as a solution to the problem of Germany is implicit in some of these passages, even though the United States was still denying its intentions to rearm Germany at this time.

19. For the history of the EDC, see Van Der Beugel, *From Marshall Aid to Atlantic Partnership* (1966), pp. 248-301. Adenauer's gains from the rearmament policy are discussed in Hanrieder, *Crisis,* p. 137. American eagerness to include West Germany within the NATO alliance was closely linked to the strong Soviet drive in this period for a negotiated settlement of the German question. It is generally acknowledged that the Russians were willing to negotiate a settlement of the German question that would have involved the neutralization of Germany. The United States was unwilling to accept this alternative because it feared that a neutral Germany would be pulled toward the East. Hinterhoff, *Disengagement* (1959), pp. 155-156; Richardson, *Germany and the Atlantic Alliance* (1966), pp. 24-27.

20. Goold-Adams, *John Foster Dulles* (1962), p. 148. The founding of the Western European Union is treated in Manderson-Jones, *The Special Relationship* (1972), ch. 7. Even after the approval of the WEU, there were fears that popular hostility to rearmament within West Germany would force the German government to abandon rearmament and the Western alliance in favor of reunification. Craig, "NATO and the New German Army" (1955).

21. Vernon, *America's Foreign Trade Policy and the GATT:* (1954); Vernon, *Trade Policy in Crisis* (1958); Camps, "Trade Policy and American Leadership" (1957). Tariff levels in the United States and the EEC, as of the early 1960s, are analyzed in Balassa, *Trade Liberalization Among Industrial Countries* (1967), especially p. 56.

22. Cited in American Assembly, *United States–Western Europe Relationships* (1951), p. 1. See pp. 1-11.

23. American Assembly, *U.S.–Western Europe,* p. 9.

24. On British and French rearmament and its consequences, see Bartlett, *The Long Retreat* (1972), pp. 60-61; Mitchell, *Crisis in Britain 1951* (1963); Osgood, *NATO: Entangling Alliance* (1962), pp. 81-83; Flamant and Singer-Kerel, *Modern Economic Crises and Recessions* (1970), pp. 88-89; Brookings Institution, *Rearmament and Anglo-American Economic Relations* (1952), pp. 26-43.

25. The "New Look," introduced by the Eisenhower administration in 1953, reduced U.S. defense spending and led to a relaxation of the pressure on Britain and France to maintain high levels of defense spending: Osgood, *NATO,* pp. 83-84. The new Conservative government in Britain had, however, already cut back Labour's ambitious rearmament plan to avert a more severe sterling crisis: Bartlett, *Retreat,* pp. 78-80.

26. Bartlett, *Retreat,* pp. 106, 268-269; Hirsch, *The Pound Sterling: A Polemic* (1965), pp. 44-45. Rearmament stimulated demand for capital goods that Germany could provide. Britain was unable to take advantage of that demand because its factories were required to turn out military hardware. Hence, the rearmament had very different consequences for the trade of the two nations.

27. Edgar Furniss made the following judgment of U.S. military aid to Europe in the 1950s: "The verdict on the accomplishments of military aid to Europe must then be that it helped the French to lose in Indochina and Algeria, helped the British and French to lose in Suez, provided a continuous and ultimately unacceptable drag on European economies, all for the purpose of introducing and maintaining direct American military and economic interest in the area." Furniss, "Some Perspectives on American Military Assistance" (1957), p. 35.

28. For more extensive analysis of trade and capital flows, see Chapter 6 below. The argument about the negative effect of military Keynesianism on the U.S. economy draws on Melman, *Our Depleted Society* (1965) and *The Permanent War Economy* (1974).

29. This danger was commented on throughout the 1950s, see for example, Brookings, *Anglo-American,* p. 44; Vernon, "Economic Aspects of the Atlantic Community" (1957), pp. 61-64.

30. The extent of U.S. influence over the EPU is discussed in Hinshaw, *Toward European Convertibility* (1958), pp. 13-14. The Treasury Department had been opposed to the European Payments Union on the grounds that it might substitute regional settlement for multilateral settlement: Manderson-Jones, *Relationship,* pp. 46-47.

31. Diebold, *Trade and Payments in Western Europe* (1952), pp. 158-171.

32. On the ECSC, see Diebold, *The Schuman Plan* (1959). It has been suggested that William Clayton was the real architect of the Coal and Steel Community: Beloff, *The United States and the Unity of Europe* (1963), pp. 55-57.

33. "Probably the principal reason for the strong and continuing American support for the 'deep' integration of the Six was the judgment that it offered the best available answer to the problems posed by a truncated but dynamic Germany. The integration of Western Germany with its neighbors made the elimination of discriminatory controls and rearmament easier for its European allies, particularly France, to accept; . . . it offered to the Germans, in the short to medium term at least, a practical and emotional alternative to reunification. . . ." Camps, *European Unification in the Sixties* (1966), p. 237.

34. Support for Little Europe provided a means to reconcile the short-term interest in more U.S. exports with the long-term interests associated with European integration as a means of overcoming the dollar gap.

35. Beloff, *Unity,* pp. 33-35, 72-75, 79-80; Van Der Beugel, *Marshall Aid,* pp. 318-319.

36. Manderson-Jones, *Relationship,* pp. 82-96.

37. Zurcher, *The Struggle to Unite Europe 1940-1958* (1958), pp. 96-109.

38. Zurcher, *Struggle*, pp. 131-132; Van Der Beugel, *Marshall Aid*, pp. 318-319.

39. The General Agreement on Tariffs and Trade was the international structure left over after the ITO failed to come into existence. It provided a forum for tariff negotiations and some ground rules, but it lacked the organizational strength that the ITO would have had. For a full account of GATT, see Curzon, *Multilateral Commercial Diplomacy* (1965).

40. Patterson, *Discrimination in International Trade* (1966), pp. 105-110. There had been similar discussions of preferential trade agreements encompassing all of Western Europe around 1950, but nothing came of them, probably because of U.S. opposition. Diebold, *Payments*, pp. 230-241.

41. Kitzinger, *The Politics and Economics of European Integration* (1963), pp. 17-20; Patterson, *Discrimination*, pp. 108-110; OEEC, *10th Annual Report*, p. 117.

42. The British proposal for a free trade area is described in Camps, *Britain and the European Community 1955-1963* (1964), pp. 130-172.

43. Camps describes how reluctant the French were to accept the liberalized trade of a common market: *Community*, pp. 28-35. Some of the loopholes in the Treaty of Rome are described in Kravis, *Domestic Interests and International Obligations* (1963), pp. 303-306. The appeal of the British plans to the Erhard wing of the Christian Democrats is noted in Camps, *Community*, p. 102.

44. The Adenauer-De Gaulle understanding is discussed in Grosser, *French Foreign Policy Under De Gaulle* 1967), p. 66; *Business Week*, October 6. 1958, pp. 103-108.

45. Camps, *Community*, pp. 195-238.

46. Camps, *Community*, p. 260.

47. Camps had warned in 1956 of the danger that EEC might become a protected high-cost area or a neutralist political force. It was because of these dangers, that she favored a sympathetic U.S. response to the British proposal for a free trade area. Camps, "The European Common Market and American Policy" (1956).

48. Wallich, *Mainsprings of the German Revival* (1955), pp. 235-240; Erhard, *Germany's Comeback in the World Market* (1954), pp. 29-33.

49. OEEC, *Report by the Secretary General* (1959), pp. 29-33.

50. The independent sterling area in the 1950s included Australia, New Zealand, India, Ceylon, Pakistan, Burma, Eire, Iceland, Iraq, Jordan, Libya, and South Africa: Tew, *International Monetary Co-operation 1945-1965* (1965), p. 135.

51. Krause, "British Trade Performance" (1968), pp. 201-222.

52. "Even in the first eight post-war years, British investment in the sterling area amounted to some £800 million in all. And from 1952 onwards, the rate of flow increased steadily." Strange, *Sterling and British Policy* (1971), p. 66.

53. See Strange, *Sterling*, ch. 6. This section draws heavily on her analysis.

54. The lack of understanding of the distinction between the reserve role and the transaction role of the pound is noted by Strange, *Sterling*, pp. 202-203. The connection between the reserve role and the transaction role of an international currency has been discussed explicitly in the case of the dollar; see, for example, Roosa and Hirsch, *Reserves, Reserve Currencies, and Vehicle Currencies: An Argument* (1966).

55. The discussions of a sterling float are recounted in Birkenhead, *The Prof in Two Worlds* (1961), pp. 283-294. The steps toward the elimination of controls are discussed in Tew, *Co-operation*, pp. 138-141; Rees, *Britain and the Postwar European Payments Systems* (1963), pp. 153-161.

56. Hinshaw, *Convertibility*, pp. 26-31.

57. *The Banker*, March 1958, pp. 143-148.

58. Furniss, *France, Troubled Ally* (1960), pp. 406-417.

59. This was not yet the final step toward convertibility. It was not until 1961 that the Europeans finally accepted the provisions of Article VIII of the Fund Agreements, meaning that they had eliminated almost all restrictions on current payments and transfers and their currencies could now be used for repayment of drawings on the Fund. Horsefield, *Fund*, II, pp. 280-291. Nevertheless, the 1958 decision was the major turning point.

60. While there is no evidence of a formal quid pro quo, the timing of the two events suggests a connection. But the U.S. shift on expansion of the fund also had an element of self-interest; an expanded fund could provide resources to defend the dollar if the U.S. deficit continued: Kenen, *Giant Among Nations* (1960), pp. 94-95.

61. This tendency for developed nations to hold currency reserves largely in gold was strengthened by the experience of the Netherlands and other countries that suffered major losses from the devaluation of the pound in 1931. Rolfe and Burtle, *The Great Wheel* (1975), pp. 33-34. The disadvantage of holding reserves in gold is that interest can be earned on holdings in reserve currencies.

62. Western Europe's gold and dollar holdings changed as follows:

Changes in Gold and Total Reserve Holdings
(in millions of $)

	France	*W. Germany*	*U.K.*	*All OEEC Countries*
1950: Total Reserves	791	274	3443	10,050
Gold	672	—	2900	6,900
1959: Total Reserves	1253	4636	3175	19,600
Gold	812	2768	2800	13,150

OEEC, *Statistical Bulletin*, July 1960. It can be assumed that the difference between gold and total reserves is almost entirely made up of dollar holdings.

63. The absence of effective international institutions that could be used to shape the EEC's evolution was noted by Vernon, "Economic Aspects" (1957), pp. 62-64.

Chapter Six. The Roots of the U.S. Deficit

1. Hirsch, *Money International* (1969), pp. 37-46, 310-318, discusses some of these problems of balance-of-payments measures. See also United States Bureau of the Budget, *The Balance of Payments Statistics of the United States, A Review and Appraisal* (1965).

2. An analysis of United States balance of payments data runs up against two problems: the accuracy of the data and the relative arbitrariness of some of the categories used by those who compile the data. Time series are particularly problematic because of the changes in the assumptions of the compilers and changes in the quality of the reports from which the data is derived. These problems seem particularly troublesome for detailed econometric analyses of changes in different balance of payments items. However, for our purposes—getting a sense of the sources of the U.S. deficit—the existing data is sufficient, so long as one maintains a healthy skepticism. For a sense of the complexity of developing balance-of-payments data, see the June issue of the *Survey of Current Business*, where the annual changes in the assumptions and techniques of analysis are reported.

3. For a discussion of the limited possibilities for further defense savings in the post-Vietnam era, see Hunter, "U.S. Defense Commitments in Europe and Asia During the 1970's" (1971).

4. The offset agreements were negotiated between the United States and Germany, the country where the largest number of U.S. troops were stationed and the country best able to pay the costs of those troops. The offsets for 1961-66 involved a German agreement to buy U.S. military equipment in the amount of the foreign exchange costs of maintaining U.S. troops in Germany. The offsets for 1967-69 included more military purchases, purchases by the Germans of medium-term U.S. government securities, and an agreement by Germany not to convert its dollar holdings into gold. In 1971 the Germans agreed to buy long-term U.S. government securities below the market rate of interest as part of the offset. Newhouse et al., *U.S. Troops in Europe* (1971), pp. 130-131.

5. The foreign military sales listed in Tables 6-A, Column 2, are only a portion of overall U.S. arms sales.

6. The amount of new grants and loans, minus the aid money spent in the United States and the repayment of earlier loans, gives only an approximation of the balance-of-payments effects of the aid program. A more precise account would require subtracting from the total aid outflow the aid money spent on services in the United States and

used for interest payments on earlier loans. When this calculation is made, it appears that the aid programs have either a negligible negative effect or a slightly positive effect on the balance of payments. See *SCB*, June 1975, Table 5—Major U.S. Government Transactions.

7. See, for example, Cooper, "The Competitive Position of the United States" (1961).

8. Wilkins, *The Emergence of Multinational Enterprise* (1970), describes this pattern.

9. The connection between Federal tax policies and direct investment flows is discussed in Kindleberger, *American Business Abroad* (1969), pp. 45-49; Barnet and Muller, *Global Reach* (1974), pp. 279-281.

10. While some studies have minimized the importance of tariffs in stimulating direct investment (Balassa, *Trade Liberalization Among Industrial Countries* [1967], pp. 126-128), there is general recognition that the combination of high tariffs and a large internal market in the EEC acted as a magnet for U.S. direct investment. See Kindleberger, *Business*, pp. 25-27.

11. This is the argument advanced by Melman, *Our Depleted Society* (1965) and *The Permanent War Economy* (1974). See also Holloman, "Technology in the U.S.: Issues for the 1970's" (1972).

12. A sense of the commodity composition of government-financed exports can be derived from the following table:

	Total Value in Dollars	Aid Financed Exports as Percent of Total Exports
All Commodities	1140	4.3
Machinery and equipment	333	5.3
Iron and steel mill products	168	24.4
Chemicals	112	5.5
Motor vehicles	91	4.6
Fertilizer	70	30.4
Nonferrous metals	72	11.5
Rubber and rubber products	33	9.6
Petroleum and products	36	7.5
Basic textiles	31	5.4
Railroad equipment	43	29.5

This data is for Agency for International Development-financed exports for 1965. It does not include those goods exported under P.L. 480 (agricultural exports) or those financed by the Export-Import Bank (which tend to be jet planes and capital goods). From Hyson and Strout, "Impact of Foreign Aid on U.S. Exports" (1965), p. 71.

13. Geiger, "A Note on U.S. Comparative Advantages" (1971); Boretsky, "Trends in U.S. Technology: A Political Economist's View" (1975).

14. The distinction between capital goods and consumer goods is only approximate, especially when it comes to the rate at which branch planting has occurred. Note also that this account tends to minimize the influence of the Vietnam War on the trade balance. I have done this in order to focus on the long-term factors involved. For an account that stresses the impact of the Vietnam War, see Ackerman and MacEwan, "Inflation, Recession and Crisis" (1972).

15. U.S. firms are estimated to have accumulated an overseas debt of $15 billion during the period of the direct investment controls. *Wall Street Journal*, January 30, 1974.

16. International Economic Policy Association, *The United States Balance of Payments: From Crisis to Controversy* (1972), and *The United States Balance of Payments: An Appraisal of U.S. Economic Strategy* (1966).

17. To realize a part of these profits, the oil companies had to invest heavily in refining and marketing capacity in Western Europe.

18. Book value refers to the value of the investment as it is carried on the books of the company. Generally, book values tend to underestimate the actual market value of

the investment. These computations are derived from IEPA, *Strategy*, pp. 171-174.

19. Calleo and Rowland, *America and the World Political Economy* (1973), p. 167.

20. Calleo and Rowland, *America*, p. 180.

21. Barnet and Muller, *Global Reach*, especially pp. 295-306.

22. A classic statement of this view is Polk et al., *United States Production Abroad and the Balance of Payments* (1966).

23. Foster, "Impact of Direct Investment Abroad by United States Multinational Companies on the Balance of Payments" (1972), p. 174.

24. However, the exchange rate realignments since 1971 have had some effect on the relative profitability of investment in the United States as compared to investment in Western Europe and Japan.

25. IEPA, *Strategy*, pp. 86-89.

26. This is the argument of Lary, *Problems of the United States as World Trader and Banker* (1963), and Despres, *International Economic Reform* (1973), chs. 16-17.

27. For the history of the Eurodollar market, see Cooper, *The Economics of Interdependence* (1968), pp. 117-122. For problems of the market, see Barnet and Muller, *Global Reach*, pp. 286-287; Meier, *Problems of a World Monetary Order* (1974), pp. 133-136; *Business Week*, October 12, 1974, pp. 112-116.

28. It was also unrealistic because of the political-economic obstacles to the domestic reorganization that the scenario calls for.

Chapter Seven. Managing the U.S. Deficit

1. The United States' obligation was to maintain the dollar-gold parity at a fixed rate, while every other country was obliged to maintain a fixed parity between its currency and the dollar.

2. Active cooperation could include short-term loans designed to allow a country to maintain its currency parity in the face of massive short-term speculative capital outflows, a willingness to continue to hold on to currency suffering from a decline in confidence, and the pursuit of domestic economic policies that relieve some of the burden on the payments balance of the beleaguered country.

3. The anticipation of devaluation or capital controls serves to intensify speculation. Any devaluation could mean major profits for those who speculate against the currency. If capital controls seem a possibility, investors tend to rush to get their capital out of the country concerned while they still have the chance.

4. On the possibility of détente in this period see Lafeber, *America, Russia and the Cold War* (1972), pp. 209-211; Osgood, *NATO: Entangling Alliance* (1962), pp. 308-313.

5. On fears of Germany turning toward the East, see Kulski, *De Gaulle and the World* (1966), p. 291. On Britain, Northedge, *British Foreign Policy* (1962), pp. 250-251. France was suspected because détente had been the dream of the Fourth Republic: Grosser, *French Foreign Policy Under De Gaulle* (1967), pp. 102-103. De Gaulle's fears of a Soviet-American understanding are mentioned in Osgood, *NATO*, p. 258.

6. The still-secret Gaither Report outlined a multibillion-dollar program for domestic fallout shelters: Huntington, *The Common Defense* (1961), pp. 106-113. See also Rockefeller Brothers Fund, *International Security, The Military Aspect* (1958).

7. Osgood, *NATO*, especially pp. 60-63; Kulski, *De Gaulle*, pp. 93-115.

8. While there was little likelihood of actual war with the U.S.S.R., the bargaining power of the various European regimes vis-à-vis the Russians would be diminished if they lacked effective defenses.

9. On the seriousness of the American-French disagreement, see Grosser, *French Policy*, pp. 36-37.

10. The historic conflicts over colonialism are discussed in Good, "The United States and the Colonial Debate" (1959). Some of the political considerations that shaped Western European aid policies are discussed in Esman and Cheever, *The Common Aid Effort* (1967), pp. 89-101.

11. For critiques of the idea of Atlantic Partnership, see Calleo and Rowland, *America and the World Political Economy* (1973); Steel, *The End of Alliance* (1964); Kissinger, *The Troubled Partnership* (1966).

12. The reorganization of the OEEC had been proposed in 1955 in Elliott, *The*

Political Economy of American Foreign Policy, pp. 317-319. On the organization of the OECD, see Cottrell and Dougherty, *The Politics of the Atlantic Alliance* (1964), pp. 152-153.

13. On the accomplishments and limitations of the Development Assistance Committee, see Esman and Cheever, *Aid Effort,* chs. 4-6.

14. The shift in U.S. policy on the overseas territories is recounted in Curzon, *Multilateral Commercial Diplomacy* (1965), pp. 280-282.

15. Krause, *European Economic Integration and the United States* (1968), pp. 188-196. "While the U.S. is not convinced that the influence of France in its former dependencies is in the U.S. interest, it has not been in any position to challenge French leadership or accept the burdens which leadership requires": p. 192.

16. On the genesis of the MLF, see Van Der Beugel, *From Marshall Aid to Atlantic Partnership* (1966), pp. 385-393; Kissinger, *Partnership,* ch. 5; Cleveland, *NATO: The Transatlantic Bargain* (1970), pp. 48-52.

17. *New York Times,* November 20 and 26, 1960.

18. On the Skybolt incident, see Sorensen, *Kennedy* (1965), pp. 564-570; Schlesinger, *A Thousand Days* (1965), pp. 783-788. It also seems that the U.S. scrapped the MLF as a concession to the Soviet Union when the United States began moving toward détente and a nonproliferation treaty: Hanrieder, *The Stable Crisis* (1970), pp. 22-26.

19. If American suppliers of a certain commodity were displaced in French markets because German goods could enter France more cheaply because of the Common Market, that is a case of trade diversion.

20. Curzon, *Commercial,* pp. 98-100; Cottrell and Dougherty, *Alliance,* p. 185.

21. The act was written with a provision eliminating all tariffs on those goods for which the EEC and the U.S. supplied 80 percent of the world's exports. With Britain not in the EEC, there were relatively few goods to which this provision applied. See Balassa, *Trade Liberalization Among Industrial Countries* (1967), pp. 30-31; Cleveland, *The Atlantic Idea and Its European Rivals* (1966), p. 108. For the direct investment logic behind the Trade Expansion Act, see Calleo and Rowland, *America,* p. 125.

22. Calleo and Rowland, *America,* p. 82.

23. Van Der Beugel, *Marshall Aid,* pp. 376-379. The Common Market crisis revolved around French resistance to a plan by the EEC's commission to link the development of a common agricultural policy, which the French strongly favored, to an extension of supranational authority in the EEC. See Newhouse, *Collision in Brussels: The Common Market Crisis of 30 June 1965* (1967); Calleo and Rowland, *America,* pp. 127-128.

24. This does not necessarily contradict the argument that U.S. branch-planting in Western Europe was originally stimulated by high tariff levels abroad. By the mid or late 1960s, multinationalization of industry had developed its own independent dynamic.

25. Ernest Preeg, quoted in Calleo and Rowland, *America,* p. 125.

26. Roosa's diplomatic offensive is described in *The Banker,* May 1962, pp. 292-300. Apparently, the Europeans followed Roosa's leadership out of respect for his dynamism and clear grasp of the problems. Roosa's program also included technical operations such as interventions in the forward exchange market that were designed to discourage speculation against the dollar.

27. The creation of the gold pool is described in Horsefield, *The International Monetary Fund 1945-1965* (1969), I, p. 485.

28. Another expansion in IMF quotas was rejected because of the difficulty that some countries would have in transferring the gold portion of their increased quotas so soon after the last quota expansion: Horsefield, *Fund,* I, p. 507.

29. The conflicts over the creation of this supplement to IMF resources are described in Horsefield, *Fund,* I, pp. 510-512; *The Banker,* October 1961, pp. 659-664; *New York Herald Tribune,* June 21, 1961.

30. On the British drawing, see Horsefield, *Fund,* I, p. 487.

31. IEPA, *The United States Balance of Payments: An Appraisal of U.S. Economic Strategy* (1966), pp. 168-169.

32. Robert Triffin advocated an international central bank with liquidity-creating

powers, similar to Keynes' original clearing union plan. See Triffin, *Gold and the Dollar Crisis* (1961), pp. 102-120. The main neo-Triffinites in the Kennedy administration were George Ball at the State Department and James Tobin at the Council of Economic Advisers. Much of the tension between the neo-Triffinites and the Roosaites occurred on the question of the appropriate level of domestic economic activity. The neo-Triffinites were frustrated by Roosa's and Dillon's insistence that a program of domestic economic expansion was impossible because of the weakness of the dollar. However, it is not clear how the kind of reforms envisioned by the neo-Triffinites would have made domestic economic expansion possible in the short term. See Schlesinger, *Thousand*, pp. 600-601; *New York Herald Tribune*, September 25, 1962 (Walter Lippmann).

33. On the Maudling plan and the U.S. response, see *The Banker*, October 1962, pp. 632-638. Roosa explains his view of the connection between the reserve role and the vehicle role of the dollar in Roosa and Hirsch, *Reserves, Reserve Currencies, and Vehicle Currencies* (1966), pp. 3-6.

34. There were other balance-of-payments measures in this period. The Eisenhower administration made efforts to economize on the costs of U.S. military efforts abroad, tied U.S. aid purchases of U.S. goods, and encouraged U.S. agencies to "Buy American." The Kennedy administration reduced the quantity of money American travelers abroad could spend on duty-free goods, encouraged foreign investment in the United States, promoted foreign tourism in the United States, and attempted to expand U.S. exports. The Kennedy administration also made an effort to lower long-term interest rates while keeping short-term rates high, to discourage the export of capital. See *New York Herald Tribune*, December 12, 1960; *The Banker*, December 1960, pp. 779-784; John F. Kennedy's Message on Balance of Payments and Gold, reprinted in Harris, ed., *The Dollar in Crisis* (1961), pp. 295-307; Sorensen, *Kennedy*, pp. 405-412.

35. Dillon's efforts in Europe are reported in *The Banker*, June 1962, p. 346. On the interest equalization tax, see IEPA, *Strategy*, pp. 86-87; *The Banker*, August 1963, pp. 519-526.

36. An empirical basis for the continued belief that the U.S. payments situation would be sound once the Vietnam involvement ended was provided in Salant et al., *The United States Balance of Payments in 1968* (1963). Unfortunately, the predictions of this Brookings study would prove misguided.

37. The heightened realism toward Western Europe was indicated by the gradual abandonment of the devil theory of De Gaulle. Henry Kissinger wrote in 1966, " . . . the difficulties in American-European relationships may be symbolized in the personality of President De Gaulle, but they are not caused by him. Instead, they reflect deep-seated, structural changes in the nature of foreign policy in the contemporary period": "America and Europe, A New Relationship" (1966), p. 11. The same kind of realism is reflected in the following: "In general, the best kind of political and military 'Europe' from an American viewpoint would be the one which De Gaulle fears and many 'Europeans' want: A 'Europe' including Britain which is insufficiently united to reach for nuclear autonomy but still unified enouch to go some way toward meeting the European desire for political identity and independence, while at the same time restricting German and French freedom of action considerably": Cleveland, *Atlantic Idea*, p. 163.

38. On the interaction between French and German détente policies, see Kaiser, *German Foreign Policy in Transition* (1968), pp. 195-200.

39. Schlesinger, *Thousand*, p. 906.

40. For the turn toward escalation in 1964, see *The Pentagon Papers* (1971), vol. ii, pp. 198-200. Even if the dramatic later escalations had not yet been envisioned, it was clear that there would be a continuing balance-of-payments drain.

41. The December 1965 tightening is reported in Levitt, *Silent Surrender* (1970), p. 10. The December 1966 tightening is reported in *The Banker*, February 1967, pp. 97-98. The 1968 controls are described in *The Banker*, February 1968, p. 100.

42. Halberstam, *The Best and the Brightest* (1972), pp. 606-610.

43. The shift from a "top currency" that is willingly held to a "negotiated currency" that is held only in response to certain incentives is analyzed by Strange, *Sterling and British Policy* (1971), ch. 1.

44. Negotiations to gain German agreement to stop redeeming dollars for gold are reported in *Wall Street Journal*, April 21, 1967. Exemptions from the interest equalization tax as a quid pro quo for Japan's agreement not to redeem its dollars is noted in Diebold, *The United States and the Industrial World* (1972), p. 63. The U.S.-Canadian arrangements are described in Levitt, *Surrender*, pp. 12-13.

45. Brittan, *Steering the Economy* (1969), chs. 5-8.

46. The data on foreign exchange costs of the foreign military presence is from Bartlett, *The Long Retreat* (1972), p. 172. Much of the analysis of the costs of the Sterling Area is drawn from Strange, *Sterling*.

47. The stop-go policy is criticized by Strange, *Sterling*, ch. 9; Calleo, *Britain's Future* (1968), pp. 28-29. It should also be re-emphasized that the rearmament decision of 1951 had a disastrous impact on Britain's export trade because it allowed Germany to displace Britain in the production of certain key industrial goods. The decline in British competitiveness is discussed in Krause, "British Trade Performance" (1968), pp. 201-227.

48. Wilson's orientation is described in Foot, *The Politics of Harold Wilson* (1968), ch. 5; Pryke, *Though Cowards Flinch* (1967), p. 12; Brittan, *Steering*, pp. 188-190.

49. Brittan, *Steering*, ch. 8.

50. On the drawing from the fund, see Horsefield, *Fund*, I, p. 569. For the rest of the chronology, see Brittan, *Steering*, ch. 8; Meier, *Problems of a World Monetary Order* (1974), pp. 48-62.

51. This is the evaluation of the defense of the pound reached by Strange, *Sterling*, ch. 9.

52. The primary interest of the Europeans was democratizing the process of international liquidity creation. They no longer wanted the United States to exercise that power unilaterally by running dollar deficits of an arbitrary size. The background to the liquidity discussions is given in Cohen, *International Monetary Reform 1964-1969* (1970), ch. 1.

53. On the 1964 quota increase, see Horsefield, *Fund*, I, pp. 574-580. Much of the bargaining revolved around European reluctance to ease the gold contribution of Britain and the United States to the increased quotas. Since Britain and the United States had the largest quotas, their gold contributions were sizable, and they wanted some relief in transferring that gold to the fund. The CRU proposal had been drawn up by E.M. Bernstein. For a description of the Bernstein version, see IEPA, *Strategy*, pp. 179-181. For the French version of the CRU, see *New York Times*, April 26 and September 10, 1964.

54. The sudden shift in U.S. policy can be seen in *New York Times*, June 14, 15, July 11, 12, 1965. Significantly, Dillon, now out of office, endorsed the policy reversal.

55. Cohen analyzes the U.S. motives in *Reform*, pp. 61-64. He does not, however, touch on the possibility of deliberate delay or diversion.

56. Cohen, *Reform*, pp. 53-60.

57. The Ossola Report grew out of earlier discussions within the Group of Ten that had been initiated by Roosa with the intention of being able to avert discussions of reforms that might be in conflict with U.S. interests. Cohen, *Reform*, p. 31. The progress of the SDR negotiations are recounted in detail by Cohen in Chs. 3-4.

58. The U.S. share in the gold pool increased from 50 percent to 59 percent after the French withdrew from the pool in 1967 as another way of putting pressure on the United States. The size of the gold loss and the U.S. counterproposals are described in Hudson, *Superimperialism* (1972), pp. 221-225. It should also be noted that the limited U.S. response to the seizing of the *Pueblo* by the North Koreans in January 1968 might have been due to fears about the weakness of the dollar: *New York Times*, January 29, 1968.

59. There were some interagency conflicts over the outlines of these proposals. The State Department favored only a 5 percent tariff surcharge, while the Treasury Department wanted 10 percent and an export rebate plan, which was considered a highly aggressive measure. These proposals are reported in *Wall Street Journal*, March 6, 1968. European responses are noted in *New York Times*, March 7 and April 10, 1968.

60. Meier, *Order*, pp. 129-131.

61. The "financial deterrent" is described in Aubrey, *Behind the Veil of International Money* (1969). Aubrey's recognition that international power lurks behind the monetary veil reflects a new American sophistication.

62. See Kindleberger, *Balance-of-Payments Deficits and the International Market for Liquidity* (1965); Despres, *International Economic Reform* (1973), especially chs. 16-17. Critiques of this position appear in Cooper, *The Economics of Interdependence* (1968), pp. 132-136; Hudson, *Superimperialism*, pp. 245-251; Halm, *International Financial Intermediation: Deficits Benign and Malignant* (1968).

63. Cleveland, *Atlantic Idea*, pp. 84-86.

64. These events are recounted in Silk, *Nixonomics* (1972), chs. 10-13.

65. Meier, *Order*, p. 182.

66. Meier, *Order*, p. 189.

67. See, for example, the statement by Jack F. Bennett, former Undersecretary of the Treasury for Monetary Affairs, "A Free Dollar Makes Sense" (1975-76). See also *New York Times*, June 13 and August 10, 1975; *Wall Street Journal*, June 16, 1975.

68. See *Business Week*, June 2, 1975, pp. 60-63.

69. This argument has been developed by Robert Mundell and Arthur B. Laffer. See Wanniski, "The Mundell-Laffer Hypothesis—A New View of the World Economy" (1975).

70. Evaluating the impact of the 1971 and 1973 devaluations is enormously complicated, especially because the vast increases in imports by the OPEC countries since the oil price rise make it difficult to sort out the impact of exchange rates on specific U.S. exports. Note also that the strength of the U.S. trade balance during 1975 has been heavily dependent on agricultural exports, which are not that sensitive to price changes.

Chapter Eight. The International Monetary Order in Crisis

1. I am arguing that inflation is the visible manifestation of the contradictions of advanced capitalism, in the same way that periodic economic crises were the indication of contradictions in classical capitalism. This means that there is no single cause of inflation, but it can be traced in a variety of ways to the contradiction of private appropriation of socially created value. This view of inflation draws on Glyn and Sutcliffe, *Capitalism in Crisis* (1972); O'Connor, *The Fiscal Crisis of the State* (1973); Morris, "The Crisis of Inflation" (1973).

2. This was the problem with Britain's stop-go policies.

3. These problems are analyzed in Cooper, *The Economics of Interdependence* (1968), especially pp. 139-147.

4. See, for example, Block and Plotke, "Food Prices" (1973).

5. See *Wall Street Journal*, September 23, 1975 (Arthur Laffer).

6. Germany has been the most important low-inflation country using these arrangements in recent years. See Wadbrook, *West German Balance-of-Payments Policy* (1972).

7. "Since restoration of international balance typically calls for a decline in total expenditures, attempts to preserve real income (and expenditure) will frustrate the currency depreciation, higher wages will lead to higher prices leading to further currency depreciation, and so on in an endless cycle." Cooper, *Interdependence*, p. 233. See also *Wall Street Journal*, January 10, 1974 (Arthur Laffer).

8. For an analysis of the inflationary consequences of recent floating rates, see Hewson and Sakakibara, *The Eurocurrency Markets and Their Implications* (1975), ch. 5.

9. Chalmers, *International Interest Rate War* (1972), documents the way in which countries raised their interest rates competitively during the 1960s. This kind of interest-rate competition has serious inflationary consequences.

10. For example, further efforts by Third World countries to improve their position within the world economy will involve renewed strains on the developed economies and the international financial structure. It is quite possible also that some underdeveloped nations will be forced to repudiate some of their foreign debts, which could have a devastating impact on international finance.

11. The coordination I am describing would have to go far beyond the rather limited cooperation developed within the OECD, the Group of Ten, and the Bank for International Settlements. It would also have to be far more extensive and elaborate than the types of coordination agreed on at the Rambouillet Summit. *New York Times*, November 19 and 23, 1975.

12. The belief that the flowering of the multinationals can overcome the tensions between nation states is a modern version of the argument made before World War I by Kautsky. Kautsky argued that the increasing interpenetration of capital across national boundaries created a kind of "ultraimperialism" that would make national conflicts fade into insignificance given the shared interests of international capital. Lenin polemicized against Kautsky's position on the grounds that uneven development would assure that any particular divisions of the spoils would sooner or later prove unsatisfactory to some imperialist powers, and a period of renewed conflict would ensue to revise the international arrangements. Kautsky, "Ultraimperialism" (1914); Lenin, *Imperialism: The Highest Stage of Capitalism* (1917). A number of recent writers have taken the development of the multinationals as evidence that the Kautskian position has finally been vindicated; the grounds for intercapitalist conflict have been eliminated. See Hymer and Rowthorn, "Multinational Corporations and International Oligopoly: The Non-American Challenge" (1970); Nicolaus, "The Universal Contradiction" (1970). My argument is much closer to the position of Lenin and of Mandel, *Europe Versus America?* (1970). The key empirical issue, however, is the degree to which present international corporations derive critical political and military support from the government of their home country.

13. The ideology of multinationals being above politics is described in Barnet and Muller, *Global Reach* (1974), pp. 56-64. The multinational utopia is effectively critiqued in Calleo and Rowland, *America and the World Political Economy* (1973), pp. 186-191.

14. Barnet and Muller, *Global Reach*, pp. 72-104. This support extends both to emergency actions, such as defense against expropriation, and the day-to-day operations of forcing foreign governments not to discriminate against a particular firm. Examples of these latter forms of influence appear occasionally in the business press. For one involving a firm that has been outspoken in its anti-nationalism, see *Wall Street Journal*, October 16, 1975.

15. The extended period during which Britain retreated from a global role would seem to indicate the difficulties in a policy of retrenchment. In fact, Britain's retreats were forced on it by a series of sterling crises. See Strange, *Sterling* (1971).

16. The fluctuations in exchange rates have been a significant obstacle to the development of closer economic integration in Western Europe, see Bloomfield, "The Historical Setting" (1973).

17. The intensity of Japanese antimilitarism is discussed in Osgood, *The Weary and the Wary: United States and Japanese Security Policies in Transition* (1972), pp. 19-23.

18. What has changed since the 1930s is that it is now recognized that governments have the capacity to restore some reasonable level of economic activity without radically altering the economic system. That this is widely understood makes it unlikely that a modern depression would last as long as the depression of the 1930s.

19. This is what happened in the German financial crisis of 1931 when France held out for political concessions as the price of cooperation in rescuing the mark.

20. In my view, it is unlikely that the critical decision to refuse to cooperate in crisis-management would be made by a country such as Iran or Saudi Arabia. These nations, despite their oil wealth, lack the muscle to take disruptive action, particularly because they are so heavily dependent on the world market. Even if they did take such action, a united front of the developed countries would be sufficient to manage the crisis. In short, a crisis that began with underdeveloped nations could escalate out of control only if it occurred simultaneously with a major division among the major developed nations.

21. These "types" are the same ones that Polanyi described as responses to the depression of the 1930s: Polanyi, *The Great Transformation* (1944), pp. 237-248.

GLOSSARY

BALANCE OF PAYMENTS—the sum of all of a nation's international economic transactions. By analyzing all the transactions in terms of a particular accounting procedure, it is decided whether a nation is in balance of payments surplus, deficit, or equilibrium.

BALANCE-OF-PAYMENTS ADJUSTMENT—the means by which a nation attempts to move from a surplus or deficit position back to equilibrium. Techniques of adjustment include alterations in the level of domestic economic activity, changes in the nation's exchange rate, and the use of a variety of economic controls on international transactions.

BALANCE OF TRADE—the sum of all of a nation's exports and imports of goods and services.

BILATERALISM—a system in which a nation balances its international accounts on a nation-by-nation basis. Surpluses earned with nation A cannot be used to overcome a deficit with nation B. Bilateralism usually involves extensive use of exchange controls and quantitative restrictions. Compare *multilateralism.*

CAPITAL CONTROLS—restrictions on the capacity of people to move capital out of a particular nation legally. Capital controls are a form of exchange controls.

CONVERTIBILITY—a property of a specific currency that permits holders of that currency to exchange it freely for a wide variety of other currencies. In short, convertibility generally refers to the absence of exchange controls.

DEFLATION—a reduction in the level of domestic economic activity, indicated by decreased production and rising unemployment.

DEVALUATION—a reduction in the exchange rate of a nation's currency. Devaluation makes a nation's exports cheaper and its imports more expensive.

255

EURODOLLARS—claims on the U.S. banking system, held in banks in Western Europe. These claims are loaned and borrowed by banks in much the same way as a currency is used within a particular nation.

EXCHANGE CONTROLS—restrictions on the uses to which foreign exchange earnings can be put. A fully developed system of exchange controls would mean that all foreign exchange earned in a particular nation would have to be handed over to the government, which would then redistribute it for particular purposes.

EXCHANGE RATE—the price of a nation's currencly relative to other currencies and/or gold. Exchange rates can be fixed at a specific price, or the currency may be allowed to float, which means that its price is determined by the market.

FOREIGN EXCHANGE—any holdings of another nation's currency or claims on that nation's currency.

FUNDING—an operation by which short-term claims are turned into long-term loans.

INTERNATIONAL LIQUIDITY—the sum of all currency and gold reserves and all readily available international credits.

MULTILATERALISM—a system in which a nation balances its international accounts with a number of different nations. Within a multilateral system, surpluses earned with nation A can be used to make up a deficit with nation B. In the text, multilateralism generally refers to the ideal that all nations would be incorporated into one payments system with all of their currencies mutually convertible.

PETRODOLLARS—dollars earned by the oil-producing nations, a large share of which have been invested in the Eurodollar market and in the United States.

QUANTITATIVE RESTRICTIONS—a type of control over imports that limits the quantity or money value of commodities from certain specified areas of the world.

RESERVE CURRENCY—a currency held by a variety of nations in substantial quantities as a form of savings available in the event of a balance-of-payments shortfall. A reserve currency must be widely acceptable as a means for settling international accounts.

SPECIAL DRAWING RIGHTS—a reserve asset created within the International Monetary Fund that can be used under specified conditions, for settling international accounts.

STERLING BALANCES—the sum of British pounds being held as a reserve currency by the governments of foreign nations.

VEHICLE CURRENCY—a currency that is used widely in private international transactions.

BIBLIOGRAPHY

1. OFFICIAL PUBLICATIONS

International Monetary Fund
 International Monetary Reform: Documents of the Committee of Twenty. Washington, 1974.
League of Nations
 Commercial Policy in the Interwar Period. Geneva, 1942.
Organization of European Economic Cooperation
 Annual Reports.
 Report by the Secretary General. Paris, 1959.
 Statistical Bulletins.
United Nations, Department of Economic Affairs
 Economic Survey of Europe in 1948. Geneva, 1949.
 Measures for International Economic Stability. New York, 1951.
 National and International Measures for Full Employment. New York, 1949.
United States
 Bureau of the Budget
  Review Committee for Balance of Payments Statistics, *The Balance of Payments Statistics of the United States, A Review and Appraisal.* Washington, 1965.
 Bureau of Foreign and Domestic Commerce
  Markets After the War. Washington, 1943.
 Commission on International Trade and Investment
  United States International Economic Policy in an Interdependent World, two volumes. Washington, 1971.
 Congress
  Bretton Woods Agreement Act, Hearings, U.S. Senate, Committee on Banking and Currency, June 12-28, 1945, 79th Congress, 1st Session.
  International Payments Imbalances and Need for Strengthening International Financial Arrangements, Hearings, Joint Economic Committee, Subcommittee on International Exchange and Payments, May 16, June 19-21, 1961, 87th Congress, 1st Session.
 Council of Economic Advisors
  The Impact of Foreign Aid upon the Domestic Economy. Washington, 1947.
 Department of Commerce
  Markets After the Defense Expansion. Washington, 1952.
  Office of Business Economics, *United States Exports and Imports Classified by OBE End-Use Commodity Categories 1923-1968.* Washington, 1970.
  Survey of Current Business.
  The United States in the World Economy (Hal B. Lary). Washington, 1943.

Department of State
  Foreign Relations of the United States.
  Postwar Foreign Policy Preparation 1939-1945 (Harley Notter).
  Washington, 1949.
  The United States Economy and the Mutual Security Programs.
  Washington, 1959.
Director of the Office of Defense Mobilization
  Report to the President, October 1, 1953.
National Advisory Council on International Monetary and Financial Problems
  Semi-Annual Reports.
National Resources Planning Board
  National Resources Development Report for 1943, Part 1. Washington, 1943.
The Pentagon Papers, Senator Gravel Edition, vol. ii. Boston: Beacon, 1971.
Report to the President on Foreign Economic Policies (Gray Report). Washington, November 10, 1950.

2. BOOKS AND PAMPHLETS

Acheson, A.L.K., et al., eds. 1972. *Bretton Woods Revisited.* Toronto: Univ. of Toronto Press.
Acheson, Dean. 1966. *Present at the Creation.* New York: New American Library.
Adler-Karlsson, Gunnar. 1968. *Western Economic Warfare 1947-1967.* Stockholm: Almquist and Wiksell.
Aldrich, Winthrop W. 1944. *Some Aspects of American Foreign Economic Policy.* New York: n.p.
Ambrose, Stephen E. 1971. *Rise to Globalism.* Baltimore: Penguin.
American Assembly. 1951. *United States-Western Europe Relationships.* New York: American Assembly.
American Bankers Association. 1945. *Practical International Financial Organization.* New York: The Association.
Amery, L.S. 1946. *The Washington Loan Agreements.* London: MacDonald.
Amin, Samir. 1974. *Accumulation on a World Scale.* 2 vols. New York: Monthly Review Press.
Arkes, Hadley. 1972. *Bureaucracy, the Marshall Plan, and the National Interest.* Princeton: Princeton Univ. Press.
Arndt, H.W. 1963. *The Economic Lessons of the 1930's.* London: Cass.
Aubrey, Henry G. 1967. *Atlantic Economic Cooperation: The Case of the OECD.* New York: Praeger.
———. 1969. *Behind the Veil of International Money.* Princeton: Princeton Essays in International Finance.
———. 1964. *The Dollar in World Affairs.* New York: Praeger.
———. 1957. *United States Imports and World Trade.* Oxford: Clarendon Press.
Backer, John H. 1971. *Priming the German Economy.* Durham, N.C.: Duke Univ. Press.
Backman, Jules, and M.R. Gainsbrugh. 1946. *Deflation or Inflation.* New York: The Conference Board.

Balassa, Bela. 1967. *Trade Liberalization Among Industrial Countries.* New York: McGraw-Hill.

Ball, George. 1968. *The Discipline of Power.* Boston: Little, Brown.

Balogh, T. 1949. *The Dollar Crisis.* Oxford: Blackwell.

Barnet, Richard J., and Ronald E. Muller. 1974. *Global Reach.* New York: Simon and Schuster.

Bartlett, C.J. 1972. *The Long Retreat.* London: Macmillan.

Baum, Warren C. 1958. *The French Economy and the State.* Princeton: Princeton Univ. Press.

Bazelon, David T. 1963. *The Paper Economy.* New York: Random House; Vintage.

Bell, Coral. 1964. *The Debatable Alliance.* London: Oxford Univ. Press.

———. 1963. *Negotiation from Strength.* New York: Knopf.

Bell, Philip W. 1956. *The Sterling Area in the Postwar World.* Oxford: Clarendon Press.

Beloff, Max. 1963. *The United States and the Unity of Europe.* Washington, D.C.: Brookings.

Bennett, Edward W. 1962. *Germany and the Diplomacy of the Financial Crisis, 1931.* Cambridge, Mass.: Harvard Univ. Press.

Benoit, Emile. 1961. *Europe at Sixes and Sevens.* New York: Columbia Univ. Press.

Bergsten, C. Fred. 1975. *Toward A New International Economic Order.* Lexington, Mass.: Heath.

Bergsten, C. Fred, ed. 1973. *The Future of the International Economic Order: An Agenda for Research.* Lexington, Mass.: Heath.

Berle, Beatrice Bishop, and Travis Beal Jacobs, eds. 1973. *Navigating the Rapids 1918-1971, From the Papers of A.A. Berle.* New York: Harcourt Brace Jovanovich.

Bernstein, Barton, ed. 1970. *Politics and Policies of the Truman Administration.* Chicago: Quadrangle.

Beyen, J.W. 1949. *Money in a Maelstrom.* New York: Macmillan.

Birkenhead, Earl of. 1961. *The Prof in Two Worlds.* London: Collins.

Birnbaum, Eugene A. 1967. *Changing the United States Commitment to Gold.* Princeton: Princeton Essays in International Finance.

———. 1968. *Gold and the International Monetary System: An Orderly Reform.* Princeton: Princeton Essays in International Finance.

Bloomfield, Arthur I. 1959. *Monetary Policy Under the International Gold Standard 1880-1914.* New York: Federal Reserve Bank of New York.

Blum, John Morton. 1959-1967. *From the Morgenthau Diaries.* 3 vols. Boston: Houghton Mifflin.

———. 1973. *The Price of Vision: The Diary of Henry A. Wallace 1942-1946.* Boston: Houghton Mifflin.

Blyth, C.A. 1969. *American Business Cycles 1945-50.* New York: Praeger.

Boarman, Patrick M. 1964. *Germany's Economic Dilemma.* New Haven: Yale Univ. Press.

Bosman, Hans, and Frans A.M. Alting von Gesau, eds. 1970. *The Future of the International Monetary System.* Lexington, Mass.: Heath.

Bowie, Robert R. 1964. *Shaping the Future.* New York: Columbia Univ. Press.

Brandon, Henry. 1967. *In the Red: The Struggle for Sterling.* Boston: Houghton Mifflin.

Brittan, Samuel. 1969. *Steering the Economy*. London: Secker and Warburg.

Brookings Institution—International Study Group. 1952. *Rearmament and Anglo-American Economic Relations*. Washington, D.C.: Brookings.

Brown, Michael Barrett. 1963. *After Imperialism*. London: Heinemann.

Brown, William Adams, Jr. 1940. *The International Gold Standard Reinterpreted*. 2 vols. New York: National Bureau of Economic Research.

———. 1950. *The United States and the Restoration of World Trade*. Washington, D.C.: Brookings.

Brown, William Adams, Jr., and Redvers Opie. 1953. *American Foreign Assistance*. Washington, D.C.: Brookings.

Buchanan, Norman S. 1945. *International Investment and Domestic Welfare*. New York: Holt.

Buchanan, Norman S., and Friedrich A. Lutz, eds. 1947. *Rebuilding the World Economy*. New York: Twentieth Century Fund.

Calleo, David. 1968. *Britain's Future*. London: Hodder and Stoughton.

Calleo, David, and Benjamin M. Rowland. 1973. *America and the World Political Economy*. Bloomington: Indiana Univ. Press.

Camps, Miriam. 1964. *Britain and the European Community 1955-1963*. Princeton: Princeton Univ. Press.

———. 1966. *European Unification in the Sixties*. New York: McGraw-Hill.

Carr, E.H. 1966. *International Relations Between the Two World Wars 1919-1939*. New York: Harper and Row.

Chalmers, Eric. 1972. *International Interest Rate War*. London: Macmillan.

Clarke, Stephen V.O. 1967. *Central Bank Cooperation 1924-1931*. New York: Federal Reserve Bank of New York.

Cleveland, Harlan. 1970. *NATO: The Transatlantic Bargain*. New York: Harper and Row.

Cleveland, Harold Van B. 1966. *The Atlantic Idea and Its European Rivals*. New York: McGraw-Hill.

Coffey, Peter, and John Presley. 1971. *European Monetary Unification*. London: Macmillan.

Cohen, Benjamin. 1971. *The Future of Sterling as an International Currency*. London: Macmillan.

Cohen, Stephen D. 1970. *International Monetary Reform 1964-1969*. New York: Praeger.

Cohen, Stephen S. 1969. *Modern Capitalist Planning: The French Model*. Cambridge, Mass.: Harvard Univ. Press.

Committee on Economic Development. 1951. *Economic Aspects of North Atlantic Security*. New York.

———. 1945. *International Trade, Foreign Investment and Domestic Employment*. New York.

———. 1945. *Toward More Production, More Jobs and More Freedom*. New York.

Committee on International Economic Policy. 1947. *Studies in World Trade and Employment*. New York: CIEP.

Condliffe, J.B. 1942. *Agenda for a Post-War World*. New York: Norton.

———. 1947. *Obstacles to Multilateral Trade*. National Planning Association Pamphlet No. 59. Washington, D.C.

Cooper, Richard N. 1968. *The Economics of Interdependence.* New York: McGraw-Hill.

Cottrell, Alvin J., and James E. Dougherty. 1964. *The Politics of the Atlantic Alliance.* New York: Praeger.

Crosland, C.A.R. 1953. *Britain's Economic Problems.* London: Cape.

Curtis, Gerald, ed. 1970. *Japanese-American Relations in the 1970's.* Washington, D.C.: Columbia Books.

Curzon, Gerard. 1965. *Multilateral Commercial Diplomacy.* London: Joseph.

Dalton, Hugh. 1962. *High Tide and After.* London: Muller.

Davis, William. 1970. *Three Years Hard Labour.* Boston: Houghton Mifflin.

Day, A.C.L. 1954. *The Future of Sterling.* Oxford: Clarendon Press.

Denton, G.R., ed. 1969. *Economic Integration in Europe.* London: Weidenfeld and Nicolson.

Despres, Emile. 1973. *International Economic Reform.* New York: Oxford Univ. Press.

Diebold, William, Jr. 1952. *The End of the ITO.* Princeton: Princeton Essays in International Finance.

――――. 1959. *The Schuman Plan.* New York: Praeger.

――――. 1952. *Trade and Payments in Western Europe.* New York: Harper.

――――. 1972. *The United States and the Industrial World.* New York: Praeger.

Divine, Robert A. 1967. *Second Chance.* New York: Atheneum.

Dobney, Frederick J., ed. 1971. *Selected Papers of Will Clayton.* Baltimore: Johns Hopkins.

Eccles, Marriner S. 1951. *Beckoning Frontiers.* New York: Knopf.

Eckes, Alfred E., Jr. 1975. *A Search for Solvency.* Austin: Univ. of Texas Press.

Eden, Anthony. 1960. *Full Circle.* Boston: Houghton Mifflin.

Edinger, Lewis. 1965. *Kurt Schumacher.* Stanford: Stanford Univ. Press.

Elliott, William Y., et al. 1955. *The Political Economy of American Foreign Policy.* New York: Holt, Rinehart and Winston.

Ellis, Howard S. 1950. *The Economics of Freedom.* New York: Harper.

――――. 1941. *Exchange Controls in Central Europe.* Cambridge, Mass.: Harvard Univ. Press.

Emmanuel, Arghiri. 1972. *Unequal Exchange.* New York: Monthly Review Press.

Emmerson, John K. 1971. *Arms, Yen and Power.* New York: Dunellen.

Epstein, Leon D. 1954. *Britain—Uneasy Ally.* Chicago: Univ. of Chicago Press.

Erhard, Ludwig. 1954. *Germany's Comeback in the World Market.* London: Allen and Unwin.

Esman, Milton J., and Daniel S. Cheever. 1967. *The Common Aid Effort.* Columbus: Ohio State Univ. Press.

Feavearyear, Albert. 1963. *The Pound Sterling.* Oxford: Clarendon Press.

Feis, Herbert. 1965. *Europe: The World's Banker.* New York: Norton.

――――. 1944. *The Sinews of Peace.* New York: Harper.

Feld, Werner. 1963. *Reunification and West German-Soviet Relations.* The Hauge: Nijhoff.

Fellner, William, et al. 1966. *Maintaining and Restoring Balance in International Payments.* Princeton: Princeton Univ. Press.

Fitch, Lyle, and Horace Taylor, eds. 1946. *Planning for Jobs.* Philadelphia: Blakiston.

Flamant, Maurice, and Jeanne Singer-Kerel. 1970. *Modern Economic Crises and Recessions.* New York: Harper and Row; Colophon.

Foa, Bruno. 1949. *Monetary Reconstruction in Italy.* New York: King's Crown Press.

Foot, Paul. 1968. *The Politics of Harold Wilson.* Harmondsworth, England: Penguin.

Fox, William T.R., and Annette B. Fox. 1967. *NATO and the Range of American Choice.* New York: Columbia Univ. Press.

Frank, Isaiah. 1961. *The European Common Market.* New York: Praeger.

Freeland, Richard M. 1972. *The Truman Doctrine and the Origins of McCarthyism.* New York: Knopf.

Furniss, Edgar S., Jr. 1960. *France, Troubled Ally.* New York: Harper and Row.

Galbraith, John Kenneth. 1946. *Recovery in Europe.* National Planning Association Planning Pamphlet No. 53. Washington, D.C.

Gardner, Lloyd C. 1970. *Architects of Illusion.* Chicago: Quadrangle.

———. 1971. *Economic Aspects of New Deal Diplomacy.* Boston: Beacon.

Gardner, Richard N. 1969. *Sterling-Dollar Diplomacy.* New York: McGraw-Hill.

Geiger, Theodore, and Harold Van B. Cleveland. 1951. *Making Western Europe Defensible.* National Planning Association Planning Pamphlet No. 74. Washington, D.C.

Gilpin, Robert. 1968. *France in the Age of the Scientific State.* Princeton: Princeton Univ. Press.

Glyn, Andrew, and Bob Sutcliffe. 1972. *Capitalism in Crisis.* New York: Pantheon.

Goold-Adams, Richard. 1962. *John Foster Dulles.* New York: Appleton-Century-Crofts.

Grosser, Alfred. 1967. *French Foreign Policy Under De Gaulle.* Boston: Little, Brown.

Halberstam, David. 1972. *The Best and the Brightest.* New York: Random House.

Halliday, Jon, and Gavan McCormack. 1973. *Japanese Imperialism Today.* New York: Monthly Review Press.

Halm, George N. 1968. *International Financial Intermediation: Deficits Benign and Malignant.* Princeton: Princeton Essays in International Finance.

———. 1945. *International Monetary Cooperation.* Chapel Hill: Univ. of North Carolina Press.

Hanrieder, Wolfram F. 1970. *The Stable Crisis.* New York: Harper and Row.

Hansen, Alvin H. 1945. *America's Role in the World Economy.* New York: Norton.

———. 1938. *Full Recovery or Stagnation?* New York: Norton.

———. 1964. *The Postwar American Economy.* New York: Norton.

Harris, Seymour. 1964. *Economics of the Kennedy Years.* New York: Harper and Row.

———. 1948. *The European Recovery Program.* Cambridge, Mass.: Harvard Univ. Press.

Harris, Seymour, ed. 1961. *The Dollar in Crisis.* New York: Harcourt, Brace and World.

———. 1948. *Foreign Economic Policy for the United States*. Cambridge, Mass.: Harvard Univ. Press.

———. 1943. *Postwar Economic Problems*. New York: McGraw-Hill.

Harrod, Roy F. 1971. *The Life of John Maynard Keynes*. New York: Avon.

———. 1958. *The Pound Sterling, 1951-1958*. Princeton: Princeton Essays in International Finance.

Haviland, H. Field, Jr., ed. 1957. *The United States and the Western Community*. Haverford, Pa.: Haverford College Press.

Hawley, Ellis W. 1966. *The New Deal and the Problem of Monopoly*. Princeton: Princeton Univ. Press.

Hawtrey, R.G. 1950. *The Balance of Payments and the Standard of Living*. London: Royal Institute of International Affairs.

———. 1949. *Western European Union*. London: Royal Institute of International Affairs.

Hayek, Friedrich August von. 1944. *The Road to Serfdom*. Chicago: Univ. of Chicago Press.

Hayter, Teresa. 1972. *Aid as Imperialism*. Harmondsworth, England: Penguin.

Hewson, John, and Eisuke Sakakibara. 1975. *The Eurocurrency Markets and Their Implications*. Lexington, Mass.: Heath.

Hickman, Bert G. 1960. *Growth and Stability of the Postwar Economy*. Washington, D.C.: Brookings.

Hinshaw, Randall. 1964. *The European Community and American Trade*. New York: Praeger.

———. 1958. *Toward European Convertibility*. Princeton: Princeton Essays in International Finance.

Hinterhoff, Eugene. 1959. *Disengagement*. London: Stevens.

Hirsch, Fred. 1969. *Money International*. New York: Doubleday.

———. 1965. *The Pound Sterling: A Polemic*. London: Victor Gollancz.

Hobsbawm, E.J. 1968. *Industry and Empire*. London: Weidenfeld and Nicolson.

Hoffman, Stanley. 1968. *Gulliver's Troubles, Or the Setting of America's Foreign Policy*. New York: McGraw-Hill.

Holbik, Karel. 1959. *Italy in International Cooperation*. Padua: Cedam.

Holbik, Karel, and Henry Myers. 1964. *Postwar Trade in Divided Germany*. Baltimore: Johns Hopkins.

Hollerman, Leon. 1967. *Japan's Dependence on the World Economy*. Princeton: Princeton Univ. Press.

Homan, Paul T., and Fritz Machlup, eds. 1945. *Financing American Prosperity*. New York: Twentieth Century Fund.

Hoopes, Townsend. 1969. *The Limits of Intervention*. New York: McKay.

Hoover, Calvin B. 1945. *International Trade and Domestic Employment*. New York: McGraw-Hill.

Horowitz, David, ed. 1969. *Corporations and the Cold War*. New York: Monthly Review Press.

Horsefield, J. Keith. 1969. *The International Monetary Fund 1945-1965*. 3 vols. Washington, D.C.: International Monetary Fund.

Hudson, Michael. 1972. *Superimperialism*. New York: Holt, Rinehart and Winston.

Hull, Cordell. 1948. *The Memoirs of Cordell Hull*. New York: Macmillan.

Humphrey, Don D. 1962. *The United States and the Common Market.* New York: Praeger.

Hunsberger, Warren S. 1964. *Japan and the United States in World Trade.* New York: Harper and Row.

Huntington, Samuel P. 1961. *The Common Defense.* New York: Columbia Univ. Press.

Hutchison, Keith. 1946. *Rival Partners.* New York: Macmillan.

International Economic Policy Association. 1972. *The United States Balance of Payments: From Crisis to Controversy.* Washington, D.C.: IEPA.

————. 1966. *The United States Balance of Payments: An Appraisal of U.S. Economic Strategy.* Washington, D.C.: IEPA.

Irving Trust Company. 1944. *International Financial Stabilization: A Symposium.* New York: Irving Trust.

Janeway, Eliot. 1968. *The Economics of Crisis.* New York: Weybright and Talley.

Johnson, Harry G. 1965. *World Economy at the Crossroads.* Oxford: Clarendon Press.

Jones, Joseph. 1955. *The Fifteen Weeks.* New York: Harcourt, Brace and World.

Kaiser, Karl. 1968. *German Foreign Policy in Transition.* New York: Oxford Univ. Press.

Kenen, Peter B. 1960. *Giant Among Nations.* New York: Harcourt, Brace and World.

————. 1963. *Reserve-Asset Preferences of Central Banks and Stability of the Gold-Dollar Standard.* Princeton: Princeton Studies in International Finance.

Kennan, George F. 1967. *Memoirs 1925-1950.* Boston: Little, Brown.

Kenwood, A.G., and A.L. Lougheed. 1971. *The Growth of the International Economy 1820-1960.* London: Allen and Unwin.

Keynes, J.M. 1925. *Economic Consequences of Sterling Parity.* New York: Harcourt.

————. 1964. *The General Theory of Employment, Interest, and Money.* New York: Harcourt, Brace and World.

Kindleberger, C.P. 1969. *American Business Abroad.* New Haven: Yale Univ. Press.

————. 1965. *Balance-of-Payments Deficits and the International Market for Liquidity.* Princeton: Princeton Essays in International Finance.

————. 1950. *The Dollar Shortage.* New York: Wiley.

————. 1966. *Europe and the Dollar.* Cambridge, Mass.: MIT Press.

————. 1967. *The Politics of International Money and World Language.* Princeton: Princeton Essays in International Finance.

————. 1973. *The World in Depression 1929-1939.* Berkeley: Univ. of California Press.

Kissinger, Henry A. 1966. *The Troubled Partnership.* Garden City, N.Y.: Doubleday; Anchor.

Kitzinger, U.W. 1963. *The Politics and Economics of European Integration.* New York: Praeger.

Kolko, Gabriel. 1968. *The Politics of War.* New York: Random House.

Kolko, Joyce. 1974. *America and the Crisis of World Capitalism.* Boston: Beacon.

Kolko, Joyce, and Gabriel Kolko. 1972. *The Limits of Power*. New York: Harper and Row.

Korbel, Josef. 1972. *Détente in Europe: Real or Imaginary?* Princeton: Princeton Univ. Press.

Kraft, Joseph. 1962. *The Grand Design*. New York: Harper and Row.

Krause, Lawrence. 1968. *European Economic Integration and the United States*. Washington, D.C.: Brookings.

Krause, Lawrence, ed. 1964. *The Common Market—Progress and Controversy*. Englewood Cliffs, N.J.: Prentice-Hall.

Kravis, Irving B. 1963. *Domestic Interests and International Obligations*. Philadelphia: Univ. of Pennsylvania Press.

Kulski, W.W. 1966. *De Gaulle and the World*. Syracuse, N.Y.: Syracuse Univ. Press.

Kuznets, Simon. 1964. *Postwar Economic Growth*. Cambridge, Mass.: Harvard Univ. Press.

Lafeber, Walter. 1972. *America, Russia and the Cold War*. New York: Wiley.

Landes, David S. 1969. *The Unbound Prometheus*. Cambridge: Cambridge Univ. Press.

Lanyi, Anthony. 1969. *The Case for Floating Exchange Rates Reconsidered*. Princeton: Princeton Essays in International Finance.

Lary, Hal B. 1963. *Problems of the United States as World Trader and Banker*. New York: National Bureau of Economic Research.

Lawson, R. Alan. 1972. *The Failure of Independent Liberalism 1930-1941*. New York: Capricorn.

Lenin, V.I. 1917. (1939). *Imperialism: The Highest Stage of Capitalism*. New York: International Publishers.

Letiche, J.M. 1948. *Reciprocal Trade Agreements in the World Economy*. New York: King's Crown Press.

Levitt, Kari. 1970. *Silent Surrender*. New York: Liveright.

Lewis, Cleona. 1948. *The United States and Foreign Investment Problems*. Washington, D.C.: Brookings.

Lindert, Peter H. 1969. *Key Currencies and Gold 1900-1913*. Princeton: Studies in International Finance.

Lippman, Walter. 1962. *Western Unity and the Common Market*. Boston: Little, Brown.

Lubell, Samuel. 1955. *The Revolution in World Trade*. New York: Harper.

Luthy, Herbert. 1955. *France Against Herself*. New York: Praeger.

Lutz, Friedrich A. 1948. *The Marshall Plan and European Economic Policy*. Princeton: Princeton Essays in International Finance.

MacDougall, Donald. 1957. *The World Dollar Problem*. New York: St. Martin's.

McGeehan, Robert. 1971. *The German Rearmament Question*. Urbana: Univ. of Illinois Press.

McKinnon, Ronald I. 1969. *Private and Official International Money: The Case for the Dollar*. Princeton: Princeton Essays in International Finance.

Machinery and Allied Products Institute. 1968. *The Case Against Balance of Payments Controls*. Washington, D.C.: MAPI.

Macmillan, Harold. 1971. *Riding the Storm 1956-1959*. London, Macmillan.

Mallalieu, William C. 1956. *British Reconstruction and American Policy 1945-1955*. New York: Scarecrow.

Mandel, Ernest. 1972. *Decline of the Dollar.* New York: Monad.

———. 1970. *Europe Versus America?* London: New Left Books.

Manderson-Jones, R.B. 1972. *The Special Relationship.* London: Weidenfeld and Nicolson.

Meier, Gerald M. 1974. *Problems of a World Monetary Order.* New York: Oxford Univ. Press.

Melman, Seymour. 1965. *Our Depleted Society.* New York: Delta.

———. 1974. *The Permanent War Economy.* New York: Simon and Schuster.

Meyer, Richard Hemming. 1970. *Banker's Diplomacy.* New York: Columbia Univ. Press.

Mikesell, Raymond F. 1954. *The Emerging Pattern of International Payments.* Princeton: Princeton Essays in International Finance.

———. 1970. *The United States Balance of Payments and the International Role of the Dollar.* Washington, D.C.: American Enterprise Institute.

———. 1952. *United States Economic Policy and International Relations.* New York: McGraw-Hill.

Mikesell, Raymond F., ed. 1962. *United States Private and Government Investment Abroad.* Eugene: Univ. of Oregon Press.

Mitchell, Joan. 1963. *Crisis in Britain 1951.* London: Secker and Warburg.

Moggridge, D.E. 1972. *British Monetary Policy 1924-1931.* Cambridge: Cambridge Univ. Press.

Moore, Ben T. 1958. *NATO and the Future of Europe.* New York: Harper.

National Foreign Trade Council. 1949. *Sterling Since the Convertibility Crisis.* New York: NFTC.

National Industrial Conference Board. 1952. *Post Defense Outlook.* Studies in Business Economics, No. 34. New York.

National Planning Association. 1944. *America's New Opportunities in World Trade.* Planning Pamphlet Nos. 37-38. Washington, D.C.

———. 1941. *Britain's Trade in the Post-War World.* Planning Pamphlet No. 9. Washington, D.C.

———. 1941. *Guides for Post-War Planning.* Planning Pamphlet No. 8. Washington, D.C.

———. 1945. *National Budgets for Full Employment.* Planning Pamphlet Nos. 43-44. Washington, D.C.

———. 1971. *United States Foreign Economic Policy for the 1970's.* Planning Pamphlet No. 130. Washington, D.C.

Neumann, Franz. 1966. *Behemoth.* New York: Harper and Row.

Newhouse, John. 1967. *Collision in Brussels: The Common Market Crisis of 30 June 1965.* New York: Norton.

Newhouse, John, et al. 1971. *U.S. Troops in Europe.* Washington, D.C.: Brookings.

Northedge, F.S. 1962. *British Foreign Policy.* New York: Praeger.

O'Connor, James. 1973. *The Fiscal Crisis of the State.* New York: St. Martin's.

Oliver, Robert W. 1971. *Early Plans for a World Bank.* Princeton: Princeton Studies in International Finance.

Osgood, Robert E. 1962. *NATO: Entangling Alliance.* Chicago: Univ. of Chicago Press.

———. 1972. *The Weary and the Wary: United States and Japanese Security Problems in Transition.* Baltimore: Johns Hopkins.

Pabst Brewing Company. 1944. *The Winning Plans in the Pabst Postwar Employment Awards*. Milwaukee: Pabst.

Parrini, Carl P. 1969. *Heir to Empire*. Pittsburgh: Univ. of Pittsburgh Press.

Patterson, Gardner. 1966. *Discrimination in International Trade*. Princeton: Princeton Univ. Press.

Payer, Cheryl. 1974. *The Debt Trap*. New York: Monthly Review Press.

Penrose, E.F. 1953. *Economic Planning for the Peace*. Princeton: Princeton Univ. Press.

Polanyi, Karl. 1944 (1957). *The Great Transformation*. Boston: Beacon.

Polk, Judd. 1956. *Sterling: Its Meaning in World Finance*. New York: Harper.

Polk, Judd, et al. 1966. *United States Production Abroad and the Balance of Payments*. New York: The Conference Board.

Price, Harry Bayard. 1955. *The Marshall Plan and Its Meaning*. Ithaca, N.Y.: Cornell Univ. Press.

Pryke, Richard. 1967. *Though Cowards Flinch*. London: MacGibbon and Kee.

Radosh, Ronald. 1969. *American Labor and United States Foreign Policy*. New York: Random House; Vintage.

————. 1975. *Prophets on the Right*. New York: Simon and Schuster.

Rees, David. 1973. *Harry Dexter White*. New York: Coward, McCann and Geoghegan.

Rees, Graham L. 1963. *Britain and the Postwar European Payments Systems*. Cardiff: Univ. of Wales Press.

Reuss, Henry. 1964. *The Critical Decade*. New York: McGraw-Hill.

Richardson, James L. 1966. *Germany and the Atlantic Alliance*. Cambridge, Mass.: Harvard Univ. Press.

Rockefeller Brothers Fund. 1958. *Foreign Economic Policy in the 20th Century*. Garden City, N.Y.: Doubleday.

————. 1958. *International Security, The Military Aspect*. Garden City, N.Y.: Doubleday.

Rolfe, Sidney E. 1966. *Gold and World Power*. New York: Harper and Row.

Rolfe, Sidney E., and James L. Burtle. 1975. *The Great Wheel*. New York: McGraw-Hill.

Roosa, Robert V. 1967. *The Dollar and World Liquidity*. New York: Random House.

————. 1965. *Monetary Reform for the World Economy*. New York: Harper and Row.

Roosa, Robert V., and Fred Hirsch. 1966. *Reserves, Reserve Currencies, and Vehicle Currencies: An Argument*. Princeton: Princeton Essays in International Finance.

Rueff, Jacques. 1972. *The Monetary Sin of the West*. New York: Macmillan.

Rueff, Jacques, and Fred Hirsch. 1965. *The Role and Rule of Gold: An Argument*. Princeton: Princeton Essays in International Finance.

Salant, Walter, et al. 1963. *The United States Balance of Payments in 1968*. Washington, D.C.: Brookings.

Salter, Arthur. 1951. *Foreign Investment*. Princeton: Princeton Essays in International Finance.

Scammell, W.M. 1961. *International Monetary Policy*. London: Macmillan.

Schlesinger, Arthur, Jr. 1965. *A Thousand Days*. Greenwich, Conn.: Fawcett.

Schmitt, Hans A. 1962. *The Path to European Union*. Baton Rouge: Louisiana

State Univ. Press.

Schumacher, E.F. 1943. *Export Policy and Full Employment*. London: Fabian Society.

Segal, Ronald. 1974. *The Decline and Fall of the American Dollar*. New York: Bantam.

Silk, Leonard. 1972. *Nixonomics*. New York: Praeger.

Skidelsky, Robert. 1967. *Politicians and the Slump*. London: Macmillan.

Sorensen, Theodore C. 1965. *Kennedy*. New York: Harper and Row.

Starobin, Joseph. 1972. *American Communism in Crisis 1943-1957*. Cambridge, Mass.: Harvard Univ. Press.

Steel, Ronald. 1964. *The End of Alliance*. New York: Viking.

Stephenson, Hugh. 1973. *The Coming Clash*. New York: Saturday Review Press.

Strange, Susan. 1971. *Sterling and British Policy*. London: Oxford Univ. Press.

Sutton, Francis X. et al. 1956. *The American Business Creed*. Cambridge, Mass.: Harvard Univ. Press.

Swann, D. 1970. *The Economics of the Common Market*. Harmondsworth, England: Penguin.

Tew, Brian. 1965. *International Monetary Co-operation 1945-1965*. London: Hutchinson.

Thorp, Willard. 1954. *Trade, Aid or What?* Baltimore: Johns Hopkins.

Triffin, Robert. 1957. *Europe and the Money Muddle*. New Haven: Yale Univ. Press.

———. 1964. *The Evolution of the International Monetary System*. Princeton: Studies in International Finance.

———. 1961. *Gold and the Dollar Crisis*. New Haven: Yale Univ. Press.

Truman, Harry S. 1955-56. *Memoirs*. 2 vols. Garden City, N.Y.: Doubleday.

Van Der Beugel, Ernst H. 1966. *From Marshall Aid to Atlantic Partnership*. Amsterdam: Elsevier.

Vatter, Harold G. 1963. *The U.S. Economy in the 1950's*. New York: Norton.

Vernon, Raymond. 1954. *America's Foreign Trade Policy and the GATT*. Princeton: Princeton Essays in International Finance.

———. 1958. *Trade Policy in Crisis*. Princeton: Princeton Essays in International Finance.

———. 1969. *United States Controls on Foreign Direct Investment—A Reevaluation*. New York: Financial Executives Research Foundation.

Wadbrook, William Pollard. 1972. *West German Balance-of-Payments Policy*. New York: Praeger.

Wallace, Henry A. 1945. *Sixty Million Jobs*. New York: Reynal and Hitchcock.

Wallerstein, Immanuel. 1974. *The Modern World System*. New York: Academic Press.

Wallich, Henry C. 1955. *Mainsprings of the German Revival*. New Haven: Yale Univ. Press.

Warnecke, Steven, ed. 1972. *The European Community in the 1970's*. New York: Praeger.

Weinstein, James. 1969. *The Decline of Socialism in America. 1912-1925*. New York: Random House; Vintage.

White, Nathan I. 1956. *Harry Dexter White—Loyal American*. Waban, Mass.: B.W. Bloom.

Wilcox, Francis O., and H. Field Haviland, Jr., eds. 1963. *The Atlantic Community*. New York: Praeger.
Wilkins, Mira. 1970. *The Emergence of Multinational Enterprise*. Cambridge, Mass.: Harvard Univ. Press.
Williams, John H. 1953. *Economic Stability in a Changing World*. New York: Oxford Univ. Press.
————. 1947. *Post-War Monetary Plans and Other Essays*. New York: Knopf.
Williams, Philip M. 1966. *Crisis and Compromise: Politics in the 4th Republic*. New York: Doubleday.
Williams, William Appleman. 1962. *The Tragedy of American Diplomacy*. New York: Dell.
Williamson, John H. 1965. *The Crawling Peg*. Princeton: Princeton Essays in International Finance.
Wilson, Joan Hoff. 1973. *American Business and Foreign Policy 1920-1933*. Boston: Beacon.
Wolfe, Martin. 1951. *The French Franc Between the Wars*. New York: Columbia Univ. Press.
Zupnick, Elliot. 1957. *Britain's Postwar Dollar Problem*. New York: Columbia Univ. Press.
Zurcher, Arnold. 1958. *The Struggle to Unite Europe 1940-1958*. New York: New York Univ. Press.
Zurcher, Arnold, and Richmond Page, eds. 1945. *America's Place in the World Economy*. New York: New York Univ. Press.

3. ARTICLES AND OTHER SOURCES

Ackerman, Frank, and Arthur MacEwan. 1972. "Inflation, Recession, and Crisis." *Review of Radical Political Economy*, 4: (Aug.) 4-37.
Bennett, Jack F. 1975-76. "A Free Dollar Makes Sense." *Foreign Policy* 21 (winter): 63-75.
Bernstein, E.M. 1945. "British Policy and a World Economy." *American Economic Review*, 35: (Dec.) 891-908.
————. 1972. "The Evolution of the IMF." In *Bretton Woods Revisited*, A.L.K. Acheson eds., et al., pp. 51-65. Toronto: Univ. of Toronto Press.
————. 1944. "A Practical International Monetary Policy." *American Economic Review*, 34: (Dec.) 771-784.
Block, Fred. 1970. "Expanding Capitalism: The British and American Cases." *Berkeley Journal of Sociology*, 15:138-165.
Block, Fred, and Larry Hirschhorn. 1972. "The International Monetary Crisis." *Socialist Revolution*, 11: (Sept.-Oct.) 138-165.
Block, Fred, and David Plotke. 1973. "Food Prices." *Socialist Revolution*, 16: (July-Aug.) 89-98.
Bloomfield, Arthur I. 1973. "The Historical Setting." In Lawrence B. Krause and Walter S. Salant, eds., *European Monetary Unification*, pp. 1-30. Washington, D.C.: Brookings.
————. 1946. "Postwar Controls of International Capital Movements." *American Economic Review*, 36: (May) 687-709.
Boretsky, Michael. 1975. "Trends in U.S. Technology: A Political Economist's View." *American Scientist*, 63: (Jan.-Feb.) 70-82.
Branson, William, and Helen B. Junz. 1971. "Trends in U.S. Trade and Competitive Advantage." *Brookings Papers on Economic Activity* 2, 285-338.

Camps, Miriam. 1956. "The European Common Market and American Policy." *Princeton Center for International Studies,* Memo 11.

———. 1957. "Trade Policy and American Leadership." *Princeton Center for International Studies,* Memo 12.

Clark, John Maurice. 1945. "Financing High Level Employment." In *Financing American Prosperity,* Paul T. Homan and Fritz Machlup, eds., pp. 71-125. New York: Twentieth Century Fund.

Cooper, Richard N. 1961. "The Competitive Position of the United States." In *The Dollar in Crisis,* Seymour Harris, ed., pp. 137-164. New York: Harcourt, Brace and World.

Craig, Gordon. 1955. "NATO and the New German Army." *Princeton Center for International Studies,* Memo 8.

Diebold, William, Jr. 1948. "East-West Trade and the Marshall Plan." *Foreign Affairs,* 26: (July) 709-722.

Eakins, David. 1969. "Business Planners and America's Postwar Expansion." In *Corporations and the Cold War,* David Horowitz, ed., pp. 143-171. New York: Monthly Review Press.

Feis, Herbert. 1947. "The Conflict Over Trade Ideologies." *Foreign Affairs,* 25 (Jan.) 217-228.

Foster, Susan B. 1972. "Impact of Direct Investment Abroad by United States Multinational Companies on the Balance of Payments." *Monthly Review, Federal Reserve Bank of New York,* 54: (July) 166-177.

Furniss, Edgar S., Jr. 1957. "Some Perspectives on American Military Assistance," *Princeton Center for International Studies,* Memo 13.

Gardner, Richard. 1972. "The Political Setting." In *Bretton Woods Revisited,* A.L.K. Acheson et al., eds., pp. 20-33. Toronto: Univ. of Toronto Press.

Geiger, Theodore. 1971. "A Note on U.S. Comparative Advantages." In *United States Foreign Economic Policy for the 1970's.* National Planning Association, Planning Pamphlet no. 130, pp. 58-64.

Good, Robert C. 1959. "The United States and the Colonial Debate." In *Alliance Policy in the Cold War,* Arnold Wolfers, ed., pp. 224-270. Baltimore: Johns Hopkins.

Hammond, Paul Y. 1962. "NSC-68: Prologue to Rearmament." In Schilling, Hammond, and Snyder, *Strategy, Politics and Defense Budgets:* pp. 271-378. New York: Columbia Univ. Press.

Hickman, Warren. 1949. "Genesis of the European Recovery Program." Unpublished Ph.D. thesis, University of Geneva.

Hirschhorn, Larry. 1974. "Toward a Political Economy of the Service Society." Institute of Urban and Regional Development, University of California, Berkeley, *Working Paper,* no. 229.

Hirschman, Albert O. 1951. "The European Payments Union." *Review of Economics and Statistics,* 33: (Feb.) 49-55.

Holloman, J. Herbert. 1972. "Technology in the U.S.: Issues for the 1970's." *Technology Review,* (June) 10-21.

Hunter, Robert. 1971. "U.S. Defense Commitments in Europe and Asia During the 1970's." In *United States Foreign Economic Policy for the 1970's.* National Planning Association, Planning Pamphlet no. 130, pp. 160-193.

Hymer, Stephen, and Robert Rowthorn. 1970. "Multinational Corporations and International Oligopoly: The Non-American Challenge," pp. 57-91. In C.P. Kindleberger, ed., *The International Corporation,* Cambridge,

Mass.: MIT Press.

Hyson, Charles D., and Alan M. Strout. 1968. "Impact of Foreign Aid on U.S. Exports," *Harvard Business Review*, 46 (Jan.-Feb.) 63-71.

Kautsky, Karl. 1914 (1970). "Ultraimperialism." *New Left Review*, 59: (Jan.-Feb.) 41-46.

Keynes, J.M. 1933. "National Self Sufficiency." *Yale Review*, 26:755-769.

Kissinger, Henry. 1966. "America and Europe, A New Relationship." In *Problems of European Integration, Proceedings of the Institute of World Affairs*, 43rd session, pp. 11-20.

Knorr, Klaus. 1953. "Strengthening the Free World Economy." *Princeton Center for International Studies*, Memo 3.

Krause, Lawrence. 1968. "British Trade Performance." In *Britain's Economic Prospects*, Richard Caves et al., eds., pp. 201-222. Washington, D.C.: Brookings.

———. 1970. "A Passive Balance of Payments Strategy for the United States." *Brookings Papers on Economic Activity*, 3:339-360.

Kuklick, Bruce. 1968. "American Foreign Economic Policy and Germany, 1934-1946." Unpublished Ph.D. thesis, Univ. of Pennsylvania.

Lary, Hal B. 1946. "Domestic Effects of Foreign Investment." *American Economic Review*, 36: (May) 672-685.

Mansfield, Lawrence P. 1960. "The Origins of the International Monetary Fund." Unpublished Ph.D. thesis, Univ. of North Carolina.

Marcuse, Herbert. 1951. "Antidemocratic Popular Movements." In *Germany and The Future of Europe*, Hans Morgenthau, ed., pp. 108-113. Chicago: Univ. of Chicago Press.

Moggridge, D.E. 1972. "From War to Peace—How Much Overseas Assistance." *The Banker*, 122:1163-1168.

———. 1972. "From War to Peace—The Sterling Balances." *The Banker*, 122:1032-1035.

Morris, Jacob. 1973. "The Crisis of Inflation." *Monthly Review*, 25: (Sept.) 1-22.

Mundell, Robert A. 1973. "The Future of the International Financial System." In *Bretton Woods Revisited*, A.L.K. Acheson et al., eds., pp. 91-104. Toronto: Univ. of Toronto Press.

Murray, Robin. 1971. "The Internationalization of Capital and the Nation State." *New Left Review*, 66: (May-June) 84-109.

Nicolaus, Martin. 1970. "The Universal Contradiction." *New Left Review*, 59: (Jan.-Feb.) 3-18.

Paterson, Thomas. 1968. "The Economic Cold War: American Business and Economic Foreign Policy." Unpublished Ph.D. thesis, Univ. of California, Berkeley.

Patterson, Gardner, and Judd Polk. 1947. "The Emerging Pattern of Bilateralism." *Quarterly Journal of Economics*, 62: (Nov.) 118-142.

Piater, André. 1957. "Business Cycles in Post-War France." In *The Business Cycle in the Post-War World*, Erik Lundberg, ed., pp. 100-121. London: Macmillan.

Plumptre, A.F.W. 1973. "Canadian Views." In *Bretton Woods Revisited*, A.L.K. Acheson et al., eds., pp. 41-45. Toronto: Univ. of Toronto Press.

Reuther, Walter. 1945. "The Challenge of Peace." *International Postwar Problems*, 2: (April) 143-164.

Robinson, R., and J. Gallagher. 1953. "The Imperialism of Free Trade."

Economic History Review, 6: (August) 1-15.

Schilling, Werner. 1962. "The Politics of National Defense: Fiscal 1950." In *Strategy, Politics, and Defense Budgets*, Werner Schilling et al., pp. 5-266. New York: Columbia Univ. Press.

Schoepperle, Victor. 1943. "Future of International Investment: Private vs. Public Foreign Lending." *American Economic Review*, 33: (March) 336-341.

Vernon, Raymond. 1957. "Economic Aspects of the Atlantic Community." In *The United States and the Western Community*, H. Field Haviland, Jr., ed., pp. 53-64. Haverford, Pa.: Haverford College Press.

Wanniski, Jude. 1975. "The Mundell-Laffer Hypothesis—A New View of the World Economy." *Public Interest*, 39: (Spring) 31-52.

White, Harry D. 1945. "The Monetary Fund: Some Criticisms Examined." *Foreign Affairs*, 23: (Jan.) 195-210.

————. 1943. "Postwar Currency Stabilization." *American Economic Review*, 33: (March) 382-387.

4. NEWSPAPERS AND PERIODICALS

The Banker   *The New York Times*
Business Week   *Politics and Money*
The Economist   *The Wall Street Journal*
The New York Herald Tribune

INDEX

275